Praise for *The Effective Software Engineer*

Don't just do things, do the right things: use this practical guide to grow your skills and impact as an engineer. The concrete steps and practical examples in this book make it a useful companion to help you increase your impact as a software engineer.

—*Lena Reinhard, VP engineering, leadership and executive coach, founder*

Osmani transforms the vague notion of "effectiveness" into concrete, actionable strategies. Essential reading for mid-level engineers wondering why their good work isn't translating into career advancement.

—*Teal Bauer, founder and MD, Starsong Consulting*

Many engineers struggle to understand how to have an impact. This book gives a map with many practical tools to help engineers increase their impact and grow in their careers.

—*Patrick Kua, founder of the Tech Lead Academy*

The book empowers every IC to think bigger, lead with influence, and elevate their technical journey. A must read!

—*Akanksha Gupta, software development manager, AWS—Amazon*

A concise guide that serves as a reminder of how individual contributors can direct their time and energy more intentionally.

—*Shawna Martell, principal engineer, Imprint*

The Effective Software Engineer

How ICs at Every Level Can Leverage AI, Prioritize High-Value Work, and Lead Beyond Their Role

Addy Osmani

O'REILLY®

The Effective Software Engineer

by Addy Osmani

Copyright © 2026 Addy Osmani. All rights reserved.

Published by O'Reilly Media, Inc., 141 Stony Circle, Suite 195, Santa Rosa, CA 95401.

O'Reilly books may be purchased for educational, business, or sales promotional use. Online editions are also available for most titles (*https://oreilly.com*). For more information, contact our corporate/institutional sales department: 800-998-9938 or *corporate@oreilly.com*.

Acquisitions Editor: David Michelson
Development Editor: Melissa Potter
Production Editor: Katherine Tozer
Copyeditor: Liz Wheeler
Proofreader: Laura K. Miller

Indexer: BIM Creatives, LLC
Cover Designer: Susan Thompson
Cover Illustrator: Susan Thompson
Interior Designer: Monica Kamsvaag

February 2026:   First Edition

Revision History for the First Edition

2026-02-11:   First Release

See *https://oreilly.com/catalog/errata.csp?isbn=9798341638174* for release details.

The O'Reilly logo is a registered trademark of O'Reilly Media, Inc. *The Effective Software Engineer*, the cover image, and related trade dress are trademarks of O'Reilly Media, Inc.

The views expressed in this work are those of the author and do not represent the publisher's views. While the publisher and the author have used good faith efforts to ensure that the information and instructions contained in this work are accurate, the publisher and the author disclaim all responsibility for errors or omissions, including without limitation responsibility for damages resulting from the use of or reliance on this work. Use of the information and instructions contained in this work is at your own risk. If any code samples or other technology this work contains or describes is subject to open source licenses or the intellectual property rights of others, it is your responsibility to ensure that your use thereof complies with such licenses and/or rights.

979-8-341-63817-4

[LSI]

Contents

| Preface vii

1 | The Foundations of Effectiveness 1

2 | Understanding the Fundamentals (Junior to Mid-Level Focus) 19

3 | Technical Depth Versus Breadth (Senior+ Focus) 29

4 | Collaboration and Cross-Functional Influence 39

5 | Anti-Patterns That Limit Individual Contributor Effectiveness 47

6 | Career Growth and Leveling Up 73

7 | Leadership as an Individual Contributor 87

8 | Strategic Thinking for Engineers 97

9 | Avoiding Burnout and Sustaining Long-Term Success 107

10 | Team-Level Effectiveness Anti-Patterns 117

11 | Thriving in Modern Work Environments 151

| **12** | The Future of Individual Contributors   167
| **13** | Practical AI for Effective Software Engineers   175
| | A Closing Note on Craft and Humanity   229
| | Index   235

Preface

In software engineering, understanding the difference between *efficiency* and *effectiveness* is crucial. As management consultant Peter Drucker famously said, "Efficiency is doing things right; effectiveness is doing the right things." Ideally, you want to excel at both. This book, *The Effective Software Engineer*, is designed to help individual contributors (ICs) at all levels maximize their impact and effectiveness, not just their output.

We often get caught up in the details of coding, focusing on speed and elegance. However, true effectiveness goes beyond technical skills. It means understanding the bigger picture, prioritizing valuable tasks, collaborating smoothly, and making decisions that align with business goals.

This book is a collection of my years of experience in the software industry, filled with lessons and practical advice. It's intended to be a resource you can revisit throughout your career, providing guidance as you grow.

We'll explore the fundamental skills every effective engineer needs, as well as the strategic thinking and leadership that distinguishes senior and staff engineers. We'll also explore the nuances of team dynamics and the necessity of continuous learning, showing you how to thrive in various environments, including remote settings.

This book is for any software engineer looking to advance their career or thrive in a new role after a promotion. Whether you're a junior engineer just starting out or a seasoned tech lead, I hope it provides valuable insights and actionable strategies to enhance your effectiveness and impact in software development.

Becoming More than Just "Efficient"

Efficient engineers do things right. Effective engineers do the right things. Ideally, do the right things right. This principle, echoing Peter Drucker's wisdom, captures where true expertise lies, and that's the journey we'll explore together.

Let's be honest. As software engineers, we're often obsessed with *efficiency*. We tweak our integrated development environments (IDEs), learn the latest keyboard shortcuts, and strive to write concise, elegant code. We pride ourselves on doing things *right*. And that's important. Nobody wants to work with messy, buggy, or incomprehensible code. Efficiency is table stakes.

> **Note**
>
> When we say "efficient code" in the context of code quality, we typically mean code that performs well computationally. In this book, we're using "efficient" more broadly to describe engineers who work productively—this distinction matters to avoid confusion.

But efficiency, on its own, isn't enough. You can be the fastest, most technically brilliant coder on the planet, churning out perfectly optimized lines of code at a breakneck pace…and still be completely *ineffective*. How? By building the wrong thing.

This book is about *effectiveness*, and the distinction is crucial.

Think about it. Have you ever poured your heart and soul into a project, meticulously crafting every feature, only to have it shelved? Or maybe you built a feature that perfectly matched the initial specs, but nobody used it? Sometimes the initial requirements (*https://oreil.ly/xo3pM*) (which are often better viewed as a starting point for collaboration rather than fixed specifications) changed, or the market shifted, or perhaps the initial problem wasn't even the *real* problem. Even when you've delivered effectively on the requirements given to you, the ultimate outcome can still fall short. That's the sting of ineffectiveness. More than a scheduling issue, this drains the creative energy and potential required to drive real results. While not every ineffective outcome is within your control—sometimes projects are shelved due to top-down organizational decisions—understanding what effectiveness means helps you navigate these situations better.

What Is Effectiveness, Anyway?

Defining "effectiveness" in software engineering can be surprisingly tricky. It's more nuanced, more contextual, and, frankly, more *human* than simple metrics.

At its core, effectiveness is about delivering value. It is about maximizing positive outcomes. It's about ensuring that your efforts, your skills, and your time are directed toward the things that actually *matter* to your team, your company, and, ultimately, your users. This applies whether you're building customer-facing features, maintaining internal tools and platforms, or supporting infrastructure. This value can manifest in many ways:

Solving the right problem
> This might seem obvious, but it's astonishing how often we get caught up in the *how* without fully understanding the *why*. Effective engineers dig deep to understand the underlying need, the root cause, and the desired outcome. They ask "why" thoughtfully—not to be obstructive or overly skeptical, but to ensure everyone is aligned on the problem being solved.

Delivering impactful work
> Not all work is created equal. Some efforts have a massive impact on user engagement, revenue, or strategic goals. Others...don't. Effective engineers can (with the help of their team and stakeholders) prioritize and focus on the work that will move the needle.

Creating sustainable solutions
> Effectiveness isn't just about the short term. It's about building solutions that are maintainable, scalable, and adaptable—what we often call engineering excellence. A quick hack might seem efficient in the moment, but if it creates a mountain of technical debt, it's ultimately ineffective. This doesn't mean over-engineering everything; it means finding the right balance between speed and sustainability for your context.

Collaborating well
> Software engineering is rarely a solo endeavor. Effective individual contributors are also strong team members. They communicate clearly, share knowledge, and contribute to a positive and productive team environment.

Optimizing the environment
> As engineers grow in their roles, effectiveness can also mean improving the broader engineering environment—removing bottlenecks and

optimizing inputs for the team. In practice, this might mean streamlining build pipelines, improving continuous integration/continuous delivery or deployment (CI/CD) reliability, or contributing to internal developer platforms that make everyone more productive. Many organizations now invest in "platform engineering" teams specifically to accelerate software delivery and improve developer experience. This becomes more relevant as you advance, though it's less of an expectation for junior engineers still building their foundational skills.

These principles form the core of an effective engineer's mindset. They guide you to not only solve technical problems, but to solve the right technical problems in a sustainable and collaborative way, which is the central theme we will explore.

The "Right Things Right" Spectrum

The phrase "do the right things right" isn't a binary switch. It's a spectrum, a continuous balancing act. Let's break it down with some examples:

Doing the wrong things wrong
> This is the worst-case scenario. You're not only building something nobody needs, but you're also doing it poorly. For example, building a complex feature that users never asked for, with buggy implementation and no tests. This is where projects go to die.

Doing the wrong things right
> This is the "polished turd" scenario. You've built something beautifully, but it's fundamentally useless. For instance, spending three months building a perfectly architected microservice for a feature that user research shows nobody wants. This is often the result of poor communication, lack of user research, or chasing shiny new technologies without a clear purpose.

Doing the right things wrong
> This is where things get interesting. You're addressing a real need, but your execution is flawed. Maybe the code is buggy, the architecture is unsustainable, or the user experience is clunky. This category also includes the "ship it fast and iterate" philosophy—sometimes the "wrong" execution is actually the right strategic choice when speed to market matters more than perfection. You'll learn from real-world usage and improve iteratively.

The good news is, this is fixable! Improving your technical skills and processes can move you toward the ideal.

Doing the right things right
> This is the sweet spot. You're delivering valuable, high-quality solutions that meet the needs of your users and your organization. This is where you want to be.

This book will provide you with tools, techniques, and mindsets to move you consistently toward that sweet spot—doing the right things right. It will be less about how to write a perfect for loop and more about, for instance, determining when you need a for loop at all.

Why This Book, and Why Now?

The software engineering landscape is constantly evolving. New technologies emerge, methodologies shift, and the demands on engineers continue to grow. In this environment, being *just* a good coder isn't enough. You need to be a strategic thinker and an effective problem solver.

This book is designed to be a practical guide for individual contributors who want to level up their impact. It's not a theoretical treatise; it's a collection of actionable insights, real-world examples, and pragmatic advice drawn from years of experience (and plenty of mistakes!) in the software industry.

What You'll Find Inside

We'll cover a range of topics, all focused on helping you become a more effective engineer:

Understanding the bigger picture
> How to connect your work to the overall goals of your team and organization.

Prioritization and focus
> How to identify the most important tasks and avoid getting bogged down in distractions.

Communication and collaboration
> How to work effectively with your team, stakeholders, and users.

Problem solving and decision making
> How to approach complex challenges and make sound technical choices.

Continuous learning and growth
  How to stay relevant and adapt to the ever-changing world of software.

Long-term value
  How to balance quality with pragmatism and avoid accumulating technical debt.

Resources and templates
  The companion website (*https://effective.addy.ie*) provides practical templates, frameworks, and resources referenced throughout the book to help you apply the concepts immediately.

This book is a starting point, not a destination. Effectiveness is a journey, not a checklist. It's a continuous process of learning, adapting, and striving to make a meaningful difference. Let's begin.

Conventions Used in This Book

The following typographical conventions are used in this book:

Italic
  Indicates new terms, URLs, email addresses, filenames, and file extensions.

`Constant width`
  Used for program listings, as well as within paragraphs to refer to program elements such as variable or function names, databases, data types, environment variables, statements, and keywords.

O'Reilly Online Learning

For more than 40 years, *O'Reilly Media* has provided technology and business training, knowledge, and insight to help companies succeed.

Our unique network of experts and innovators share their knowledge and expertise through books, articles, and our online learning platform. O'Reilly's online learning platform gives you on-demand access to live training courses, in-depth learning paths, interactive coding environments, and a vast collection of text and video from O'Reilly and 200+ other publishers. For more information, visit *https://oreilly.com*.

How to Contact Us

Please address comments and questions concerning this book to the publisher:

O'Reilly Media, Inc.
141 Stony Circle, Suite 195
Santa Rosa, CA 95401
800-889-8969 (in the United States or Canada)
707-827-7019 (international or local)
707-829-0104 (fax)
support@oreilly.com
https://oreilly.com/about/contact.html

We have a web page for this book, where we list errata and any additional information. You can access this page at *https://oreil.ly/the-effective-software-engineer*.

For news and information about our books and courses, visit *https://oreilly.com*.

Find us on LinkedIn: *https://linkedin.com/company/oreilly-media*.

Watch us on YouTube: *https://youtube.com/oreillymedia*.

Acknowledgments

With special thanks to Stephen Covey, Daniel Clifford, Jeff Dean, Titus Winters, Hyrum Wright, Ben Collins-Sussman, Sarah Drasner, Fernando Loizides, Malte Ubl, Timothy Jordan, Richard Seroter and the many engineering leaders who inspire me.

The Foundations of Effectiveness

Software engineering isn't just about writing code; it's about delivering value that matters. In an industry where technical competency is sometimes measured by features shipped, tickets closed, or even by lines of code written (an especially problematic metric, though still used in some organizations), the most impactful engineers distinguish themselves through a fundamentally different approach. They focus relentlessly on solving the right problems and achieving meaningful outcomes, rather than simply maximizing their visible output.

This distinction between effectiveness and efficiency represents one of the most crucial mindset shifts that separates good engineers from exceptional ones. While "productivity" is often used to describe raw output (shipping code quickly), this book focuses on *effectiveness*—achieving meaningful results, not just completing tasks. Throughout this book, we'll explore how this foundational principle applies to every aspect of an individual contributor's career, from writing maintainable code to leading cross-functional initiatives. But first, we must establish what effectiveness truly means and why it matters more than raw output.

The journey toward becoming an effective engineer begins with understanding that our role extends far beyond the technical act of programming. We go beyond simple problem-solving to act as strategic drivers of organizational success. This chapter will provide the conceptual framework that underlies all subsequent chapters, establishing the mental models that effective engineers use to navigate complex decisions and prioritize their efforts.

Outcomes Versus Outputs: Solve the Right Problem

The software industry has a measurement problem. We often celebrate engineers who deliver quickly and frequently—those who close the most tickets, ship the most features, or even contribute the most code. While velocity and consistent delivery are valuable, these metrics capture activity rather than actual impact, fundamentally missing what matters most: whether that work creates meaningful value.

Peter Drucker articulated this principle (*https://oreil.ly/ECu4j*) decades ago when he observed that "there is nothing so useless as doing efficiently that which should not be done at all." In software-engineering terms, you could implement a perfectly architected, thoroughly tested feature that solves a problem no user actually has. Despite the technical excellence, such work contributes minimal value to the organization or its customers.

To put this principle into practice, we must first learn to distinguish between the work we do (outputs) and the results we create (outcomes). While outputs are the tangible deliverables (code, features, documentation), outcomes are the changes in user behavior, business metrics, or system capabilities that result from those outputs. This section will explore this crucial distinction through three lenses: defining what a true outcome looks like, examining real-world examples of impact, and outlining the skills required to consistently align technical work with genuine needs.

UNDERSTANDING TRUE OUTCOMES

Dan North, the originator of behavior-driven development, emphasized this distinction between outputs and outcomes when he noted that "the goal of software development is not to produce stuff, the goal of software development is to impact the business in some way." This perspective reframes every engineering decision through the lens of business and user value.

Effective engineers consistently ask themselves these fundamental questions before, during, and after their work:

Before starting
> Is this the right problem to solve? What evidence suggests this problem matters to users or the business? How does this align with our broader strategic objectives? (While you'll often collaborate with product managers [PMs], designers, and other stakeholders who own these questions,

understanding the answers helps you be more effective in your implementation and helps you identify potential concerns early.)

During execution
How can I validate that this solution addresses the core problem? What's the minimum viable approach that will provide meaningful feedback?

After completion
How will I know this work was successful? What metrics or user behaviors should change as a result?

This outcome-focused approach requires engineers to develop comfort with ambiguity and to actively seek context beyond their immediate technical tasks. It means regularly engaging in cross-functional collaboration with product managers, designers, customer support teams, and even end users to understand the broader ecosystem their code operates within. The goal isn't to second-guess every decision, but to ensure you understand the "why" behind the work so you can make better technical choices and raise concerns when appropriate.

THE SPECTRUM OF ENGINEERING IMPACT

Consider four engineers working on different aspects of an ecommerce platform: *engineer A* spends three weeks building a sophisticated recommendation algorithm that improves product suggestions by 12%. However, after checking with product analytics, they discover the feature is buried deep in the user interface where few customers discover it. Despite the technical achievement, conversion rates remain unchanged. (Note: This could have been directed by leadership or product, but the lack of usage validation still makes it ineffective work.)

Engineer B notices that the checkout process times out frequently during peak traffic periods, causing cart abandonment. They spend two days implementing a simple queue system that reduces timeout errors by 85%. Revenue from completed purchases increases measurably within the first week.

Engineer C identifies that customer support receives hundreds of tickets about users forgetting their passwords. Rather than building a more complex password recovery system, they implement one-click sign-in via existing social media accounts. Support ticket volume drops by 40%, and user satisfaction scores improve significantly.

Engineer D observes that the deployment pipeline is slow and unreliable, causing delays for the entire team. Though there's no direct user request for this maintenance work, they refactor the build process and add better caching.

Deployment time drops from 45 minutes to 8 minutes, and the team can ship fixes and features much faster, ultimately improving their ability to respond to user needs. This illustrates how high-impact work doesn't always come from explicit customer requests—sometimes operational excellence and infrastructure improvements deliver tremendous value.

Each engineer demonstrated technical competence, but their impact varied dramatically. Engineers B, C, and D focused on observable problems with measurable consequences—whether user-facing or internal. Engineer A, while technically sophisticated, worked on something that didn't reflect actual usage patterns. The key takeaway is that effectiveness isn't determined by the complexity of the code, but by the value of the outcome. Engineers B, C, and D were more effective because they delivered simpler solutions that had a direct and measurable positive impact.

Connecting Your Code to User Sentiment

A major challenge for individual contributors (ICs) is understanding the real-world impact of their work. While not yet common practice at many organizations, AI has the potential to bridge this gap by analyzing qualitative user feedback at scale. After you ship a feature or a fix, an AI model could be pointed at sources like support tickets, app store reviews, or social media mentions related to that feature.

Important caveat: Before using AI tools to analyze any company or customer data, always check your organization's data privacy policy and get proper approvals. Uploading proprietary or customer information to unapproved AI services could expose your company to significant risk and potentially violate confidentiality agreements or data protection regulations.

In organizations with the proper infrastructure in place, AI can perform sentiment analysis to answer questions like: "After the v2.1 release, did user sentiment regarding the checkout flow improve?" or "What are the most common frustration keywords associated with the new dashboard?" This automates the tedious task of sifting through hundreds of user comments, providing a clear, data-driven link between your engineering output (the feature) and the business outcome (improved user satisfaction). This helps you and your team prioritize future work based on what truly matters to users.

DEVELOPING PROBLEM-SOLUTION ALIGNMENT

Effective engineers develop an intuitive sense for problem-solution alignment—the degree to which their technical work addresses genuine user or business needs. This skill emerges through deliberate practice in several areas:

Customer understanding
> Regularly interacting with user feedback, support tickets, and analytics data to understand how people actually use the software. This might involve sitting with customer support representatives, reviewing user session recordings, or conducting informal user interviews.

Business context
> Understanding the economic model, competitive landscape, and strategic priorities that drive product decisions. Effective engineers can articulate how their technical contributions connect to revenue, cost reduction, or market positioning. Learn about competitors by reviewing their engineering blogs, exploring their public APIs and documentation, examining their product roadmaps, and conducting product comparisons to understand how your system stacks up.

Data literacy
> Developing comfort with metrics, A/B testing, and experimental design to validate assumptions and measure impact. This doesn't require advanced statistical knowledge, but rather a habit of seeking evidence over intuition.

Collaborative curiosity
> Actively engaging with cross-functional partners to understand their perspectives and constraints. Product managers, designers, sales teams, and support representatives all possess insights that can inform better technical decisions.

The common thread connecting these engineers and skills is a shift in perspective. Instead of seeing their role as simply implementing technical specifications, effective engineers see themselves as partners in solving business and user problems. They cultivate the curiosity and context needed to question assumptions, validate impact, and ensure their technical efforts are directed at goals that truly matter. This proactive, outcome-oriented approach is the first and most critical step toward becoming a truly effective engineer.

While focusing on outcomes rather than outputs provides the foundation for effectiveness, truly impactful engineers must also develop the ability to think strategically about their work's broader implications.

Thinking Beyond Tasks: Long-Term Impact

While solving the right immediate problems provides the foundation for effectiveness, truly impactful engineers also develop the ability to think strategically about their work's broader implications. This requires expanding your time horizon beyond the current sprint or quarter to consider how today's decisions will affect future capabilities, team velocity, and system maintainability. Cross-functional collaboration plays a critical role here—working closely with your product manager, designers, and team members helps shape the engineering foundation and ensures technical decisions align with broader product strategy.

UNDERSTANDING SYSTEMIC CONSEQUENCES

Every line of code you write becomes part of a larger system that will evolve over months and years. Effective engineers consider not just whether their current solution works, but how it will interact with future changes, scale with increased usage, and enable or constrain future development.

This long-term thinking manifests in several practical ways:

Architecture with evolution in mind
> Designing systems that can gracefully accommodate new requirements without requiring complete rewrites. This doesn't mean over-engineering for hypothetical future needs, but rather building with clean interfaces and avoiding tight coupling that makes change difficult.

Documentation and knowledge sharing
> Creating clear explanations of design decisions, trade-offs, and assumptions that will help future developers (including yourself) understand and modify the system. Good documentation improves team maintainability and velocity, as engineers don't need to reverse-engineer decisions from code alone. This includes both formal documentation and informal knowledge transfer through code comments, design documents, and team discussions.

Technical debt management
> Recognizing when short-term expedient solutions create long-term maintenance burdens, and advocating for periodic investment in system health.

Effective engineers can articulate the business case for refactoring, improved testing, or architectural improvements in terms of future development velocity and system reliability.

Mastering these prioritization skills transforms an engineer from a passive task-executor into a strategic partner. It is this judgment—the ability to look beyond the immediate backlog and invest effort where it will generate the most long-term value—that truly distinguishes an effective engineer.

STRATEGIC PRIORITIZATION IN PRACTICE

Effective engineers don't just accept task assignments passively; they actively participate in shaping their team's priorities based on their unique technical perspective. This requires developing judgment about which efforts will yield the highest long-term return on investment (ROI).

Consider these common prioritization scenarios that effective engineers navigate skillfully:

Balancing new features with system health

When product managers push for rapid feature development, effective engineers can articulate when technical investments are necessary to maintain a sustainable development pace. They present these arguments in business terms, showing how current technical debt slows future feature delivery or increases operational costs.

Choosing depth over breadth

Rather than trying to contribute to every project, effective engineers often achieve greater impact by focusing deeply on fewer initiatives. They develop expertise in critical system components and become trusted advisors for complex technical decisions in their area of focus.

Proactive problem identification

Instead of waiting for issues to become urgent, effective engineers monitor system health, user feedback, and team productivity to identify emerging problems before they become critical. They bring potential solutions to leadership rather than simply flagging problems.

THE COMPOUND EFFECT OF QUALITY

One of the most profound ways engineers create long-term impact is through consistent attention to code quality, testing, and maintainability. While these practices may slow initial development, they create compound benefits that accelerate future work.

Quality-focused engineers understand that software systems are living entities that evolve continuously. A codebase with comprehensive tests enables confident refactoring and rapid iteration. Well-documented APIs reduce integration time for new team members. Clear architectural patterns make it easier to add new features without introducing bugs.

The challenge lies in balancing quality investments with delivery pressure. Effective engineers develop intuition for when quality shortcuts are acceptable (prototypes, time-sensitive fixes) versus when they create unacceptable long-term costs (core business logic, frequently modified code paths).

Ultimately, thinking beyond immediate tasks is about stewardship. Effective engineers recognize that they are not just building features for today, but are also contributing to a system that must live, adapt, and serve users for years to come. By balancing immediate needs with long-term system health, strategic prioritization, and a commitment to quality, they create a foundation that enables sustained velocity and impact for the entire team. This long-term perspective is a defining characteristic that separates good engineers from great ones.

Productive Versus Effective: A Comprehensive Framework

While we all want to be productive, in software engineering, it's important to shift our focus toward being *effective*. After all, we can produce a lot that's not ultimately benefiting our organizations. To make the distinction between productivity and effectiveness more concrete, consider how these different approaches manifest across various aspects of software engineering work. Understanding these patterns helps engineers recognize when they're optimizing for the wrong metrics and adjust their approach accordingly:

Feature development comparison

Productive approach: Accept feature requirements at face value and implement them exactly as specified. Focus on completing the work quickly and moving to the next task. Measure success by meeting deadlines and matching acceptance criteria.

Effective approach: Engage with product managers and designers to understand the underlying user problem. Propose alternative solutions that might better address the core need. Question requirements that seem misaligned with user data or business objectives. Measure success by user adoption and business impact.

Bug-fixing strategies
> *Productive approach*: Fix the immediate symptoms quickly to resolve user-reported issues. Focus on getting tickets out of the backlog and maintaining high closure rates.
>
> *Effective approach*: Investigate root causes to prevent similar issues from recurring. Consider whether bugs indicate deeper architectural problems or gaps in testing strategy. Use bug patterns to identify areas where preventive investments would reduce future maintenance burden.

Code review philosophy
> *Productive approach*: Provide quick feedback focused on obvious errors and style issues. Approve changes rapidly to avoid blocking other developers' progress.
>
> *Effective approach*: Use code reviews as opportunities to share knowledge, identify potential architectural issues, and ensure changes align with long-term system goals. Balance thoroughness with development velocity based on the risk and complexity of changes.

Learning and skill development
> *Productive approach*: Focus primarily on tools and technologies directly relevant to current assignments. Learn new skills reactively when specific needs arise.
>
> *Effective approach*: Develop both deep expertise in core areas and broad awareness of adjacent technologies and business domains. Invest time in understanding user needs, business context, and emerging industry trends that might influence future technical decisions.

To help identify whether you're operating in a productive or effective mode, regularly ask yourself questions in the following domains:

Impact measurement
> Can I articulate the specific user or business value my recent work has created? Do I have evidence that my contributions have made a measurable difference?

Problem ownership
> Do I understand why the problems I'm solving matter to users and the business? Have I questioned whether the solutions I'm building address the root causes?

Future implications
> How will my current technical decisions affect the team's ability to develop and maintain this system six months from now? Am I creating or reducing complexity?

Collaborative engagement
> Am I actively participating in cross-functional discussions about product direction and technical strategy? Do my colleagues view me as a trusted advisor for technical decisions in my areas of expertise?

Learning trajectory
> Am I developing skills and knowledge that will enable me to tackle increasingly complex and impactful problems? Is my learning aligned with the evolving needs of my team and organization?

This framework isn't meant to suggest that productivity is unimportant. Deadlines are real, and delivering work is essential. Instead, it serves as a diagnostic tool. By regularly asking these questions and comparing your actions against these patterns, you can identify when you might be defaulting to an output-focused "factory" mode. Recognizing these moments is the first step toward consciously shifting your approach to one that prioritizes lasting, meaningful impact.

Building an Effectiveness Mindset

Transitioning from a productivity-focused to an effectiveness-focused approach requires more than intellectual understanding—it demands developing new habits, communication skills, and mental models for evaluating your work. This transformation often challenges conventional wisdom about what makes engineers valuable to their organizations.

CULTIVATING STRATEGIC THINKING

Effective engineers operate with a broader context than their immediate technical tasks. They understand their company's business model, competitive position, and strategic objectives well enough to make informed decisions about technical trade-offs and prioritization.

This strategic awareness develops through several practices:

Regular business context gathering
   Schedule periodic conversations with product managers, sales teams, and customer support representatives to understand how technical decisions affect business outcomes. Subscribe to company-wide communications and attend all-hands meetings to stay informed about organizational priorities.

Industry awareness
   Follow relevant industry publications, attend conferences, and participate in professional communities to understand broader technological and market trends that might influence your company's technical strategy.

Competitive analysis
   Understand how your company's technical capabilities compare to competitors. This knowledge helps inform architectural decisions and identify opportunities for technical differentiation. Start by reading your competitors' engineering blogs, reviewing their public APIs and documentation, analyzing their product roadmaps (from press releases or investor documents), and discussing with your product team what features customers often compare against competitors.

Customer journey mapping
   Develop a detailed understanding of how users interact with your systems, including pain points, workflow patterns, and success metrics. This knowledge enables you to prioritize technical improvements that meaningfully impact user experience.

The key takeaway is that shifting from productivity to effectiveness requires moving beyond the code and actively cultivating a strategic mindset. By consistently gathering business context, staying aware of the industry, and deeply understanding the customer journey, an engineer transforms from a simple implementer of tasks into a valuable partner who can make informed decisions that align technical work with broader organizational success.

DEVELOPING INFLUENCE WITHOUT AUTHORITY

As an individual contributor, your ability to drive effective outcomes often depends on influencing decisions and priorities without formal authority over other team members. This requires developing strong communication skills and building credibility through consistent delivery and strategic thinking.

Effective engineers build influence through several approaches:

Technical credibility
Consistently delivering high-quality solutions that work reliably and maintainably. When you have a strong track record of good technical judgment, others are more likely to trust your recommendations about priorities and approaches.

Clear communication
Presenting technical concepts and trade-offs in language that nontechnical stakeholders can understand. This includes translating technical complexity into business terms and helping others understand the implications of different technical decisions. For learning resources on clear technical communication, consider books like *The Pyramid Principle* by Barbara Minto (Pearson Education) for structuring arguments or courses on business writing for engineers.

Collaborative problem solving
Engaging with cross-functional partners as peers rather than service providers. Rather than simply implementing specifications, effective engineers participate in problem definition and solution design discussions.

Data-driven advocacy
Supporting recommendations with evidence from user analytics, system metrics, and business data. When you can show concrete evidence that supports your technical opinions, stakeholders are more likely to adjust priorities accordingly.

Ultimately, influence is the currency of effectiveness for an individual contributor. By combining technical credibility with clear, collaborative, and data-informed communication, engineers can shape decisions and guide their teams toward more impactful outcomes, ensuring the best ideas win, regardless of where they originate.

MANAGING EFFECTIVENESS AT DIFFERENT CAREER STAGES

The application of effectiveness principles evolves as engineers progress through different career levels, but the core focus on outcomes over outputs remains constant. I introduce these career levels here because the scope of an engineer's influence and the complexity of the problems they face change over time. An early-career engineer demonstrates effectiveness by delivering well-defined work, while a senior engineer does so by shaping strategy across teams. As you move forward through this book, I will occasionally reference these levels to highlight how certain skills, such as mentorship or architectural design, become more critical at different stages. This framework will help you identify the specific capabilities you need to develop to increase your impact as you grow in your career:

Early career (junior to mid-level, ~0–3 years)
> Effectiveness often means asking clarifying questions about requirements, proposing simpler solutions that address core user needs, and learning to estimate and communicate about technical trade-offs. Junior engineers can demonstrate effectiveness by preventing over-engineering and ensuring their work integrates smoothly with existing systems.

Mid-level (established contributor, ~3–5 years)
> Effectiveness expands to include technical leadership within project teams, identifying architectural improvements that enable future development, and mentoring junior team members. Mid-level engineers often serve as bridges between senior technical leadership and implementation teams.

Senior+ (experienced leader, 5+ years)
> Effectiveness involves driving technical strategy across multiple teams, identifying and solving complex organizational problems, and representing engineering perspectives in business strategy discussions. Senior engineers are often responsible for the long-term health and capability of large technical systems.

Throughout this progression, the fundamental principle remains the same: focus on solving important problems well rather than simply completing tasks efficiently. The key takeaway is that growth is not just about deepening technical skills, but about expanding the scope of your effectiveness, from a single task, to a project, to the long-term health of entire systems and the organization itself.

Developing an effectiveness mindset is an active, ongoing process. It involves moving from being a passive task-taker to an active problem-solver who understands the business, communicates clearly, and builds trust across functions. While the specific application of these skills may change as you advance in your career, the underlying principle of leveraging your technical expertise to influence broader outcomes remains the key to growing your impact.

Measuring and Developing Effectiveness

Unlike productivity metrics, which are often straightforward to quantify, effectiveness requires more nuanced measurement approaches. Developing these assessment capabilities helps engineers self-regulate their focus and demonstrate their value to organizations in meaningful ways.

PERSONAL EFFECTIVENESS METRICS

Why track your effectiveness? Because what gets measured gets improved. Personal metrics help you identify patterns in your impact, make informed career decisions, and communicate your value during performance reviews and promotion discussions. Unlike vanity metrics (lines of code, tickets closed), effectiveness metrics focus on outcomes that matter to your team and organization.

Effective engineers develop personal systems for tracking their impact beyond simple task completion. These might include the following:

Business impact tracking
> Maintain records of how your technical contributions affected user behavior, system performance, or business metrics. For example: "Implemented lazy loading for images → reduced page load time from 3.2s to 1.1s → increased mobile conversion rate by 8%." Use a simple spreadsheet or note-taking app with the following columns: Date, Project, Technical Change, Measured Impact, and Business Outcome. This might involve tracking conversion rates before and after your changes, monitoring error rates and performance improvements, or documenting user feedback related to your work.

Knowledge sharing impact
> Measure how your documentation, mentoring, and technical guidance affects team productivity and capability. This could include tracking how frequently your documentation is referenced, monitoring the success of engineers you mentor, or assessing whether architectural patterns you establish get adopted across the organization.

Problem prevention
> Document issues you identified and addressed before they became critical, including technical debt reduction, security improvements, and performance optimizations that prevented future problems.

Cross-functional collaboration success
>Track the quality of your relationships and communication with product managers, designers, and other stakeholders. For example, measure things like the following: How often do PMs proactively seek your input on requirements? Do designers ask you to review prototypes before full implementation? Have you received positive feedback like "Your explanation helped me understand the technical trade-offs" or "You flagged that edge case early, saving us two weeks of rework"? Track instances where your collaboration prevented problems or accelerated decisions.

These personal metrics are not for performance reviews; they are for self-awareness. They help you build a narrative of your work centered on impact, enabling you to articulate your value and intentionally focus your efforts on activities that truly matter.

ORGANIZATIONAL CONTEXT AND FEEDBACK

Effectiveness cannot be assessed in isolation—it requires understanding how your contributions fit within broader organizational needs and priorities. Regular feedback gathering from multiple sources provides essential context for calibrating your efforts. These sources could include the following:

Manager feedback
>Regular one-on-one discussions about strategic priorities, long-term career development, and opportunities to increase impact. Effective engineers use these conversations to align their individual efforts with team and company objectives.

Peer feedback
>Input from other engineers about code quality, technical leadership, and collaborative effectiveness. This feedback often reveals blind spots and opportunities for improvement that aren't visible from individual work.

Cross-functional feedback
>Insights from product managers, designers, and other collaborators about your communication effectiveness, problem-solving approach, and strategic thinking. This feedback helps engineers understand how their technical perspective contributes to broader product and business decisions.

Downstream feedback
> Feedback from teams that depend on your work, like site reliability engineering, operations, customer support, and customer success. They experience the operational reality of your code—is it observable, debuggable, resilient? Support teams can tell you if your features are intuitive or generate confusion. This feedback is invaluable for understanding the full lifecycle impact of your work.

User and stakeholder impact
> When possible, solicit direct feedback from users or internal stakeholders about how your technical contributions have affected their experience or capabilities.

The central theme here is that effectiveness is not self-defined; it is validated by the ecosystem around you. Actively seeking and integrating feedback from these varied sources provides a 360-degree view, ensuring your work remains aligned with the broader needs of the team, the business, and your users.

CONTINUOUS IMPROVEMENT PRACTICES

Effectiveness is not a destination but rather a capability that requires ongoing development and refinement. What this looks like varies by experience level: junior engineers might focus on building consistent coding and communication habits, while senior engineers work on strategic influence and architectural thinking. Regardless of level, successful engineers establish systematic practices for improving their effectiveness over time:

Regular reflection
> Periodic assessment of recent work to identify patterns in what created significant impact versus what consumed time without meaningful results. This might involve monthly or quarterly reviews of completed projects and their outcomes.

Experimentation mindset
> Treating different approaches to prioritization, communication, and technical decision making as experiments to be evaluated based on their results. This includes being willing to adjust strategies that aren't producing desired outcomes.

Skill gap analysis
> Regularly assessing which capabilities would most improve your ability to drive meaningful outcomes and creating development plans to address those gaps. A simple formula for this might be to create three columns: Current Skills, Target Role/Impact, and Gap to Close. For example, if you want to lead architectural decisions, you might identify gaps in distributed systems design, technical writing for requests for comments (RFCs), or presenting to senior leadership. This might include technical skills, business knowledge, or communication abilities. (See the book's companion website (*https://effective.addy.ie*) for a skill gap analysis template.)

Network and mentorship
> Building relationships with more experienced engineers who can provide guidance on strategic thinking, career development, and effectiveness improvement. Learning from others' experiences accelerates your own development.

Measuring and developing effectiveness is a journey of self-awareness and intentional practice. Unlike counting tickets or lines of code, it requires a qualitative and holistic view of your contributions. By creating personal systems for tracking impact, actively seeking multi-faceted feedback, and committing to continuous improvement, you transform effectiveness from an abstract concept into a tangible, career-defining skill.

Setting the Foundation for Advanced Skills

This focus on effectiveness provides the conceptual foundation for all the advanced skills we'll explore in subsequent chapters. Whether you're mastering technical fundamentals, developing cross-functional influence, or leading complex initiatives, the principle of prioritizing meaningful outcomes over visible activity will guide your approach.

In Chapter 2, we'll examine how effectiveness principles apply to core engineering practices like code quality, testing, and documentation. Chapter 3 will explore how to balance technical depth and breadth to maximize your long-term impact. Chapter 4 covers collaboration and cross-functional influence. Chapters 5 and 6 address anti-patterns and career growth. Chapter 7 explores leadership as an IC, including the ethical considerations and responsibilities that come with technical influence.

Throughout this journey, remember that becoming an effective engineer is ultimately about developing the judgment and skills to consistently solve important problems well. This requires technical competence, strategic thinking, collaborative ability, and a persistent focus on creating value for users and organizations.

The engineers who advance to senior levels and drive significant organizational impact are those who master this balance between technical excellence and strategic effectiveness. They write great code not as an end in itself, but as a means to deliver meaningful value. They collaborate effectively not to be well-liked, but to ensure their technical perspective contributes to better product and business decisions.

As you progress through the remaining chapters of this book, carry this effectiveness mindset with you. Let it guide your decisions about which skills to develop, how to prioritize your efforts, and how to measure your success as an individual contributor. The specific techniques and strategies will evolve with your career, but this fundamental orientation toward creating meaningful impact will remain your most valuable asset.

Understanding the Fundamentals (Junior to Mid-Level Focus)

Early in your career (typically corresponding to junior and mid-level roles, sometimes designated as L3–L4 in large tech companies, or roughly zero to four years of experience, depending on the organization), effectiveness comes from technical excellence and good engineering habits. By understanding fundamental skills—writing clean code, debugging effectively, testing, using version control, and basic design—you set yourself up to deliver reliably and learn faster. This chapter covers those basics and why they matter.

Clean, Maintainable, and Readable Code

Code is read far more often than it's written. You or someone else will maintain this code for years. If it's sloppy or unclear, that maintenance will be slow and error-prone. Clean code—code that is easy to understand, modify, and maintain—is a force multiplier because it accelerates everyone who works with it. Clean code creates a transparent environment where bugs are obvious and development velocity remains high for everyone on the team. The term "clean code" was popularized by Robert C. Martin (Uncle Bob) in his influential book of the same name (*Clean Code* [Pearson]), and refers to code that reads almost like well-written prose.

Characteristics of clean code include the following:

Clarity

Use meaningful names (functions, variables). Write code that others (and future you) can understand without needing deep domain knowledge or extensive context. When you do add comments, focus on explaining *why* rather than *what*—the code itself should show what it does. If you have to add a comment explaining what a section of code does, consider rewriting that code more clearly or extracting a well-named function instead.

Simplicity

Follow KISS—*keep it simple, silly*. Don't use an elaborate pattern if a straightforward loop suffices. Avoid premature generalization. Solve the problem at hand; resist adding YAGNI (*you aren't gonna need it*) features. Simple code is easier to understand, test, and debug. Complexity should only be introduced when it solves a real, present problem. Simplicity matters because simple code has fewer places for bugs to hide, requires less documentation, and allows new team members to become productive faster. When faced with a choice between a clever solution and a simple one that both work, choose simple every time.

Consistency

Adhere to team style guides and conventions. Consistency reduces cognitive load because engineers know what to expect. Google's guides say, "On matters of style, the style guide is the absolute authority." It's better to be consistent than to have your personal ideal style everywhere.

Refactorability

Strive for code structure that allows change. This includes the *single responsibility principle* (each component has one job) and minimizing tight coupling. If adding a new feature requires touching 10 unrelated files, that's a sign the code isn't clean. Clean code is modular and organized logically.

Your AI-Powered Pair Programmer for Clean Code

Writing clean code is a fundamental skill, and AI tools now act as a real-time pair programmer to help you build this habit. Modern code editors with integrated AI, like GitHub Copilot, do more than just autocomplete; they can be configured to learn from your team's style guides.

As you type, modern AI tools can suggest variable names that align with existing conventions, refactor a complex block of code into a cleaner, more readable function, or even automatically generate documentation and comments that explain what your code does. Beyond inline autocomplete, agent-based AI tools (like Claude, GitHub Copilot Chat, and Google Gemini) enable iterative, collaborative code improvement through conversation. Think of these as automated code review assistants that help catch issues before you even commit. This frees up human reviewers to focus on higher-level logic and design, while the AI helps maintain cleanliness and consistency.

Here are some good practices to adopt now:

Follow core design principles.
Principles like *single responsibility* (each component has one job), *high cohesion* (related code stays together), and *loose coupling* (minimize dependencies between components) help create maintainable code. SOLID principles from object-oriented programming can be useful guidelines, though focus on the broader goal: making your code easy to understand and modify. SOLID is an acronym for five object-oriented design principles: single responsibility, open/closed, Liskov substitution, interface segregation, and dependency inversion. These principles aim to create maintainable, flexible, and scalable software by guiding how classes and modules should be structured. Applying them helps reduce coupling and increase cohesion, and makes code easier to understand and extend. Some specific SOLID principles may feel less relevant in modern architectures like microservices or functional programming, but the underlying ideas of clarity and modularity remain valuable.

Eliminate dead code and fix "todos."
Leaving junk in the codebase accumulates "code debt," which can confuse or trip up future work. When you spot it, address it, or at least flag it clearly.

Learn your language's idioms.
Write Pythonic Python, not Java-ish Python, etc. Code that leverages language features well is often clearer and more concise.

Let's take a look at a clean code example: Suppose you have some complicated conditional logic that's hard to follow. This often signals underlying complexity in your business logic or state model. A junior might write it all in one giant `if` block with complex conditions. A cleaner approach might be to break it into multiple well-named functions that make the logic explicit, or `if/else` sections with explanatory condition names. However, if you find yourself with truly complex conditional logic, consider whether the underlying model can be simplified—sometimes the best solution is to address the root cause rather than just reorganizing the code.

Clean code leads to fewer bugs (since it's easier to reason about and spot errors), faster onboarding of new team members (they can read and grasp code quickly without extensive explanation), and more agility (making changes doesn't require untangling complex dependencies). These benefits compound over time—what saves 10 minutes today might save hours or days for your team down the road. As a junior, building a habit of leaving code better than you found it will serve you throughout your career and make you a valued team member.

Testing and Quality Mindset

Early-career engineers sometimes see testing as a chore. But establishing a quality mindset now will save you so much pain later. Effective engineers don't just get things working; they ensure things stay working. There are a few things you can do to ensure quality.

First, write tests for your code. If your team doesn't have a strong testing culture, be the change. Start with basic *unit tests* (tests that verify individual functions or components in isolation) for critical logic. When feasible in your codebase, use *integration tests* (tests that verify multiple components working together) to ensure key flows work end-to-end—though recognize that adding integration tests to an existing codebase can be challenging and may require architectural support. Aim for a good balance of coverage without going overboard (100% test coverage isn't a goal unto itself because not all code is equally critical, and some code, like simple getters/setters, adds little value when tested; focus on testing important business logic, edge cases, and error conditions).

You can also use AI assistants to help generate initial test scaffolding or suggest edge cases you might have overlooked. For example, after writing a function, you might ask an AI tool to propose test scenarios—but treat these as starting points, not finished tests. You still need to review the suggestions, ensure they match your requirements, and verify the tests actually catch bugs. AI-generated tests are a time-saver for boilerplate, not a replacement for thoughtful test design.

Testing is beneficial as it does the following things:

Prevents regressions
    You know if something you change breaks old functionality immediately.

Facilitates refactoring
    If you have a safety net of tests, you can improve code structure with confidence.

Documents intent
    A test shows examples of how code is supposed to work. Future readers can see, "Ah, given input X, we expect Y," without digging into the implementation.

Next, automate what you can. Learn how to run tests locally and in your continuous integration (CI) pipeline. If running the test suite is burdensome, discuss with your team about speeding it up or splitting tests to run in parallel. Engineers often skip tests if they're slow or flaky. Investing time to fix that is high leverage.

Quality is not just about tests; it's also about code reviews and static analysis:

Code reviews
    Embrace them (Chapter 4 covers collaboration, including reviews). As a junior, you'll learn tons from feedback. Over time, you'll also sharpen your ability to spot issues in others' code (and thus in your own).

Linters/static analysis
    These tools catch common mistakes (unused variables, possible null dereferences, style issues). Examples include ESLint for JavaScript, Pylint for Python, and RuboCop for Ruby. Use them! They offload trivial bug-catching from your brain so you can focus on more complex problems.

Lastly, we need to talk about bug fixing. When you do encounter bugs (and you will), adopt a practice: whenever you fix a bug, add a test case to cover it if possible. This prevents that bug from sneaking back. It's a quick way to continuously improve your test suite based on real-world scenarios.

Time spent testing is paid back many times over by time *not* spent debugging issues in production or fighting fires at midnight. As a less experienced engineer, you might worry that writing tests slows you down. In truth, it speeds up the *whole team* over the project life. It also builds your reputation as someone whose code is solid.

Consider two engineers who both deliver features at the same pace initially, but one writes tests. Three months later, that engineer's features have far fewer issues and are easier to extend, so they're now delivering faster (not being bogged down by maintenance), while the other engineer is stuck fixing old bugs. Quality is a long-term speed boost.

> **Tip**
>
> Treat your test code with the same care as production code—use clear naming, avoid copy-paste, and keep tests maintainable. Poorly written tests become a maintenance burden rather than an asset.

Version Control and Debugging Discipline

Version control and debugging discipline might seem like separate topics, but they boil down to being systematic and disciplined, key traits of effective engineers.

VERSION CONTROL (E.G., GIT)

The most transformative habit you can develop with version control is thinking of commits as storytelling. Each commit should tell a clear, focused story about one change to your codebase. Consider adopting conventional commit formats (like `feat:`, `fix:`, `docs:`), or use your team's commit message style guide to make your history even more readable. When you commit early and often with logical, self-contained changes, you're not just saving your work; you're creating a historical narrative that future developers (including yourself) can follow. The difference between "Add search API" and a massive commit that also refactors three unrelated functions is the difference between a clear chapter in a book and a confusing jumble of plot threads.

Your commit messages are love letters to your future self. Six months from now, when you're using `git blame` to track down a mysterious bug, you'll either thank yourself for writing "Fix off-by-one error in pagination logic (index should start at 0)" or curse yourself for "Fix stuff." The extra 30 seconds to write a descriptive message can save hours of archaeological work later. Think of it as documentation that travels with your code.

Fluency in git features like branches, rebasing, and `git revert` provides the safety net required to code without fear, turning complex version control into a reliable foundation. The certainty of recovery gives you the freedom to refactor and innovate boldly. This psychological safety is the defining trait of engineers who push boundaries.

The real magic happens when things go wrong and you need to use version control's debugging features like `git bisect` (which works similarly in other version control systems like Mercurial, Fossil, and Perforce). This tool can pinpoint exactly which commit introduced a bug by doing a binary search through your history. But it only works well if your commits are small and focused. Each commit becomes a potential debugging checkpoint, which is why disciplined version control practices pay dividends during crisis moments when you need to find problems fast.

DEBUGGING

Debugging is fundamentally detective work, but too many engineers approach it like archaeology—digging randomly and hoping to stumble upon artifacts. The most effective debuggers I know treat it as a scientific discipline. They start by gathering evidence: What are the exact symptoms? Can you reproduce the problem consistently? What changed recently? This systematic approach prevents the wild goose chases that can consume entire afternoons.

Modern engineers can even leverage AI assistants for debugging—inputting error logs or stack traces into tools like ChatGPT to hypothesize potential causes. Used wisely, these can accelerate the evidence-gathering phase, though you still must verify all suggestions through testing. The same scientific approach applies: clear symptoms in, useful insights out.

The scientific method isn't just for laboratories; it's your debugging superpower. Form a specific hypothesis like "I think the authentication token is expiring before the API call completes" rather than vague hunches like "something's wrong with the login." Then design tests to prove or disprove that hypothesis. Use logging strategically, set targeted breakpoints, or write a quick unit test that isolates the suspected component. This methodical approach feels slower initially, but it's actually far more efficient than the scatter-shot debugging that many developers default to.

Your relationship with debugging tools—debuggers, profilers, browser dev tools—determines how much time you spend in frustration versus a flow state. Every minute you spend learning keyboard shortcuts, understanding call stacks, or mastering conditional breakpoints is an investment that pays compound interest. The engineers who seem to have a sixth sense for finding bugs aren't actually psychic; they've just automated the mechanical parts of debugging so they can focus their mental energy on the logical puzzle-solving.

DOCUMENTATION AND NOTE-TAKING

The most undervalued debugging skill is externalized thinking through notes. When you're deep in a complex bug, your working memory fills up quickly with hypotheses, test results, and dead ends. Writing down what you've observed and tested isn't just a good practice; it's cognitive offloading that frees your brain to see patterns and connections you might otherwise miss. I've seen experienced engineers solve problems simply by reviewing their debugging notes and noticing something they'd overlooked.

When you discover those peculiar environment quirks or system gotchas, documenting them is an act of engineering consideration for your teammates. That weird Secure Sockets Layer (SSL) certificate issue that took you two hours to figure out? The next developer who encounters it shouldn't have to retrace your entire investigative journey. A simple comment in the code or a wiki entry transforms your hard-won knowledge into team knowledge. This documentation—written while the solution is fresh—is what separates good engineers from great ones: great engineers optimize for the team's collective efficiency, not just their own immediate productivity.

Strong version control means fewer lost changes, easier collaboration, and quickly identifying which commit introduced a bug. A disciplined debugging approach means less time stuck and fewer "I have no idea what's happening" moments. Together, these fundamentals ensure you spend more time coding features and less time dealing with self-inflicted problems or floundering with broken code.

Documentation and Communication (Even as a Junior)

You might think documentation is something only senior folks worry about, but that's a misconception—engineers at all levels, including junior engineers, are expected to produce high-quality documentation, especially in larger tech companies. In fact, documenting while learning is one of the best ways to solidify your understanding. Building good documentation habits now will amplify your effectiveness:

- Write down key decisions or assumptions about your code (in code comments or team docs). This helps future maintainers (which could be you in six months).

- If you find the onboarding docs or runbook lacking as you ramp up, volunteer to improve them while the experience is fresh. This not only helps others, but forces you to solidify your understanding.
- Communicate early if you are stuck or if requirements seem fuzzy. Asking good questions is a strength, not a weakness. It prevents working hard on the wrong thing.

Remember, being easy to work with is part of being effective. If you write amazing code but nobody understands it or you never share how to run it, the value is diminished. Clear code, clear tests, clear docs, clear communication—these fundamentals create a foundation so that as you take on bigger challenges, you do so with confidence and the support of your team.

By understanding how to write clean code, ensure quality, use tools effectively, and communicate clearly, you set yourself apart as a reliable engineer. These skills might not be as flashy as designing an entire system or inventing an algorithm, but they enable you to eventually do those bigger things successfully. Moreover, they boost team productivity and trust in your work, which accelerates your growth opportunities. Invest in good habits now; they'll pay dividends throughout your career.

Once you have a firm grasp of these fundamentals, your career growth will depend on new strategic considerations, such as balancing the depth and breadth of your technical knowledge, which is what we'll cover in Chapter 3.

| 3

Technical Depth Versus Breadth (Senior+ Focus)

As you grow into a senior engineer role (typically five or more years of experience, sometimes designated as L5 and above in large tech companies), you'll face a strategic career question: should you develop deep expertise in a particular domain or maintain broad knowledge across many areas? The reality is that effective senior ICs often need both depth *and* breadth—they complement each other. This chapter explores how to balance becoming an expert in something (depth) with staying versatile and informed (breadth), and how each contributes to designing scalable systems and managing technical debt.

The Value of Depth: Becoming an Expert

When you reach senior engineer level and beyond, having at least one area of deep expertise dramatically increases your impact. Depth means the following:

- You understand the intricate details and nuances of a technical domain (e.g., databases, machine learning, frontend frameworks, distributed systems). While some engineers also develop deep expertise in business or product domains, this chapter focuses on technical depth.
- You can solve complex problems in that domain faster and more elegantly than others because you've seen many patterns and pitfalls.
- You can mentor others in this area and lead major projects related to it.

A deep expert can often provide what's colloquially known in the industry as 10x value in that specific area. Kate Matsudaira (a respected engineering leader) wrote that while broad skills are useful, "it is important to go deep in at least one area, and it is almost always better to hire people who have a solid depth of experience in the tools and technology they are using." In other words, teams benefit greatly from having go-to experts—be one of those. You can look at this as a three-step process:

1. *Choose a specialty*: By mid-career, notice what technology or domain you gravitate toward or what the company needs:
    - Perhaps you find performance optimization fascinating—dive into algorithms and become the performance guru.
    - Or you love data and analytics—become the data engineering expert who designs efficient pipelines.
    - Maybe security is neglected at your company—learning it deeply could make you indispensable.

   Sometimes your specialization picks you (through project assignments or a critical problem that needs solving). Other times, you pick it (because you see high demand for a skill and it's interesting to you). Both paths are equally valid—what matters is developing genuine expertise rather than surface-level familiarity.

2. *Commit to depth*: Depth requires continuous learning. Read books, take advanced courses, attend conferences or meetups in your domain. Work on challenging problems in that field, even if as side projects. Depth often comes from solving many variations of a problem. *An expert has failed before and so can avoid mistakes, and if there's a library or prebuilt code, they are probably aware of it.* That comes from exposure and experience.

3. *Leverage your depth*: Once you have deep knowledge, use it:
    - Lead design reviews in your domain.
    - Volunteer or advocate to take on projects in that space.
    - Mentor colleagues wanting to learn it.
    - Write internal docs or give tech talks to spread that expertise (this not only helps others but also reinforces your own knowledge).

Depth not only makes you more effective (you can handle the hardest issues in that domain), it also builds your reputation. At promotion time, it helps to be known as "the person who figures out our hardest scaling problems" or "the go-to database performance expert." That kind of brand often aligns with senior/staff expectations (leading technically, influencing others).

The Importance of Breadth: Being Versatile

Breadth means having a working knowledge of multiple domains, technologies, or parts of the stack. While you might not be the deepest in each, you understand how they fit together. This breadth proves invaluable because software systems are inherently complex, involving many interconnected components, such as where a frontend change might affect the backend, or a database choice might impact UI capabilities. When you have breadth, you can foresee these interactions and design more holistically, preventing the tunnel vision that afflicts deep specialists who lack broader perspective.

For example, consider a database expert with narrow focus investigating a slow-loading page. They might immediately dive into query optimization, adding indexes and tweaking SQL. However, an engineer with breadth might recognize that the page is making 50 separate database calls that could be batched, or that a simple Redis cache could eliminate 90% of the database hits entirely, or even that the UI is requesting unnecessary data that could be lazy-loaded. Breadth opens your eyes to multiple solution angles, often allowing you to find simpler and more effective approaches than doubling down on a single domain.

This wider perspective becomes especially critical in technical leadership roles at the staff level and above, where you need to arbitrate between teams and review designs across different tech stacks. Your breadth enables you to contribute meaningfully across many contexts, bridging conversations between specialists who might otherwise talk past each other. People often describe this as being "T-shaped"—deep in one thing (the vertical bar) while broad across many (the horizontal bar). Your deep skill might evolve over time, or you might even develop multiple areas of depth, but maintaining breadth remains essential.

As Gergely Orosz noted in interviews (*https://oreil.ly/d41_Q*) about his podcast *The Pragmatic Engineer*, broad-skilled engineers often find more opportunities and face less career risk because they can adapt as technology changes or business needs shift. On the job, this breadth allows you to bridge between teams during feature discussions, suggesting solutions like "If the frontend does X, we could simplify the backend logic, which might be easier overall." You can pick up tasks outside your main area of expertise when needed, making you invaluable in pinch situations, and you can empathize with other engineers' challenges, improving collaboration in situations like when you understand why frontend caching might be tricky or why the mobile team is concerned about battery drain.

Developing Breadth

An early career often gives you breadth by necessity through varied tasks, but even as you specialize, allocate time to stay aware of adjacent areas. If you're a backend expert, learn frontend framework basics. If you're a machine learning (ML) specialist, understand the software engineering needed to integrate models into production. Learn the vocabulary and key concerns of other areas. You don't need to code a mobile app from scratch, but know terms like "async storage" or "view lifecycle" if your backend supports mobile clients. Work cross-functionally sometimes: pair with a site reliability engineer (SRE) on deployment issues, or shadow a product manager in user research. Breadth includes understanding not just technical domains but the broader context of building products, which makes you a stronger individual contributor because you can anticipate non-code constraints and needs.

Designing for Scale: Applying Depth and Breadth

One of the hallmarks of senior engineers is designing systems that scale in terms of performance, maintainability, and team ownership. Doing this well requires both depth (to know how to optimize and design robust components) and breadth (to see the whole picture and how components interplay). Here's a simple way to think about it: depth is knowing a lot about something, and breadth is knowing something about a lot of things.

SCALING SYSTEMS (TECHNICAL DEPTH)

Let's say you're tasked with scaling an architecture 10x. Depending on the area of focus, depth of knowledge will make it easy for you to recognize solutions:

- For databases, maybe you need to partition (shard) or add read replicas. You know the queries to optimize or the indexing strategy because you've seen similar problems before.

- For backend services, you recognize a CPU-bound service where adding threads or switching to async could increase throughput, or perhaps you identify where vertical scaling hits a limit, and it's time to move to horizontal scaling with load balancers.
- For web apps, maybe you implement caching or content delivery networks (CDNs) effectively, or split the app by domain (micro-frontends).

Your deep knowledge helps you understand how to best fix the specific bottleneck within your domain—the optimal indexing strategy, the right caching approach, or the appropriate concurrency model.

Accelerating Architectural Decisions with AI-Driven Research

Making sound architectural decisions requires evaluating multiple potential solutions, a process that can involve hours of research for engineers at all levels. AI can drastically speed up this discovery phase, increasing developer velocity by handling mundane, repetitive information-gathering tasks. Instead of manually searching for articles and documentation, you can task a large language model (LLM) with the research:

> **Prompt:** *Compare and contrast using a message queue (like RabbitMQ) versus a streaming platform (like Kafka) for an ecommerce order processing system. Summarize the key trade-offs in terms of scalability, latency, and data persistence. Provide links to two case studies for each.*

The AI can synthesize information from countless sources in minutes, presenting a structured summary of the pros and cons. This doesn't replace the engineer's critical thinking—you still need your depth of experience to evaluate the trade-offs in your specific context. But it handles the routine work of information gathering, allowing you to spend your time on the high-impact task of making the right design choice.

SCALING THE TEAM/CODEBASE (BREADTH)

Breadth helps engineers design the system to be worked on by many engineers without conflicts. Here are a few examples:

- You break the system into clear modules or services (and since you understand each part's basics, you set good boundaries). This prevents a monolithic ball of mud that only you could navigate.
- You consider frontend needs while designing the API, maybe creating more granular endpoints to avoid one mega-endpoint becoming a choke point for all development.
- You involve SREs early, understanding deployment pipelines, so the system is designed with proper observability (logs/metrics/traces). In smaller companies without dedicated SRE or quality assurance (QA) teams, you handle these responsibilities yourself, making this breadth even more critical. A narrow-minded coder might omit that, focusing only on functionality, but your breadth reminds you that maintainability in production is crucial.

Effective scale design often requires trade-offs: e.g., "Should we denormalize the database to reduce expensive joins, at the cost of some redundancy?" Depth helps engineers analyze the performance trade-off; breadth helps them consider impacts on data integrity and multiple app features that use the data.

For example, a staff engineer with deep performance knowledge might identify that the database is the bottleneck and propose introducing a caching layer (depth: knowing how to implement caching correctly). Their breadth allows them to realize the cache will introduce eventual consistency issues that will affect how the frontend renders data (so they coordinate with frontend engineers on a loading state UX to handle slightly stale data). They also consult with the data analytics team to ensure the cache doesn't hide data updates they rely on. The result is a solution that scales (addressing technical concerns) and works well across all uses (addressing broad context).

This balance of depth and breadth not only makes you a better architect but also a more effective collaborator, capable of influencing decisions across teams—a skill we will explore in the next chapter.

Managing Technical Debt: Depth Versus Breadth Perspective

Technical debt is inevitable, but how you manage it will distinguish you as an effective senior engineer. Here, depth helps you see *where* code or design is suboptimal and how to fix it properly; breadth helps you judge *when* to pay debt down based on overall priorities.

Ward Cunningham coined the debt metaphor (*https://oreil.ly/ROeMR*): "Shipping first time code is like going into debt…The danger occurs when the debt is not repaid. Every minute spent on not-quite-right code counts as interest on that debt." Senior engineers have a sense of that interest accumulating.

Depth can help you identify and fix debt. With deep experience, you recognize code smells and pitfalls:

- "This module has grown huge and difficult to change; it's a refactoring candidate."
- "We're copy-pasting code in multiple services (cut corners to deliver fast). If we abstract that into a shared library now, it'll reduce bug fixes by half."
- Deep knowledge of design patterns might tell you that introducing, say, an event-driven approach could simplify what is now tangled logic.

Because of your expertise, you can plan a debt paydown effectively (rather just deleting stuff blindly). You also know what debt is tolerable versus truly hazardous. For instance, you might say "Yes, we have some global variables in that script [debt], but it's a build tool only used by two people—interest is low. But the tightly coupled auth and user modules are causing lots of bugs—interest is high; let's address that first."

Breadth helps you align debt work with business needs. It reminds you to consider the bigger picture. Here are some examples:

- You weigh if a rewrite will delay features the business really needs (sometimes living with some debt is OK if it's not hurting much right now).
- You communicate to nonengineers in their terms. Instead of "Module X is ugly code," you say "Module X's code debt is causing every new feature to take two times longer (impacting our ability to roll out improvements)."
- You look at cross-team benefits: maybe cleaning up a core service will accelerate many teams, making it easier to justify than a cleanup in an isolated corner.

- You coordinate debt work with other roadmap items: perhaps you convince PMs to let the team spend one sprint on "engineering health" tasks. To do so, you articulate how this sprint of cleanup will make the following quarter of feature dev smoother.

Let's look at an example: A senior engineer sees that the code handling payments is very brittle (lots of quick patches done during a rushed launch). They have deep knowledge of robust payment systems from a prior job, so they know exactly how they'd redesign it (depth). But they don't just start refactoring in a vacuum. Using breadth, they note upcoming plans to add new subscription options. Doing the redesign first will actually enable those features to be built faster. They present a plan: spend two weeks refactoring the payment module (paying down debt) which will reduce bugs (important for finance) and make new pricing models easier to implement. They also acknowledge that an ongoing marketing promotion means no changes can be deployed for one week (breadth: awareness of business calendar), so they schedule the deployment carefully around that. The debt is addressed with minimal disruption and clear value.

In sum, to be effective at higher levels, cultivate *T-shaped skills*: one or a few areas of true technical depth where you excel, plus a broad understanding across the tech stack and business context. Depth makes you a powerful problem solver and authority; breadth makes you a wise architect and collaborator. Together, they enable you to design systems that are technically sound and fit-for-purpose and to make strategic decisions about where to focus your (and your team's) engineering efforts for maximum benefit.

How to Decide on Depth/Breadth Investment

Start by going deep in one area that aligns with your interests and your team's needs—this gives you credibility and a foundation. As you grow, gradually expand your breadth by working on adjacent systems, attending architecture reviews outside your domain, and asking questions during cross-team discussions. The balance shifts over time: junior engineers benefit from going deep first to build expertise; mid-level engineers start expanding breadth while maintaining depth; senior and staff engineers continuously refresh both, letting some depth areas fade as new ones emerge based on organizational priorities. You never truly stop learning in either dimension—the key is being intentional about where you invest your learning time based on career goals and current gaps.

Developing a T-shaped profile—balancing deep expertise with broad versatility—provides you with the raw capability to solve complex engineering problems and design robust systems. However, in a senior role, identifying the "right" technical solution is often only half the battle; the other half is convincing the organization to build it. Your technical leverage is ultimately multiplied—or limited—by your ability to communicate, align, and collaborate with others. As we move from individual expertise to organizational impact, the focus shifts from how you interact with code to how you interact with people.

Chapter 4 explores the essential soft skills required to make your hard skills matter, detailing how to influence stakeholders, partner with product teams, and drive technical consensus without formal authority.

| 4

Collaboration and Cross-Functional Influence

No matter how technically skilled you are, your effectiveness is limited if you can't work well with others. Software is a team sport. As an IC, especially at senior levels, you often need to influence decisions without having formal authority. This chapter covers how to collaborate with key roles (PMs, designers, managers) and how to gain influence across teams.

Working Effectively with Product and Design

Great products emerge from close collaboration between engineering, product management, and design. Cross-functional collaboration with product managers (who own product strategy and roadmap) and designers (who own user experience and interface) is particularly critical for effective engineers. Yet sometimes engineers and PMs/designers can feel at odds—engineering wanting simplicity/tech purity, PMs/design wanting more features or a pixel-perfect UI. Effective engineers bridge that gap. To do so, and to foster a strong partnership, effective engineers adopt several key practices:

Understand the "why" behind requirements.
    Don't just take a task from your ticket tracker and execute blindly. Ask your product manager what user problem a feature is solving, or what metric it aims to move. This context lets you make smart trade-offs during development. For example, if you know a feature is an experiment to see if engagement increases, you might build it in a scrappy way to test quickly

(knowing it'll be thrown out if it fails). If it's core to the business, you might invest more in robustness.

Bring technical insight to product discussions.

PMs own *what* and *why*, but you own *how*. It's your job to surface technical constraints or opportunities. For example, "We can implement variant A in two days, but variant B will take two weeks due to backend complexity" or "We have an existing service that almost does this—if we tweak it, we can get this feature with 10% of the effort." This shapes product decisions with reality. Good PMs appreciate this input because it helps them weigh the ROI. It's part of influencing without authority—they decide, but your information influences their decision.

Be solution-oriented.

If a PM asks for something that seems technically infeasible or very hard, don't just say, "No, can't be done." Explain *why* and work with them on alternatives. Maybe, "We can't deliver real-time search results at our scale easily, but we can update every five seconds, which I think achieves the same user benefit." Or, "Doing X will cause latency issues; what if we try Y approach, which I can do faster and might fulfill the need?" This turns a potential conflict into a collaboration. You're essentially doing product brainstorming with an engineering lens.

Respect the constraints of each domain and educate one another.

Sometimes PMs or designers may not understand why something that seems small (change field validation rules) is actually complex (because it touches several systems). Take time to educate them on the technical side. Conversely, try to understand basic UX or business principles so you can appreciate why a seemingly trivial UI change ("just make that button blue") might be important for conversion or branding. When each side appreciates the other's challenges, cooperation improves.

Get involved early.

Try to get involved in the ideation phase, not just after specs are done. Talk to your PM and ask to participate in planning or design sprints. Many organizations support this via sprint planning or including engineers in design sprints. Early involvement means you can steer solutions toward technically feasible ones (saving time) and you understand context better (leading to a better implementation).

Be reliable and communicative.
Deliver on promises so PMs/designers trust you. If something slips, let them know *early* so plans can adjust. This builds your credibility, so when you later say, "We should do X, not Y," they trust your judgment.

Influencing product direction as an IC.
As you become senior, you might see product directions that concern you (perhaps adding a feature that will increase tech debt significantly). Use your influence by providing data or prototypes to sway decisions. For example, build a quick proof-of-concept to show an alternate (better) approach, or gather data on system limits to show why a proposed feature might break something. This is influencing without authority—you're not the PM, but you can drive the group toward a better outcome using evidence and reasoning.

Getting Up to Speed with AI-Generated Document Summaries

Effective cross-functional collaboration requires understanding documents from other domains, like long product requirements documents (PRDs) or detailed user research findings. Instead of spending an hour reading a 20-page document, an engineer can use an AI tool to get the gist in minutes.

Simply feed the document into an LLM and ask for a summary tailored to your needs.

> **Prompt:** *Summarize this PRD from an engineering perspective. Focus on the core user problems to be solved, the key features required, and any stated technical constraints or performance goals.*

The AI extracts the most relevant information, allowing you to walk into a planning meeting already understanding the context and goals.

> **Warning**
>
> Always verify critical details by scanning the original document—AI summaries can miss nuances or misinterpret technical constraints. Use summaries for initial understanding, then dive deeper into sections that matter most for your implementation. This automates the pre-reading and synthesis, freeing you up to use the meeting for high-value discussion and problem solving with your PM and designer counterparts.

Influencing Without Authority: Leading as an Individual Contributor

As a senior IC, you're expected to exhibit leadership, often over things and people you don't directly control. How do you cause changes or rally people when you're not "in charge"? Here are a few suggestions:

Build trust through competence and understanding.

People listen to those who have proven they know their stuff and who consider others' perspectives. If you consistently produce good work, help others, and credit your teammates, you'll develop a reputation. Then, when you speak up with a suggestion or concern, people take it seriously. This trust is your informal authority.

Identify key stakeholders and understand their motivations.

Say you believe the team should invest in a new infrastructure tool. Stakeholders might include your manager (concern: team output), a PM (concern: feature timeline), and other engineers (concern: learning curve, coolness of tech). To influence them:

1. With your manager, frame it as "This will enable us to deliver features more quickly in the long run/reduce operational burdens" (tie to their goal of productivity).

2. With the PM, "Doing this now will reduce bugs and maintenance on feature X, so we won't be distracted when we try to scale to more users next quarter" (tie to reliability for upcoming launch).

3. With peers, maybe appeal to technical merit: "This addresses the pain points we've all felt with the current system, and it's a chance to learn a modern tech many of us are interested in."

By aligning the benefits of your proposal with what each stakeholder cares about, you make it a win for them.

Use data and prototypes.
As noted in earlier chapters, evidence is powerful. Instead of saying "I think we should refactor this," you might demonstrate that refactoring a small piece improved performance by 30%, implying doing more will yield gains. Or if you want to adopt a new library, maybe create a sample integration to show that it's feasible and solves a problem. Now you're not asking people to take your word on faith—you have proof of concept.

Lead by example.
If you want to change the team's process (say, add code reviews or improve documentation), start doing it yourself in a helpful, nonjudgmental way. Others often follow suit, especially if they see it working well. For instance, start writing design docs for your own features; when others see how it helped catch issues early and made implementation smoother, they may try it, too. It's much easier to influence behavior by *doing* than by just telling.

Mentor and build goodwill.
Influence often comes from people respecting and liking you. Take time to help others—mentor a junior, assist a teammate stuck on a bug (even if it's not "your responsibility"). This creates goodwill. People are naturally more inclined to go along with suggestions from someone who has helped them in the past. (This isn't manipulation; it's just human nature and building positive team culture.)

Pick your battles and be willing to compromise.
If you object to everything or are rigid, people will start to tune you out. Save your influencing capital for things that matter. And sometimes you won't get your way—that's OK. Support the decision and make it succeed if possible. This will show you're a team player, not just pushing an ego agenda, which in turn gives more weight to your future inputs.

Use communication skills.
The key to influence is communicating clearly and persuasively. Structure your arguments; use visuals if helpful (draw architecture diagrams of both options for comparison); speak confidently but listen to concerns. Consider taking an influencing or negotiation workshop if offered—these skills can be learned. For improving business writing and structured communication, resources like *The Pyramid Principle* by Barbara Minto (Prentice Hall) or business writing courses can help you craft more compelling arguments.

Let's look at an example: imagine you're a senior engineer convinced the codebase needs a major refactor to support new features. Even without authority, you can take some actions likely to influence the outcome:

1. Write a brief document outlining the current problems (with data: e.g., "Feature A took four weeks due to intertwining logic; similar feature at my last company with better separation took one week").
2. Propose a phased refactor plan that allows delivering user value in parallel (so the PM is less scared).
3. Show a small refactor you did in one module that already cut its code size in half and reduced one class of bugs to zero (proof it works).
4. Discuss it one-on-one with a few teammates to incorporate their feedback and quietly get allies ("What do you think of this approach?").
5. Then present to the team and manager collectively, focusing on how it benefits everyone (less on how it's *your* idea, more on "our code will be easier to work with, we all hate how hard feature X was...This will help").

Chances are, you'd successfully influence the team to undertake the refactor. This is leading as an IC—seeing a needed change, and rallying people to pursue it, through persuasion, not command.

Managing Up: Collaborating with Management

The term *managing up* means proactively working with your manager to align on goals, communicate progress, and build a strong working relationship. This is a crucial skill for ICs, as it helps you gain the trust and autonomy needed to be truly effective.

For junior engineers, this often starts with clear communication and a proactive approach to seeking feedback. For senior engineers, it evolves into a more strategic partnership focused on influencing team priorities and direction.

Here are several ways ICs at all levels can practice managing up effectively:

Communicate proactively.
> Keep your manager in the loop on progress and issues—don't make them chase you for status updates. If you foresee a deadline slip, tell them early (with a plan to mitigate, if possible). This builds trust; they know you won't let them be blindsided.

Understand your manager's goals.
Is your manager concerned about team velocity? System stability? Hitting a key deadline? If you know their pressures, you can tailor your influencing tactics accordingly (as above) and choose where to spend extra effort. For example, if stability is a big worry, you might prioritize that refactoring story that improves reliability. Show that you consider their priorities. This effectively "manages up" by making your manager's job easier (they don't have to nag you to do the important but unglamorous things).

Ask for feedback and act on it.
Show your boss you're trying to grow. Managing up isn't just about getting your way; it's about forging a good working relationship. If they suggest you improve in some area (e.g., "I'd like you to involve the new engineer more in design"), do it. Then let them know the positive results ("I paired with Alex on the API design; she picked it up quickly and delivered ahead of time"). Now your manager sees you as low-maintenance and someone who "gets it." That often means they'll give you more influence naturally (because they trust your judgment).

Make your manager's life easier.
In many ways this sums it up. Senior ICs often informally do "tech lead" duties: coordinating tasks among the team, resolving minor disagreements without manager involvement, mentoring juniors. When you do this, you're managing up by handling things at your level that otherwise the manager might have to step into. Then you can approach your manager not with problems, but with solutions or well-analyzed options. For example, instead of saying, "The team disagrees on approach X," you say "The team was split on X, so we did a quick proof-of-concept and found Approach A is more performant, so we're going with that unless you object." Most managers will say "Great!" and appreciate you taking leadership.

Respect boundaries and chain of communication.
Part of managing up is knowing when to escalate something versus handling it yourself, and understanding your manager's style. Some managers like detailed daily updates; others prefer you run with things and just notify them on major events. Adapt to their style. This, again, fosters a smoother relationship.

If your manager respects and trusts you, they'll often advocate for your ideas higher up or let you run with experimental projects. Building this trust means you can influence team priorities while avoiding becoming a "yes-person" who simply agrees with everything—the goal is a constructive partnership where you bring data and context to help make better decisions together. If they constantly worry about you or have to course-correct for you, they'll be more hesitant to endorse your innovative suggestions (because they're not confident those suggestions will pan out). Essentially, being in sync with management gives you leverage to push for bigger changes while maintaining your independent judgment.

Collaboration and influence are at the heart of an IC's role, especially as you become more senior. Technical skill might get you to mid-level, but beyond that, leadership and teamwork skills determine a huge part of your effectiveness. By learning to work well with PMs/designers, to lead peers without formal power, and to manage upward, you amplify the impact of your technical talents. These are skills that turn a good engineer into a *great* one within an organization. After all, the most brilliant code solves nothing if it isn't integrated into a product people use—which takes working with others. Effective ICs embrace that and excel at it.

By honing these collaborative skills, you amplify your effectiveness. However, even skilled engineers can fall into habits that undermine their impact. In Chapter 5, we'll explore common anti-patterns that limit an IC's effectiveness and how to avoid them.

| 5

Anti-Patterns That Limit Individual Contributor Effectiveness

Even smart, hardworking engineers can fall into habits that undermine their effectiveness. This chapter will shine a light on common *anti-patterns* that can affect engineers at different career levels, and how to avoid them. While some patterns, like knowledge silos, can emerge at any level, others, like over-engineering and delegation challenges, are more common as engineers gain seniority (mid-level to senior), and visibility issues often become critical when pursuing staff-level roles.

The anti-patterns we'll explore include the following:

- Knowledge silos and code hoarding
- Hero complex ("white knight syndrome")
- Over-engineering versus YAGNI (pragmatism over perfection)
- Inability to delegate (bottlenecking yourself)
- Poor communication and visibility (invisible work)
- Analysis paralysis (overthinking without action)
- Not-invented-here syndrome (rejecting external solutions)
- Perfectionism and gold-plating (never shipping)
- Context-switching addiction (lack of deep focus)
- Scope creep enablement (the inability to say no)

- Technical debt denial (ignoring system health)
- Meeting overload (time mismanagement)
- Feedback resistance (closed to input)
- Tool obsession (chasing shiny objects)
- Imposter syndrome paralysis (fear-driven inaction)

Studies like those from Code Climate (*https://oreil.ly/9EjNS*) have shown that addressing knowledge-sharing practices alone can increase development productivity by 50%. Recognize any of these patterns in yourself? It's OK—we all have blind spots. But addressing them can supercharge your impact and your team's success.

Knowledge Silos: Share What You Know

One engineer becomes the sole authority on a piece of code or a domain such as the build system, payment logic, or legacy infrastructure. They might guard that territory, whether intentionally due to a job security mentality or unintentionally because they lack time to document or teach. Information isn't shared, and a *knowledge silo* forms around critical systems.

This pattern creates significant problems for team effectiveness. If only one person knows how something truly works, that component becomes a bottleneck. The team slows down whenever work touches that area. The *bus factor* is a risk measurement technique that determines how vulnerable a project is to losing key team members. The term is a humorous and dark metaphor for how many people could be "hit by a bus" (or leave the team for any reason) before a project stalls or fails. The bus factor in this case drops to one, meaning if the expert is sick or leaves, the team is stuck. It also burdens that person with all bugs and questions in that area, often leading to stress or burnout.

Using AI-Powered Repository Analysis to Detect Knowledge Silos

Knowledge silos are often invisible until a key person goes on vacation. AI-powered engineering intelligence platforms can make these risks visible by analyzing your version control history. These tools can automatically scan your codebase contributions over time to identify which engineers are the sole or primary contributors to critical modules.

The AI can generate a "bus factor" report, highlighting parts of the system where knowledge is not well-distributed. For example, it might flag: "The 'billing-service' has had 95% of its commits authored by a single engineer in the past six months, indicating a potential knowledge silo." This transforms a vague team concern into a concrete, data-backed insight, allowing your team to take proactive steps—like scheduling pair programming or documentation sessions—to distribute that knowledge before it becomes a problem.

ANTI-PATTERN SIGNS

You often hear phrases like, "Oh, Alice owns that, you'll have to ask her" or "We avoid changing that part; it's Dave's baby." In code reviews, only one person can meaningfully review certain code because nobody else understands it. Team members route all questions about specific systems to the same individual.

For engineers who find themselves as the knowledge holder, letting go can feel deeply uncomfortable. There's often an identity crisis when you stop being the go-to person in a given area. This discomfort is natural but also a sign of growth. While it can feel unsettling to share your specialized knowledge, it's worth celebrating this transition as it represents your evolution from individual contributor to team enabler.

REMEDY

Sharing knowledge scales your impact far beyond what hoarding ever could. Effective engineers make themselves more valuable by spreading knowledge, not by hoarding it. If you find yourself in a silo, start by writing documentation, or at least high-level README files about that component—what it does, how to work with it, and common troubleshooting steps.

Onboard a backup person by pairing with a teammate on a few tasks in that area so they learn the ropes. For example, next time a bug comes in, instead of just fixing it yourself in an hour, pair program with another engineer for two hours so they learn the system. Encourage code reviews from others by explaining the code patiently. It takes longer initially, but it trains the team and prevents future interruptions.

If you feel you don't have time to document or teach, realize that every time you answer a one-off question or fix something alone, that's actually more time wasted long-term. Teaching once prevents answering fifty questions later.

CULTURE FIX

Teams can combat silos through frequent rotation of ownership areas during sprints and establishing rules that at least two people must be familiar with any given system. Some organizations implement knowledge-sharing sessions where domain experts present their areas to the broader team, creating multiple backup experts over time.

BENEFIT

Sharing knowledge makes you more indispensable, not less. When you enable five other engineers to work in an area, you free yourself to tackle new challenges and become the person who builds teams, not just code. Management recognizes this as a leadership trait, often rewarding it in performance reviews and promotion decisions.

The "Hero" Complex: Don't Be the Lone Savior

An engineer repeatedly steps in to "save the day" through heroic efforts—pulling all-nighters, single-handedly fixing critical bugs at the last minute, owning every major issue personally. They may enjoy the recognition of being the savior, and the team and managers might even praise them initially. However, this "white knight" anti-pattern creates a culture of dependency and burnout.

This pattern damages team dynamics in multiple ways. The hero becomes a single point of failure, similar to knowledge silos but focused on high-pressure situations. It often signals systemic issues—why are emergencies cropping up that need heroics? Is planning inadequate? Are others being shut out of complex work? The pattern discourages teamwork, as others may think, "Why bother, the hero will swoop in anyway," leading to learned helplessness or lack of growth opportunities. Eventually, the hero themselves will burn out, as consistent crunch time is unsustainable.

ANTI-PATTERN SIGNS

One person is always on pager duty, officially or unofficially. Firefighting is consistently done by a small subset of go-to people. Team retrospectives—recurring meetings where teams reflect on recent work—mention, "We're relying too much on X." The hero figure resists delegating critical work, believing only they can handle it properly.

REMEDY

Spread the load and the knowledge rather than maintaining hero culture. If you notice yourself doing heroics, ask whether each crisis could have been prevented by better planning or technical debt resolution earlier, then advocate for those changes going forward.

Next time there's a late-night bug, invite another engineer to join the troubleshooting call. You not only share the burden but train them, breaking the habit of "only I fix things." This mentoring approach builds team capability while distributing the load. Push for sustainable practices like proper on-call rotation, monitoring systems that catch issues during working hours, and post-mortems that help the team learn from emergencies and share knowledge of solutions.

Manage expectations with leadership. If projects are consistently scoped so tightly that only heroics meet deadlines, bring data showing overtime hours logged and quality impacts. Sometimes you need to negotiate with cross-functional partners and say, "We can't meet that date with high quality without crunch. How about we trim scope or adjust the timeline?" It's scary to push back, but good leaders will listen, and this builds trust and demonstrates leadership that's more sustainable than repeated crisis management.

CULTURE FIX

If your team has a hero but it's not you, encourage knowledge transfer rather than always leaving the toughest tasks to them. Volunteer for challenging work, asking for their guidance. This converts hero culture into mentor culture. Celebrate team successes in retrospectives and team communications. Individual heroics should be acknowledged as symptoms of team dysfunction that need addressing, rather than celebrated as ideal behavior—the goal is building resilient teams, not creating dependency on individuals.

BENEFIT

A team without hero syndrome is more resilient and less stressed. Work becomes predictable rather than firefighting-driven. You avoid burnout and become a leader who enables others rather than overshadowing them. Leadership recognizes this sustainable approach as more valuable than sporadic heroics.

Over-Engineering: When More Isn't Better

An engineer designs an elaborate, future-proof solution for a problem that doesn't yet exist, or builds an overly generic framework when a simple function would suffice. The code is super clever—maybe too clever—and hard for others to understand. Engineers might also implement performance optimizations in parts of the system that aren't bottlenecks.

This pattern wastes effort and creates maintenance burdens. Time spent building complexity that isn't needed could have been spent delivering features or fixing known issues. Over-engineered solutions have more code and more abstraction layers, thus more potential bugs and more difficulty in onboarding new developers. While you spend extra weeks making something super configurable for future scenarios that may not happen, users aren't getting value from delayed features. Complex systems often have hidden bugs or performance issues of their own, while simpler code is easier to reason about and test.

ANTI-PATTERN SIGNS

Design documents or pull requests are pages long for seemingly straightforward tasks. Teammates often ask, "Why are we adding this complexity? Do we need it now?" The engineer justifies their work with, "I'm just considering future requirements," but those requirements are speculative. Code reviews frequently have "This is very hard to follow" comments, or the style is overly abstract, with many patterns layered on top of each other.

REMEDY

Embrace pragmatism and incremental design by practicing YAGNI. Build what is needed now, with the ability to extend later if needed, but don't overbuild today. For example, don't implement multi-tenancy until you have a plan to add a second tenant.

If you're worried about future changes, leave a comment or small hook rather than fully implementing unused flexibility. Use iterative development by delivering a simple solution, then refining if requirements indeed expand. Often, by the time they do, you'll have more information to make a better design anyway.

Seek feedback early in design reviews by explicitly asking, "Am I over-engineering this?" Encourage peers to call it out. Time-box research and development or fancy optimizations. If you think a complex approach might be worth it, prototype it within a fixed time; if no clear benefit emerges, revert to simpler approaches.

CULTURE FIX

Teams can establish design review practices that specifically evaluate complexity versus current needs. Some organizations use complexity budgets or require justification for abstractions beyond immediate requirements. Regular code reviews should include discussions about whether solutions are appropriately scoped to current problems.

BENEFIT

Simpler systems are easier to maintain and extend in reality, even if they're theoretically less "powerful." By focusing on present needs, you deliver value faster. The team can understand your work, so others can contribute, preventing knowledge silos. You also free up time for other impactful work instead of polishing features users might never appreciate.

Inability to Delegate: The "I'll Just Do It Myself" Trap

A senior engineer personally tackles almost every critical task, even ones that could be done by others. They may say, "It's faster if I do it," or they don't trust others to do it right. They keep control over implementation details when they could empower a junior team member. Essentially, they become a bottleneck, and the team's growth is stunted because one person hoards the challenging work.

This pattern creates multiple problems. You become overloaded and frustrated that you're doing "all the work." Team members miss learning opportunities, so the bus factor for critical skills stays low. As projects scale, one person can't do everything, so either quality slips or deadlines slip, or both. Morale suffers as others feel relegated to less interesting tasks, so they disengage or don't develop, which leaves more work on your plate—creating a vicious cycle.

An African proverb states: "If you want to go fast, go alone. If you want to go far, go together." Early on, going alone might seem fastest, but in a team environment, enabling others is how you scale up output over time.

ANTI-PATTERN SIGNS

You often say or think, "I'll just handle this, it'll be done quicker." You rarely delegate even small tasks. You feel stress from having too much to do but also feel uncomfortable letting anyone else handle critical pieces. Teammates stop volunteering for hard tasks because they assume you will take them over anyway.

REMEDY

Shift from a pure doer to a coach and leader mindset as you become senior. Start small with delegation by having a less-experienced engineer implement part of a feature. Let them do it their way, within reason, and resist the urge to rewrite it for them. Code review it and give suggestions, but allow them to incorporate the feedback. Observe that often they do fine, even if it's not exactly how you would have done it.

Use pair programming if you struggle to let go completely. This approach shares knowledge and lets you guide quality without taking over. Empower through guidelines rather than micromanagement. Instead of doing all the important coding, share your vision and standards with the team so others can execute to that standard. Design the module interfaces, then let a teammate fill in the implementation.

Remember that growing others is part of your job as a senior engineer. Your output is not just the code you personally write, but how the whole team performs. Delegating and mentoring can multiply the team's output. Manage perfectionism by accepting that 90% right and done by someone else plus freeing you up is often better than 100% right but only you can do it.

CULTURE FIX

Create an environment where delegation is viewed as a development opportunity rather than dumping work. If you're buried in tasks, communicate with your manager: "I have too much on my plate; I'd like to hand off X to someone else so I can focus on Y." That's not weakness; it's prioritization. Managers want you working at a sustainable pace on the most important things, and delegating some tasks could be an opportunity for a junior that the manager can frame as growth.

BENEFIT

When you delegate effectively, you multiply your impact. Instead of completing five tasks in a week, maybe you do two and mentor three others to each complete one. End result: five tasks done, plus three teammates got stronger. Long term, those teammates handle similar tasks independently, and you can take on bigger challenges or multiple projects as a technical leader.

Lack of Visibility: Make Your Work Known

You quietly do excellent work, but you don't communicate it effectively. Maybe you don't write status updates or talk about your accomplishments. You assume people notice what you delivered, but in the busyness of a company, they don't. You have low visibility, which creates risks for both your career and project success.

This pattern creates several problems. Decisions about project direction or promotions may overlook your contributions because decision makers aren't aware of them. It can lead to duplicated work or misunderstandings if others aren't aware of what you accomplished. During performance reviews, you may struggle to recall or compile your achievements because you didn't track them along the way.

ANTI-PATTERN SIGNS

In meetings, someone suggests building something you already implemented, indicating they weren't aware of your work. You feel underappreciated or that others take credit, but realize you never documented or announced what you achieved. Your manager is surprised by project details during reviews because you didn't inform them earlier.

REMEDY

Increase the visibility of your work in a factual, professional manner. Share updates by posting short messages in a team chat or status emails when you finish significant tasks. For example: "Deployed the new caching mechanism today—seeing approximately 40% reduction in load on the database. This should make things snappier." This keeps the team and stakeholders informed and associates the achievement with you and your collaborators. For more senior or complex work, consider setting up one-on-ones with senior engineers and technical leaders to share your work and advocate for its importance.

Write down accomplishments by keeping a personal achievement journal, even in bullet point format. It's much easier to refine these notes during review time or when updating your resume. Share these highlights with your manager in one-on-one meetings, as good managers will communicate these successes up the chain.

Demo your work by taking advantage of demo days or sprint reviews to show what you built. People remember visual demonstrations and associate them with you. If your team doesn't have these, propose a casual lunch-and-learn where you can showcase tools you wrote that others could use.

COMMUNICATION FIX

Address concerns about self-promotion by focusing on tone and facts. Stick to what you did and why it matters, such as "Implemented an automated test generator, which cut bug regression by approximately 30%," rather than "I'm a rockstar coder and I built a brilliant test system." The first approach presents truth and impact in an appropriate, professional manner.

Remember that visibility is not vanity; it's ensuring your work has the influence it should have. Invisible work often goes unrecognized and unmanaged, leading to unfair evaluations. It's in your interest and your team's interest for important contributions to be known.

BENEFIT

When others are aware of what you've accomplished, you're more likely to be consulted for relevant projects, chosen for interesting tasks, and credited appropriately in evaluations. It reduces duplicate work, saving company time, and frankly, it feels good to have your hard work acknowledged. This ensures your effort translates into recognized value and enables better collaboration.

Analysis Paralysis: Overthinking Without Action

An engineer becomes trapped in endless analysis, research, and planning without moving forward with implementation. They gather requirements, research technologies, create detailed architectural documents, and debate edge cases, but struggle to begin building or make decisions. This pattern often stems from perfectionism or fear of making the wrong choice, but it prevents progress and frustrates stakeholders who are waiting for results.

This anti-pattern significantly impacts delivery timelines and team momentum. While thorough analysis has value, excessive deliberation without action creates bottlenecks. Stakeholders lose confidence when they see lots of discussion but no tangible progress. The engineer may feel busy and productive because they're working hard on research, but they're not delivering the value the business needs. Meanwhile, market conditions or requirements may change, making the extensive analysis obsolete.

ANTI-PATTERN SIGNS

You spend weeks creating detailed design documents but haven't written a line of implementation code. You repeatedly say, "I need to research this more before we can start." Meetings become circular discussions of theoretical scenarios rather than practical next steps. You have extensive notes and research but struggle to make concrete technical decisions. Stakeholders frequently ask about timelines and progress, expressing frustration about the lack of visible advancement.

REMEDY

Use time-boxed research for analysis and research phases. For example, allocate two days for initial research, then commit to starting implementation regardless of whether you have perfect information. Build small prototypes early to test assumptions rather than trying to solve all problems theoretically. This approach provides real data to inform decisions and often reveals that many concerns were premature.

Create forcing functions by committing to deadlines with your team. Share a simple prototype or proof of concept within a week, even if it's incomplete. This creates accountability and momentum. When facing decisions, adopt a "two-way door" mentality. Many technical choices can be reversed later if needed, so optimize for learning rather than perfect initial decisions.

Practice rapid experimentation by building multiple small approaches rather than one perfect solution. This helps you gather real data about what works rather than getting lost in theoretical considerations. Remember that in most cases, a good solution implemented quickly beats a perfect solution delivered too late.

CULTURE FIX

Teams can establish standard time limits for research phases and require prototypes or implementation to begin within defined timeframes. Regular check-ins can help identify when analysis is becoming counterproductive. Some organizations use *spike time-boxes* where research and experimentation have explicit limits, after which implementation must commence.

BENEFIT

Moving from analysis to action generates real feedback and learning opportunities that pure research cannot provide. You build momentum with stakeholders by showing visible progress. Early implementation often reveals which research questions actually matter versus theoretical concerns that never materialize. This approach builds confidence in your ability to deliver while still maintaining appropriate technical rigor.

Not-Invented-Here Syndrome: Rejecting External Solutions

An engineer consistently chooses to build custom solutions rather than adopting existing tools, libraries, or frameworks that could meet their needs—essentially "reinventing the wheel." They may rationalize this by claiming existing solutions are "not quite right" for their use case, or they prefer the control and understanding that comes with custom code. However, this pattern often leads to significant time investment in recreating functionality that already exists and is well-tested.

This anti-pattern drains team resources and introduces unnecessary risk. Building custom solutions requires significant time for development, testing, documentation, and maintenance. The engineer becomes responsible for ongoing support and bug fixes for code that could have been outsourced to library maintainers. Custom implementations often lack the robustness that comes from widespread use and community testing. Security vulnerabilities, edge cases, and performance issues that have been solved in mature external solutions may resurface in custom code.

ANTI-PATTERN SIGNS

You frequently say, "That library doesn't do exactly what we need" without exploring whether the differences matter. Your projects consistently include significant custom infrastructure that replicates functionality available in established tools. You spend substantial time debugging issues that would have been solved by using mature external dependencies. Code reviews reveal reinvention of common algorithms, data structures, or design patterns that are available in standard libraries.

REMEDY

Before building custom solutions, thoroughly evaluate existing options with a bias toward adoption rather than rejection. Create explicit criteria for what constitutes a sufficient match rather than requiring perfect alignment with your vision. Ask whether the differences between an existing solution and your ideal solution actually impact user value or system functionality.

Adopt a build-versus-buy decision framework that considers total cost of ownership, including development time, maintenance burden, security risks, and opportunity cost. Factor in the expertise and resources that external maintainers bring to mature solutions. Consider whether you could contribute improvements to existing projects rather than building from scratch.

When custom development is truly necessary, start with existing solutions as a foundation and extend them, rather than building entirely new implementations. This approach leverages proven components while adding the specific functionality you need. Document your decision-making process to help future team members understand why custom solutions were chosen and when they should be reconsidered.

CULTURE FIX

Teams can establish guidelines requiring evaluation of at least three existing solutions before custom development begins. Code reviews should include discussions about whether custom implementations are necessary. Some organizations maintain lists of approved libraries and tools to encourage reuse and reduce the tendency to build everything in-house.

BENEFIT

Leveraging existing solutions allows you to focus your technical effort on problems that are truly unique to your domain rather than solving generic technical challenges. You benefit from the collective expertise and testing that comes with mature tools. Maintenance burden decreases as external dependencies handle updates, security patches, and bug fixes. Your development velocity increases as you can build on proven foundations rather than starting from zero.

Perfectionism and Gold-Plating: Never Shipping

An engineer continuously refines and improves their work without shipping it to users. They may add features that weren't requested, optimize performance beyond requirements, or endlessly polish the user interface. While attention to quality is valuable, perfectionism becomes counterproductive when it prevents delivery of functional solutions that could provide immediate value to users.

This pattern creates significant opportunity costs and frustrates stakeholders. Users cannot benefit from functionality that remains unshipped, regardless of how polished it might eventually become. Market opportunities may be missed while features undergo endless refinement. Stakeholders lose confidence when they see development effort but no user-facing results. The engineer may also miss valuable feedback that could come from real usage, instead optimizing for theoretical scenarios.

ANTI-PATTERN SIGNS

You consistently miss deadlines because you're adding "just one more feature" or making "small improvements." Stakeholders frequently ask when features will be available to users. You spend significant time on aspects of the system that users may never notice or care about. Code reviews reveal functionality far beyond what was originally scoped. You feel anxiety about shipping work that isn't complete according to your internal standards.

REMEDY

Define explicit definition-of-done (DoD) criteria before beginning work and stick to those boundaries. This helps distinguish between essential functionality and nice-to-have additions. Practice shipping minimal viable functionality and gathering user feedback rather than trying to anticipate all possible needs. Real user behavior often differs significantly from assumptions, making early feedback more valuable than theoretical perfection.

Create forcing functions by committing to ship dates with your team and stakeholders. Use feature flags or beta programs to gradually release functionality rather than waiting for complete perfection. This approach allows you to gather feedback while continuing to improve. Separate current requirements from future enhancements, keeping a backlog of improvements that can be prioritized based on actual user needs.

Remember that shipped code with minor imperfections that users can benefit from immediately is more valuable than perfect code that remains unreleased. Many successful products launched with limited functionality and improved based on user feedback rather than trying to solve all problems before launch.

CULTURE FIX

Teams can establish regular release cycles with hard deadlines that prevent endless polishing. Sprint planning should include explicit scope boundaries and criteria for considering work complete. Some organizations use "good enough" standards that define acceptable quality levels for different types of features, preventing over-optimization.

BENEFIT

Shipping early and frequently provides real user feedback that guides further development more effectively than internal speculation. You build momentum with stakeholders by demonstrating consistent delivery. Users begin receiving value immediately rather than waiting for theoretical perfection. You can iterate based on actual usage patterns rather than assumptions, often leading to better final outcomes.

Context-Switching Addiction: Lack of Deep Focus

An engineer constantly jumps between different tasks, projects, or technologies without dedicating sustained attention to any single effort. They may check messages frequently, attend numerous meetings, or volunteer for multiple initiatives simultaneously. While adaptability has value and some engineers (particularly neurodivergent individuals who may be overrepresented in tech) can thrive with varied work, excessive unplanned context-switching can reduce productivity for many and prevent the deep focus necessary for complex problem solving.

This pattern can reduce the quality and efficiency of technical work for those who work best with sustained focus. Complex engineering problems often require building up context about systems, requirements, and implementation details. Frequent interruptions force repeated context rebuilding, wasting time. The constant switching can also increase the likelihood of errors as details from different contexts become confused. However, it's important to note that context-switching is a reality of engineering work that everyone must learn to manage—the goal is to find what works for your working style and minimize unproductive switching.

ANTI-PATTERN SIGNS

You have difficulty remembering what you were working on when you return to a task after interruptions. Your daily schedule includes back-to-back meetings with different projects scattered throughout. You respond to messages immediately rather than batching communication activities. Multiple projects are perpetually "almost done" but never reach completion. You feel busy but struggle to point to significant completed work.

REMEDY

Implement time-blocking strategies that protect extended periods for focused work. Schedule specific times for checking and responding to messages rather than maintaining constant availability. Practice saying no to additional commitments when your current workload already requires full attention. Create physical and digital environments that minimize distractions during focus periods.

Batch similar activities together rather than switching between different types of work throughout the day. For example, dedicate morning hours to coding, afternoon blocks to meetings, and specific times for email and administrative tasks. Use techniques like the Pomodoro (*https://pomodorotechnique.com*) to maintain sustained attention on individual tasks while still allowing for planned breaks.

Communicate your focus periods to teammates and stakeholders so they understand when you're available for interruptions and when you need uninterrupted time. This helps set appropriate expectations while still maintaining collaboration. Track how you spend your time to identify patterns and opportunities for better focus.

CULTURE FIX

Teams can establish "focus time" periods where interruptions are minimized and meetings are avoided. Some organizations implement "no meeting" days or specific hours when deep work is prioritized. Communication norms can be adjusted to reduce expectations of immediate responses during designated focus periods.

BENEFIT

Extended focus periods enable you to tackle complex problems that require sustained mental effort. Your code quality improves as you maintain better context about system design and implementation details. Overall productivity increases significantly as you spend less time rebuilding mental context. You experience greater job satisfaction from completing meaningful work rather than feeling perpetually fragmented.

Scope Creep Enablement: The Inability to Say No

An engineer consistently agrees to additional requirements, feature requests, or timeline compressions without adjusting other commitments or pushing back on unrealistic expectations. They may fear disappointing stakeholders or believe they should accommodate all requests. However, this pattern leads to overcommitment, missed deadlines, and reduced quality as the engineer attempts to satisfy ever-expanding requirements.

This anti-pattern creates a cycle of unrealistic expectations and delivery failures. Stakeholders learn that they can successfully request additional work without consequences, encouraging further scope expansion. The engineer becomes overwhelmed trying to meet all commitments, often working unsustainable hours or cutting corners on quality. Original project goals become diluted as effort spreads across numerous additions. Team morale suffers as realistic planning becomes impossible.

ANTI-PATTERN SIGNS

Project scope regularly expands beyond initial requirements without corresponding timeline adjustments. You frequently work overtime to accommodate additional requests that weren't part of original planning. Stakeholders casually add "small" requests that accumulate into significant additional work. You feel anxiety about disappointing people when considering whether to accept new requests. Original project deadlines are consistently missed due to additional work.

REMEDY

Develop clear criteria for evaluating new requests against current commitments and project goals. Practice responding to scope changes with questions about priorities rather than automatic acceptance. For example: "I can add that feature, but it will require two additional weeks. Should we adjust the deadline or remove something else from the current scope?"

Create explicit change management processes that require stakeholders to consider trade-offs when requesting additions. Document the impact of scope changes on timelines, resource requirements, and other commitments. This helps stakeholders make informed decisions rather than assuming additions are free.

Learn to frame pushback in terms of project success rather than personal limitations. Explaining how scope creep threatens overall delivery goals often resonates better with stakeholders than simply saying you're too busy. Offer alternatives when declining requests, such as future iteration plans or reduced-scope versions of requested features.

CULTURE FIX

Teams can establish formal change control processes that require stakeholder approval for scope modifications. Sprint planning and project kickoffs should include explicit discussions about how scope changes will be handled. Some organizations use "scope buffer" time to accommodate reasonable adjustments without derailing primary objectives.

BENEFIT

Managing scope effectively allows you to deliver high-quality results within realistic timeframes. Stakeholders develop more realistic expectations about development effort and timeline impacts. Your credibility increases as you consistently meet commitments rather than overpromising and underdelivering. Work stress decreases as you maintain sustainable workloads rather than constantly playing catch-up.

Technical Debt Denial: Ignoring System Health

An engineer consistently prioritizes new feature development over addressing technical debt, code quality issues, or system maintenance needs. They may rationalize this by focusing on immediate business value or claiming that technical improvements can wait. However, this pattern allows technical debt to accumulate until it significantly impacts development velocity and system reliability.

This anti-pattern creates compounding problems that become increasingly expensive to address. Accumulated technical debt slows down future feature development as engineers spend more time working around problematic code. System reliability decreases as shortcuts and quick fixes accumulate without proper resolution. Developer morale suffers as working with poorly structured code becomes frustrating and error-prone. Security vulnerabilities and performance issues may emerge from deferred maintenance.

ANTI-PATTERN SIGNS

You insistently prioritize any feature request over code refactoring or system improvements. Technical debt items remain on backlogs indefinitely without being addressed. Debugging and feature development takes progressively longer as the codebase becomes more complex. Team members express frustration about working with certain parts of the system. System outages or performance problems occur due to deferred maintenance.

REMEDY

Allocate explicit time for technical debt reduction in sprint planning and project schedules. Many successful teams dedicate a percentage of each sprint to technical improvements rather than treating them as optional activities. Track technical debt systematically and communicate its impact to stakeholders in business terms, such as development velocity reduction or increased maintenance costs.

Make technical debt visible by documenting problematic areas and their impact on development efficiency. Create simple metrics that demonstrate how technical improvements enable faster feature delivery. For example, measure how long similar features take to implement in well-maintained versus debt-heavy parts of the system.

Integrate technical improvements into feature work when possible rather than treating them as separate activities. Refactoring code while adding new functionality often provides opportunities to address debt without separate time allocation. This approach demonstrates how technical improvements directly enable business objectives.

CULTURE FIX

Teams can establish policies requiring technical debt assessment and planning in every project. Some organizations use technical debt *interest payments*—tracking how much extra time is spent working around problematic code—to justify improvement investments. Regular architecture reviews can identify debt accumulation before it becomes critical.

BENEFIT

Proactive technical debt management maintains development velocity over time rather than allowing it to degrade. System reliability improves as maintenance issues are addressed systematically. Developer productivity and satisfaction increase as they work with well-structured, maintainable code. Long-term project costs decrease as technical improvements prevent expensive rewrites or emergency fixes.

Meeting Overload: Time Mismanagement

An engineer attends numerous meetings without carefully evaluating their necessity or contribution. They may feel obligated to participate in every discussion where they might have relevant input, or they may struggle to decline meeting invitations. However, excessive meeting attendance severely reduces time available for focused technical work and often provides diminishing returns in terms of actual contribution or information gained.

This pattern significantly impacts individual productivity and can signal broader team efficiency issues. Engineers need substantial uninterrupted time for complex problem solving, design work, and implementation. Fragmented schedules filled with meetings prevent the deep focus necessary for high-quality technical work. Many meetings include participants who contribute little or could receive information through other channels. The engineer may feel busy but accomplish little meaningful technical progress.

ANTI-PATTERN SIGNS

Your calendar shows back-to-back meetings with little time for focused work. You attend meetings where you rarely speak or contribute meaningfully. Multiple meetings discuss similar topics with overlapping participants. You feel constantly busy but struggle to complete technical tasks. Teammates comment that you're difficult to reach for technical discussions because you're always in meetings.

REMEDY

Evaluate each meeting invitation against specific criteria: Do you have essential input? Will you gain information not available elsewhere? Can your perspective be represented by someone else already attending? Practice declining meetings where your contribution is marginal or where information can be shared asynchronously.

Request agendas in advance and assess whether your participation is necessary for all agenda items. Consider attending only portions of meetings where your input is required. Suggest alternative communication methods for information sharing that doesn't require real-time discussion.

Block specific times in your calendar for focused technical work and protect those periods from meeting scheduling. Many engineers find that scheduling focused work periods like meetings helps ensure they receive appropriate priority. Communicate these protected times to teammates so they understand when you're available for collaboration.

CULTURE FIX

Teams can establish meeting-free periods or days to protect focus time. Meeting organizers should be encouraged to clearly define objectives and required participants, rather than defaulting to large invitation lists. Some organizations implement policies requiring explicit justification for recurring meetings or meetings longer than specific durations.

BENEFIT

Reduced meeting attendance provides more time for meaningful technical work and deep problem solving—though be mindful of staying connected to avoid missing critical information or being perceived as disengaged. Your contributions to remaining meetings become more valuable as you have more context and energy to engage effectively. Overall work satisfaction increases as you spend more time on activities that directly utilize your technical skills and create tangible value.

Feedback Resistance: Closed to Input

An engineer consistently responds defensively to feedback during code reviews, design discussions, or performance conversations. They may argue against suggestions, provide extensive justifications for their approaches, or dismiss concerns raised by teammates. While having technical convictions is valuable, excessive resistance to input prevents learning and improvement while damaging team collaboration.

This pattern limits both individual growth and team effectiveness. Code reviews become contentious rather than collaborative learning opportunities. Team members may stop providing meaningful feedback to avoid conflict, reducing overall code quality. The engineer misses opportunities to learn from teammates' experiences and perspectives. Design discussions become debates rather than constructive problem-solving sessions.

ANTI-PATTERN SIGNS

Code reviews, architecture discussions, and technical design sessions frequently involve lengthy discussions where you defend every implementation decision. You immediately respond to suggestions with reasons why they won't work rather than considering their merit. Teammates seem hesitant to provide feedback or critique your work. You rarely incorporate suggestions from others without extensive discussion. Performance reviews mention areas for improvement that you've heard before but haven't addressed.

REMEDY

Practice receiving feedback with curiosity rather than defensiveness. Start by asking clarifying questions about suggestions rather than immediately explaining your reasoning. Consider whether feedback reveals assumptions or constraints you hadn't considered. Thank people for their input even when you ultimately decide not to implement their suggestions. Pair programming can also help by making feedback a natural, continuous part of the development process rather than a formal review event.

Separate your work from your identity. Remember that criticism of your work, while it can feel personal, is focused on improving outcomes. Adopt a growth mindset that views feedback as opportunities to learn rather than attacks to defend against. Consider that teammates who provide feedback are investing their time to help improve the work and outcomes.

When you disagree with feedback, explain your reasoning calmly and ask for others' perspectives rather than dismissing their concerns. Often, productive discussions emerge when different viewpoints are explored openly. Sometimes you'll discover valid points you hadn't considered; other times you'll help others understand important constraints or considerations.

CULTURE FIX

Teams can establish norms around giving and receiving feedback that emphasize learning and improvement rather than evaluation or criticism. Training on effective feedback delivery helps ensure suggestions are presented constructively. Some organizations use structured feedback frameworks, like *radical candor* (developed by Kim Malone Scott, this emphasizes caring personally while challenging directly) or the Center for Creative Leadership's SBI (Situation-Behavior-Impact) model, that separate different types of input and make expectations clear.

BENEFIT

Openness to feedback accelerates your professional development as you learn from teammates' diverse experiences and perspectives. Code quality improves through collaborative review processes. Team relationships strengthen as colleagues feel heard and valued. Your reputation develops as someone who is easy to work with and committed to continuous improvement.

Tool Obsession: Chasing Shiny Objects

An engineer frequently adopts new tools, frameworks, or technologies without clear business justification or sufficient evaluation. They may be motivated by curiosity about emerging technologies, desire to keep their skills current, or belief that newer tools are inherently better. However, constant tool switching creates significant overhead and can distract from delivering actual business value. Additionally, third-party (3P) tools often come with licensing costs, vendor dependencies, and compliance considerations that first-party (1P) solutions don't have.

This pattern creates numerous problems for both the engineer and their team. Each new tool requires learning time that could be spent on feature development or problem solving. Team members must also learn new tools, multiplying the impact of each switch. Projects may be delayed while everyone adapts to new technologies. The engineer may never develop deep expertise in any particular tool as they constantly move to the next new option. Technical debt can accumulate as partially implemented solutions are abandoned for newer approaches.

ANTI-PATTERN SIGNS

Your projects use many different tools and frameworks without clear justification for the variety. You frequently suggest replacing existing tools with newer alternatives. Teammates express frustration about keeping up with tool changes. Project documentation becomes outdated quickly as toolchains evolve. You spend significant time researching and experimenting with tools rather than solving business problems.

REMEDY

Establish clear criteria for tool adoption that include factors beyond novelty or technical appeal. Consider maintenance burden, team learning curve, community support, and alignment with existing infrastructure. Require explicit business justification for tool changes rather than adopting technologies simply because they seem interesting or modern.

Practice deep expertise in a smaller set of tools rather than surface knowledge of many options. Command of fewer tools often provides more value than familiarity with numerous alternatives. When evaluating new tools, create small, timeboxed experiments rather than committing to major changes without validation.

Consider the total cost of ownership for tool adoption, including team training time, migration effort, ongoing maintenance, and potential future changes. Sometimes older, well-established tools provide better overall value than cutting-edge alternatives despite being less exciting to work with.

CULTURE FIX

Teams can establish technology adoption processes that require evaluation and approval before introducing new tools. Some organizations maintain approved technology stacks to balance innovation with stability. Regular architecture reviews can assess tool choices against current needs and future plans.

BENEFIT

Focused tool usage allows you to develop deep expertise that enables more sophisticated problem solving and better technical decisions. Team productivity increases as everyone becomes proficient with a stable toolset. Technical debt decreases as tools are chosen for long-term value rather than short-term appeal. You can focus mental energy on business problems rather than constantly learning new technologies.

Imposter Syndrome Paralysis: Fear-Driven Inaction

An engineer becomes paralyzed by self-doubt and fear of making mistakes, leading them to avoid challenging tasks or opportunities for growth. They may believe they're not qualified for their role or that their successes have been due to luck rather than skill. This pattern prevents them from taking on responsibilities that would advance their career and contribute to team success.

This anti-pattern significantly limits both individual growth and team effectiveness. The engineer avoids stretch assignments that would develop their skills and demonstrate their capabilities. They may over-research decisions due to fear of being wrong rather than making reasonable choices and learning from outcomes. Team members may not realize the engineer's full potential because they consistently avoid challenging work. Innovation and risk-taking decrease as fear dominates technical decision making.

ANTI-PATTERN SIGNS

You consistently volunteer for familiar tasks while avoiding assignments that would stretch your abilities. You spend excessive time verifying decisions or seeking approval from others before taking action. You dismiss your accomplishments as luck or attribute success primarily to external factors. You feel anxiety when asked to present your work or explain technical decisions to others. Teammates seem surprised when you demonstrate capabilities they hadn't observed before. Note that while imposter syndrome can be an internal struggle, external factors like an unpredictable manager, inconsistent leadership, or toxic team culture can also trigger or worsen these feelings.

REMEDY

Recognize that imposter syndrome is common among engineers at all levels and doesn't reflect actual competence. Keep a record of your accomplishments, positive feedback, and successful projects to reference when self-doubt emerges. Practice taking on slightly challenging tasks that push your boundaries without being overwhelming.

Reframe mistakes as learning opportunities rather than evidence of incompetence. Most experienced engineers have made numerous errors throughout their careers and view them as essential parts of the learning process. Focus on growth and improvement rather than trying to appear perfect or avoid all risks.

Seek mentorship from senior engineers who can provide perspective on normal career development and help you assess your skills objectively. Often, external viewpoints reveal capabilities and progress that are difficult to see from your own perspective. Consider that your current role suggests others believe in your abilities, even when you doubt yourself.

CULTURE FIX

Teams can create psychological safety that encourages risk-taking and learning from mistakes rather than avoiding them. Regular discussions about challenges and failures help normalize the learning process. Some organizations implement mentorship programs that pair engineers with experienced guides who can provide confidence and perspective.

BENEFIT

Overcoming imposter syndrome enables you to pursue growth opportunities that advance your career and increase your impact. Taking on challenging work develops new skills and demonstrates your capabilities to colleagues and management. Confidence in your abilities allows you to make reasonable technical decisions without excessive deliberation. You become a more valuable team member as you contribute your full potential rather than holding back due to self-doubt.

Moving Forward

These anti-patterns can creep in unintentionally, but recognizing and addressing them is what distinguishes effective engineers. Each pattern has specific remedies, but the overarching theme is balance: share knowledge while building expertise, collaborate without becoming a bottleneck, design thoughtfully without over-engineering, delegate while maintaining accountability, communicate impact without overselling, act decisively while considering consequences, leverage existing solutions while innovating when needed, ship iteratively while maintaining quality, focus deeply while staying adaptable, manage scope while remaining flexible, embrace feedback while maintaining conviction, choose tools strategically while staying current, and build confidence while staying humble.

The specific patterns we've covered—knowledge silos, hero complex, over-engineering, delegation issues, lack of visibility, analysis paralysis, not-invented-here syndrome, premature optimization, context-switching, scope creep, technical debt avoidance, meeting overload, feedback resistance, tool obsession, and imposter syndrome—represent the most common obstacles to individual effectiveness. By actively working to avoid these patterns, you clear the path for making meaningful technical contributions.

Cultivating the opposite positive habits will not only make you more effective, but also make work more enjoyable and your team more successful. These patterns form the foundation for career advancement, which leads us naturally to our next topic: understanding how to navigate career growth and level up as an IC.

Chapter 6 explores career growth and leveling up, examining how becoming an effective engineer goes hand-in-hand with advancing in your career. As you consistently deliver results and take on more responsibility, you have opportunities to progress from mid-level to senior engineer. Progression to staff engineer is not automatic or universal—it's a fundamentally different role that's not the right fit for everyone. Promotions don't happen automatically with time served; they require consistently demonstrating skills at the next level. We'll look at how to navigate your career progression as an individual contributor, including understanding promotion criteria, avoiding common pitfalls in mid-to-senior transitions, deciding whether to go into management or stay technical, and advocating for yourself effectively. Career growth can also mean lateral moves into different domains or roles, not just upward progression.

| 6

Career Growth and Leveling Up

Becoming an effective engineer goes hand-in-hand with advancing in your career. As you consistently deliver results and take on more responsibility, you have opportunities to progress from mid-level to senior engineer. Note that progression to staff engineer is not automatic or the right path for everyone— it represents a fundamentally different type of work focused on organizational impact and technical leadership. Promotions don't happen automatically with time served; they require consistently demonstrating skills at the next level. This chapter looks at how to navigate your career progression as an IC, including understanding promotion criteria, avoiding common pitfalls in mid-to-senior transitions, deciding whether to go into management or stay technical, and advocating for yourself. Remember that career growth isn't only vertical—it can also mean moving into different technical domains, roles, or areas of expertise.

How Promotions Work (and Why Tenure Isn't Enough)

In tech, impact and scope drive promotions, not just tenure. You may have seen a relatively new engineer zoom ahead in levels because they solved high-impact problems, or someone with many years of experience plateau because they kept doing the same things.

Tenure isn't enough to land a promotion. Instead, you must demonstrate readiness for the next level by showing you are already executing on expectations of that level. This could include stepping up to lead critical projects and mentoring junior team members.

Here are some tips:

Understand your company's ladder.
Most tech companies have defined expectations for each level (often shared in a rubric or leveling guide). Get a copy of that if you can. It'll say things like "Senior Engineer: leads medium-sized projects end-to-end; mentors others; designs systems with moderate complexity; expertise in at least one domain; operates with minimal oversight," etc. Use this as a checklist for yourself. Are you already doing those things? If not, those are growth areas.

Show, don't tell.
To get promoted, you generally need to already be operating somewhat at that next level. For example, if you want to be promoted to senior, start taking on some senior responsibilities: propose technical solutions, handle tasks without being asked, guide a newer engineer, improve a process on the team. Then when promotion discussions happen, it's easy for your manager to make the case: "Alice is essentially already a senior engineer."

Conversely, simply being in the role a long time or doing a good job at your current level isn't usually enough. Consistently exceeding your current level's expectations and occasionally doing work of the next level is the typical threshold.

Communicate with your manager.
Express your career goals. A good one-on-one conversation sounds something like this: "I'm interested in growing to senior engineer. What skills or accomplishments do I need to demonstrate to reach that?" Managers appreciate when you take your growth seriously (it makes their job easier to help you). They can assign you more challenging tasks or leadership opportunities to build that evidence.

Also, ask for feedback. If you get passed over for a promotion you expected, ask what you could improve. Maybe they see a gap (e.g., "You do great work but haven't shown mentorship" or "We need to see you drive a project independently"). Then make a plan to close that gap and ask for another review in six months.

Track your accomplishments.
Throughout the year, maintain a doc of achievements, especially those that had significant outcomes (e.g., "Optimized search, improving response times by 50% and boosting conversion by 5%"). This not only helps with

promotion packets and performance reviews, but it ensures *you* realize what you've done. Sometimes we forget our contributions. Keeping track also lets you see if you're short on certain kinds of achievements the next level expects. (E.g., no instances of mentoring? Then take on a mentee.)

Tenure does have some value.
With years often comes deeper system knowledge, domain expertise, and influence in the org. But tenure alone is insufficient. If you find yourself with many years but no promotion, consider whether you've been actively expanding your scope or just doing more of the same. You might need to deliberately step out of your comfort zone (volunteer for a cross-team effort, etc.). Also talk to your manager—some companies have unfortunate bureaucracy, where people can get stuck due to budget or level caps. If you're consistently performing above your level and not getting promoted, you might need to gently escalate or, in the worst case, consider other opportunities where you'll be recognized.

Creating Your "Brag Document" with an AI Assistant

Documenting your accomplishments for performance reviews or promotion packets is critical but tedious. AI can serve as a personal assistant to automate the creation of your "brag document." You can feed an AI a list of your completed Jira tickets, pull request links, and design documents from the past quarter:

> **Prompt:** *Review my contributions from the last quarter. For each major item, write a bullet point using the STAR method (Situation, Task, Action, Result). Emphasize the business impact, such as improved performance, new user features, or reduced technical debt.*

The AI will transform your raw list of tasks into a narrative focused on impact, which is exactly what managers and promotion committees look for. This saves you hours of work and helps you advocate for yourself effectively by framing your contributions in the most compelling way.

The Unwritten Rules of Progression

Beyond the formal criteria, there are subtle unwritten rules that often influence career progression. Recognizing these can help you avoid frustration:

More than coding

> At higher levels, things like communication, leadership, and impact on others become huge. An unwritten rule is that you must demonstrate leadership (even without title) to go from mid to senior, and organizational influence to go from senior to staff. This might mean taking initiative in meetings, being the one who clarifies goals, or helping coordinate cross-team work. If you only ever quietly code what you're assigned, you might top out at mid-level even if your code quality is superb.

Personal brand

> This doesn't mean becoming a social media influencer; it means within your company, be known for something positive. For example, "Oh, Bob, he's the one who always fixes the hardest bugs" or "Chitra always comes up with solid designs." Being known for consistent excellence or a key contribution helps in promotion discussions. This is often achieved by volunteering for and delivering on some high-visibility tasks.

Visibility (again)

> In larger organizations, higher-ups might not know everything each engineer does. A senior promotion might be calibrated not just by your manager, but by a committee. Make sure your significant contributions are visible to more than just your immediate peers. That might mean presenting at an internal tech forum or writing an article on the intranet about a project. Unfair as it is, sometimes those who network a bit and ensure their work is known get ahead faster than quiet contributors who assume merit alone will shine (especially true at bigger companies).

Mentors and sponsors

> An unwritten rule of promotions is that having someone senior who will say, "Yes, this person is operating at the next level" in the promotion meeting is extremely valuable. Cultivate relationships with staff engineers or managers beyond your boss if possible. How? Doing good work that interacts with their domain, or asking one to mentor you (most are flattered and willing). Then, when promotion time comes, your manager can gather supporting evidence from them. We'll explore the roles of *mentors* (people

who advise you) and *sponsors* (people who advocate for you) in more detail in Chapter 7.

Consistency matters
If you had one great project but otherwise are average, that might not suffice. Many orgs want to see sustained next-level performance. So keep the momentum after a big win—don't slack off, figuring it's "in the bag." Conversely, if you had one slip-up among a bunch of successes, you're usually fine (we all make mistakes or occasionally deliver late). Learn from it and maintain your high standard going forward.

Attitude and professionalism
Unwritten but real: if someone is toxic or very hard to work with, companies often hesitate to promote them into roles where they'd have even more influence. On the flip side, being a positive force (helpful and reliable with a growth mindset) makes leadership more comfortable putting you in a higher role, where others may emulate you.

In short: deliver great work, ensure people know about it, help others along the way, and communicate ambition to your boss. Do that consistently, and you'll significantly improve your chances of advancement—though remember that external factors like economic conditions, company growth, and organizational changes also play a role.

Mid-Level Versus Senior Versus Staff: What Changes?

Understanding the expectations at different career levels is key to navigating your growth. While every company's ladder is slightly different, the progression from mid-level to senior and then to staff generally involves an expanding scope of impact, autonomy, and leadership. Let's explore the typical shifts at each stage with concrete examples of what success looks like.

MID-LEVEL ENGINEER

As a mid-level engineer (often around two to four years of experience, sometimes designated as L4 in large tech companies), you've moved beyond the junior phase where you needed constant guidance and are now a reliable contributor who can work independently on well-defined tasks. Your primary focus is on executing features and fixes within existing systems, typically working on implementation-level problems (as opposed to architecture or cross-system design) that have clear requirements and acceptance criteria. You might own small to medium-sized features, such as implementing a new API endpoint, building a user interface component, or optimizing a specific database query.

At this level, your impact radius centers on your own work and immediately adjacent code. You're the person who consistently delivers quality code on time, catches edge cases in your own work, and helps teammates by reviewing their pull requests thoughtfully. You understand the codebase well enough to navigate it efficiently and can make informed decisions about implementation details without needing to escalate every technical choice to your senior colleagues.

Mid-level engineers are expected to write clean, maintainable code that follows established patterns and conventions. You should be comfortable with the team's development workflow, from writing comprehensive tests to deploying your changes safely. When bugs arise in areas you've worked on, you can diagnose and fix them independently. You also start to think about the broader implications of your code, considering performance, security, and maintainability, even if you're not yet driving architectural decisions.

Communication at this level involves clearly describing your progress in standups, asking thoughtful questions when requirements are unclear, and providing accurate estimates for your work. You participate in code reviews by offering constructive feedback and explaining your implementation choices when asked. While you may not yet be leading technical discussions, you contribute meaningfully to them by sharing relevant insights and asking clarifying questions.

SENIOR ENGINEER

A senior engineer (typically five to eight years of experience, sometimes designated as L5 in large tech companies) represents a significant step up in responsibility and impact. The transition from mid-level to senior isn't just about having more experience; it's about fundamentally changing how you approach problems and your role within the team. Seniors are expected to not just execute tasks, but to define, drive, and deliver complex projects while elevating the capabilities of those around them.

The scope of a senior engineer's work expands dramatically. Instead of implementing features from detailed specifications, you're often given high-level business requirements (working closely with the product team) and expected to break them down into technical tasks, design the solution, and coordinate its implementation. For example, you might be asked to "improve our checkout flow conversion rate" and be responsible for analyzing the current system, identifying bottlenecks, proposing solutions, coordinating with product and design teams, and implementing the changes across multiple services.

Leadership becomes a core part of your role, even if you don't manage people directly. You mentor junior and mid-level engineers, not just by answering their questions, but by teaching them how to think about problems systematically. You might lead a small feature team or serve as the technical lead for a project, making architectural decisions and ensuring the team stays aligned on technical direction. This includes making judgment calls during development without constantly escalating to your manager, and being able to navigate ambiguous situations where the requirements aren't perfectly clear.

Your technical thinking expands beyond individual features to consider system-wide implications. You actively work to improve code quality, reduce technical debt, and enhance development processes. You might propose and champion the adoption of new tools, advocate for refactoring legacy systems, or design new services that better serve the product's needs. You understand not just how to build features, but how they fit into the larger technical ecosystem and business context.

Communication responsibilities grow significantly as you become a bridge between engineering and other functions. You present technical proposals at architecture reviews, discuss trade-offs with product managers and designers, and can represent engineering perspectives in cross-functional meetings. You're trusted to communicate directly with stakeholders about technical feasibility, timelines, and constraints. When production issues arise, you can quickly assess the situation, coordinate the response, and communicate status to both technical and nontechnical audiences.

Reliability becomes one of your defining characteristics. You're the person teammates turn to when they encounter complex problems or need guidance on technical decisions. You can troubleshoot production issues under pressure, make sound judgment calls when time is critical, and provide technical leadership during incidents. Your estimates are trusted because you understand both the technical complexity and the potential obstacles that might arise.

As Gergely Orosz notes, "Senior is when you start to exert influence beyond your own work...mentoring others and taking initiative to improve team processes." You begin to shape not just the code, but the engineering culture and practices of your team.

STAFF ENGINEER

Staff engineering (typically eight or more years of experience, sometimes designated as L6 or higher in large tech companies) represents the first true technical leadership level, where your impact extends far beyond individual contribution to organizational influence and strategic technical direction. While you're still an individual contributor, this role requires a fundamental shift from a focus on individual features to a broader consideration of outcomes and strategy, while remaining deeply technical.

> **Note**
>
> It's important to note that not everyone will or should progress to a staff engineering role—it's a fundamentally different type of work that emphasizes organizational impact and technical leadership, similar to how management is a different career path. Many excellent senior engineers find tremendous satisfaction and impact continuing to deepen their expertise at the senior level.

Your scope expands to multiple teams or entire product areas, where you tackle the most complex and ambiguous technical challenges. Staff engineers often work on cross-cutting concerns that affect many teams, such as designing a new data platform, leading the migration from monolith to microservices, or establishing security standards across the organization. You might architect systems that several senior engineers implement, coordinate technical decisions across multiple teams, and ensure that different parts of the engineering organization work together effectively.

The influence of a staff engineer extends throughout the engineering organization and often beyond. You might spearhead the adoption of new frameworks or technologies across teams, establish coding standards and best practices, lead post-mortem processes for major incidents, and drive company-wide technical improvements. Your technical opinions carry significant weight, and you often serve as the final arbiter on complex technical decisions that affect multiple teams.

Staff engineers demonstrate exceptional autonomy by identifying important problems before they become critical and rallying the necessary people and resources to solve them. This often involves *leading without authority*—influencing and coordinating across teams where you don't have direct management responsibility. You might recognize that the company's deployment process is becoming a bottleneck and take the initiative to design and implement a solution that involves multiple teams and requires executive buy-in.

Technical breadth becomes crucial at this level. While you likely maintain deep expertise in one area, you need sufficient knowledge across the stack to make informed decisions about complex systems. You understand the frontend, the backend, infrastructure, data, and security well enough to oversee projects that span all these domains. This breadth allows you to see connections and opportunities that others might miss.

Mentorship and culture shaping become formal responsibilities. You typically mentor multiple engineers across different levels and teams, helping to develop the next generation of technical leaders. You influence engineering culture through both direct mentoring and by setting examples in how you approach problems, communicate, and collaborate. Staff engineers act as force multipliers, amplifying the capabilities of their peers while serving as recognized technical authorities across the organization.

The key distinction in progression becomes clear: a mid-level engineer focuses on completing features correctly and on time; a senior engineer ensures entire projects are delivered successfully while improving team capabilities; a staff engineer ensures the right projects are being worked on in alignment with business strategy and that multiple teams can execute them effectively. It's an evolution from code-focused to outcome- and strategy-focused work, requiring both technical depth and organizational awareness.

Understanding these progressively expanding expectations helps in planning your career growth. For example, if you're currently at mid-level and aiming for senior, start seeking opportunities to lead small projects, mentor newer team members, and participate more actively in technical design discussions. If you're targeting staff level from senior, look for cross-team initiatives, propose technical improvements that affect multiple teams, and begin building relationships across the broader engineering organization, always with your manager's support and guidance.

Individual Contributor Versus Management: Two Paths

As you grow, you might wonder: should I stay on the IC track, possibly progressing to a staff engineering role, or become an engineering manager (EM)? This is a pivotal career decision many face around senior level.

The key differences are that managers focus on people and project delivery (hiring, one-on-ones, team coordination, reporting to upper management), while ICs focus on technical solutions and direct contributions (designing systems, coding, technical mentorship).

Neither is a "promotion" from the other; they're parallel paths (a company should value a staff engineer similarly to an engineering manager in terms of their level). It's more about your strengths and what you enjoy:

- *Stay IC if* you love coding and technical problem solving, you prefer to influence via technical ideas rather than personnel decisions, you enjoy flow time, and you don't mind that your impact is measured by technical outcomes and influence rather than team performance metrics.

- *Go EM if* you feel a pull toward organizing and growing others, making sure the "machine" of the team works well. You find satisfaction in others' success more than writing the code yourself. You want to shape execution at a higher level and don't mind (or even enjoy) the meetings and planning that come with it. Strong interpersonal skills and investment in others' growth are core to being an effective manager.

It's OK not to know immediately. Some companies have "tech lead manager" roles where you can try a bit of managing while still coding, to see which aspects you gravitate to. And it's increasingly common to move from management back to IC as well as the reverse; there's a pendulum phenomenon that can occur.

There are also a few unwritten considerations to think about:

- Managers usually have more immediate influence on promotions and project assignments. If you want to shape team composition or roles, a management position gives that authority, whereas an IC influences indirectly.

- The IC track at junior to mid-levels often allows deeper focus and usually a more flexible schedule since writing code can often be done with fewer meetings. However, note that senior, staff, and higher-level ICs will need to do significant cross-collaboration work, which involves many meetings and interactions with other teams.

- At senior levels, compensation and title can reach similar heights on both tracks, though there are usually fewer staff engineers than managers (and managers also have their own progression levels, with different team sizes and responsibilities).

With either path, leadership skills matter. A manager needs technical understanding to guide the team; an IC needs people skills to lead without authority.

If you think you might want to try management, talk to your manager about opportunities (maybe you can fill in for them during their vacation or manage an intern). If you're not interested, let them know you're aiming for the staff engineer path so they can groom you accordingly (giving you technical leadership opportunities rather than team management ones).

However, it's important not to chase management just for promotion. Many companies have strong IC ladders now because they realized they lost great engineers who became mediocre managers and were unhappy in that role, just because it was the only way to advance. If your company doesn't, that might influence your decisions. But ideally, choose based on what work you find fulfilling.

Remember, you can switch. Many do a stint as an EM and then go back to being IC with an enriched perspective on big-picture and team dynamics, which often makes them even better staff engineers. The reverse is true too—former ICs can become great EMs because they understand what engineers need.

Advocating for Yourself: Navigating Promotions and Raises

Finally, a part of leveling up is making sure your contributions are recognized. This section will walk through a few different ways to advocate for yourself, including specific actions you can take around review time.

KEEP A BRAG DOCUMENT

As suggested by Julia Evans in her popular post on brag documents (*https://oreil.ly/aFO-f*), maintaining a living document of your accomplishments is a powerful career tool. I mentioned this in "Lack of Visibility: Make Your Work Known" on page 54, but it's particularly useful for performance reviews and promotion packets. This isn't just about bragging but providing an objective record of facts and feedback about your work.

Throughout the year, note key successes with metrics if possible (e.g., "Designed and launched new onboarding flow, improving Day 7 retention by 4 percentage points"). When review or promotion time comes, compile those into the requested format. Many engineers hate the idea of "self-promotion," but think of it as reporting facts. Some of us value humility a lot, and we can counter that by telling ourselves to "go ahead and brag." Managers (especially if they manage many direct reports) rely on these documents to remember your accomplishments and advocate effectively for you during calibration and promotion discussions.

ASK FOR WHAT YOU WANT

If you believe you're performing at the next level, explicitly ask your manager, "Can we target a promotion next cycle? I'd like to know what I should focus on to achieve that." Make it a collaborative plan. Some companies require you to act at level for six or more months before promoting, so signal when you feel ready to start that clock. Similarly, for raises or high performance ratings, don't assume they're automatic; ensure your manager knows your work and impact (which is why discussing it in one-on-ones helps).

USE 360 FEEDBACK

If your company gathers peer feedback, consider whom to seek it from. People whom you helped or who can speak to your leadership or cross-team impact are great. Provide thoughtful feedback for others; often, they'll reciprocate. This peer recognition can strongly support promotion cases. (E.g., a staff engineer writes, "Jane has been effectively leading our service architecture revamp—I consider her a tech lead on it.")

BE PATIENT BUT PERSISTENT

Promotions often have timing considerations (budgets, annual cycles). If you don't get it this time, take the feedback, show improvement, and revisit it in the next cycle. I've seen people miss once, then get it six months later after showing growth in the highlighted areas. If you consistently get vague deferrals, that could be a sign to get more concrete feedback or a red flag about your organization; perhaps it's time to look elsewhere to advance.

CONSIDER LATERAL MOVES FOR GROWTH

If your current team doesn't offer chances to demonstrate certain skills needed for promotion (like leadership opportunities), you might need to switch teams or projects to get that experience. For instance, if you need to lead a project end-to-end and your current team has a dominant tech lead that always does that, you might go to a new product line where you can take point on something. It's an internal mobility strategy to set yourself up for the promotion criteria.

STAY ETHICAL AND HUMBLE

Self-advocacy doesn't mean taking credit for others' work or boasting. Your brag document is for you—and don't take the term too literally. Always acknowledge teammates and circumstances. For example, instead of "I single-handedly delivered Feature X," say "I led the effort to deliver Feature X, coordinating a team of three—we shipped on time and achieved a 15% adoption increase." It's clear you were central, but you aren't dismissing others. Managers and promo committees can smell exaggeration or arrogance, and it can backfire. Confidently state facts and results; let them conclude you're awesome.

KNOW WHEN MANAGEMENT/HR PROCESSES HAPPEN

It's important to note when HR changes happen. For example, if promotions are only decided in Q4, make sure by Q3 you and your manager have explicitly discussed your readiness so they can put you up for it. If raises are done after performance reviews in June, don't wait until July to mention you feel underpaid.

LEVERAGE MENTORS OR SPONSORS

If you have a mentor or a higher-level person who supports you, they can sometimes nudge management. For example, a staff engineer might say in an annual or quarterly performance review, "I've noticed Sarah has really stepped up technically on Project Y; I think she's operating at senior level." That external validation can push a borderline case over. You often facilitate this by asking them for feedback and expressing your aspirations; people often will go to bat for you if they believe in you and know you want it.

In summary, treat your career growth like an engineering project:

- Gather requirements (level expectations)
- Implement features (develop skills, take on scope)
- Test and iterate (get feedback, adjust)
- Market the release (showcase your contributions)
- Ensure customer acceptance (manager and peers agree you're at the next level)

Do that, and you'll keep leveling up, not by accident, but by design, all while becoming a more effective engineer at each step, ready to tackle new challenges.

Navigating your career path successfully, especially toward senior and staff roles, requires more than just technical skill; it demands leadership. In Chapter 7, we'll explore what it means to be a leader as an individual contributor, even without a formal management title.

7

Leadership as an Individual Contributor

You don't need a manager title to be a leader. Senior ICs are often expected to provide technical leadership and influence outcomes across the team or even the organization, all without direct authority. This chapter is about leading from the IC position: how to guide others, drive initiatives, mentor teammates, and shape culture when you're not "the boss."

Leading Without Authority

By the time you're a senior engineer, you'll frequently find yourself in situations where you need to coordinate or influence people who don't report to you. Perhaps you're the tech lead on a project with engineers from other teams, or you're proposing a new engineering standard that others would have to adopt. This is where influencing skills and informal leadership come in (as I previewed in Chapter 4).

We'll discuss a few key techniques for leading without direct power:

Build credibility.
> As repeated throughout the book, consistently delivering quality work earns you respect. If colleagues trust your technical expertise and judgment, they'll be more open to following your lead on future decisions. This credibility is like currency for leadership. Engineers often naturally follow those with a track record of smart decisions and helpful behavior.

Communicate vision and rationale.
> People need to understand the "why" to get on board. If you're leading a project, articulate the goals and how your plan meets them. For instance, "We need to handle 10× load—my proposal to implement caching and

refactor the query logic addresses this by..." Paint the picture of success. When others see a clear destination and logical path, they're more likely to go with you. If you just issue directives ("We must refactor X because I said so"), you'll get pushback or apathy.

Invite input and listen.

Leadership isn't just telling people what to do. Involve the team in decisions. If someone objects to part of your plan, hear them out fully. Maybe they have a point you missed. By incorporating others' ideas and acknowledging their concerns, you make them invested in the plan. They'll feel it's "our plan," not just your plan. Also, if people feel heard, they're more willing to follow even if their idea isn't chosen, because the process was respectful.

Coordinate and facilitate.

As a technical leader, you often act as the organizer. That might mean setting up meetings to get alignment, writing down the plan and who's doing what, tracking progress, and clearing roadblocks. Essentially, you're doing some project management. Many engineers shy from this as it's "not coding," but it's crucial. A great tech lead ensures all parts of the machine are moving in sync. For example, you notice two developers duplicating effort—stop and realign tasks. Or the backend is waiting on API specs from the frontend—facilitate that discussion. Good coordination prevents inefficiency and frustration, which is a huge leadership contribution.

Mentor and share knowledge.

An IC leader raises the team's level. If someone is less experienced with a part of the tech, you might host a quick knowledge session or pair them with someone who can help. Take time to mentor engineers on the team at all levels—from juniors learning architecture patterns to peers seeking advice on design reviews—giving them guidance that educates and empowers. This builds goodwill (people see you care about their growth, not just the project) and increases team capability (less for you to handle alone next time). Chapter 5 emphasizes sharing knowledge versus creating knowledge silos—this is one manifestation of that at the leadership level.

Resolve conflicts objectively.

In tech discussions, disagreements happen (architecture choices, priorities, etc.). A leader guides resolution by focusing on facts and goals, not ego. You might propose an experiment to settle a debate (e.g., "Let's prototype option A and B for a day each and measure"). Or bring in data (maybe performance metrics favor one side). Sometimes just clearly laying out pros and cons in writing helps people converge. And if truly deadlocked, an IC leader might escalate to an engineering manager or architect for a tie-breaker, phrasing it as, "We have two viable options; we're seeking a fresh perspective to choose." Being seen as fair and not dictatorial in conflicts builds trust and makes people more likely to support your leadership on future decisions.

Earn authority by what you do, not what you're called. There's a leadership principle: leadership is earned, not given. As an IC, you can't rely on a title to make people listen. But if you consistently show technical know-how, clear vision, inclusive decision making, and personal integrity, people will *want* to follow your lead. This sometimes even leads to formal authority (e.g., being asked to be a team tech lead or an engineering manager), but even in the IC role, it is incredibly valuable.

Consider this example scenario: you are a senior engineer on Project Z with no official tech lead role, but the project is somewhat stalled. Instead of waiting, you step up: organize a design session to finalize decisions, volunteer to write the design doc, assign parts (after asking who wants which piece), and set up a Slack channel or regular check-ins. You also notice one member is struggling with a component; offer to pair program for an hour to help them. Soon, things get back on track. The team sees you as the de facto lead now. Next time there's a tricky integration issue, they naturally ask you to help arbitrate. You didn't need a title for this; you led through action.

Driving Large Initiatives Without Direct Reports

As you reach staff-engineer level, you may lead initiatives that span multiple teams or the whole org—still without being a manager. Chapter 4 covers influencing without authority; here, we'll focus on the mechanics of large-scale IC leadership.

Let's look at the following scenario: the company needs to overhaul its infrastructure (say move from on-prem to cloud). It's a multi-team effort. They appoint you, a staff engineer, as the tech lead architect for it. You have no direct reports, but you must align five teams and 50 engineers toward this common goal over six months.

Here's how you can succeed:

Form a working group.
Bring representatives (maybe the most senior or knowledgeable ICs) from each team into a working group. Establish clear roles—maybe one person coordinates networking changes, another databases, etc., under the overall plan. Now you have point people to collaborate with instead of dealing with 50 individuals. This group will be your go-to for disseminating info and gathering status. It's classic "matrix" leadership: you lead these people regarding the initiative, even though they report elsewhere.

Develop and communicate a plan.
Create the technical vision (target architecture) and a phased migration plan. Communicate this widely: present at engineering all-hands, write an arch doc for Confluence, etc. People need to see the whole map, not just their piece, so they understand how their work ties into the larger project. Use visual diagrams and timeline charts if it helps. As the leader, you'll maintain and update this plan as things evolve.

Project management (yes, you do some PM work).
Identify dependencies between teams and make them explicit. For example, Team A must deliver a new API by February for Team B to switch in March. Track progress (using spreadsheets or a project management tool). Follow up in sync meetings. Senior ICs often partner with an engineering manager or technical program manager (TPM) on this, but sometimes you have to do a lot of it. The key is ensuring no team is blocked, or if they are, it's surfaced and resolved.

Technical oversight.
While you can't code everything, you should review key designs from each team for alignment. Perhaps set up a weekly migration design review where each team presents what they're doing next and any challenges, and as the initiative lead, you ensure it all fits together or give advice if one team is approaching something suboptimally. You don't micromanage (teams need autonomy), but you gently guide. Think consultant more than boss.

Unified standards and tools.
For a big initiative, having common approaches accelerates progress. If each team writes its own migration scripts differently, it's chaos. You, as leader, might propose, "Let's all use X tool for infrastructure-as-code."

Provide a template or example others can copy. This reduces duplicate work and fosters shared expertise (everyone can help each other because approaches are similar). It also cements your leadership role by providing helpful resources.

Cross-team communication.
Ensure wins and discoveries are shared across teams. Maybe set up a Slack channel (say, "#cloud-migration") for any gotchas found, so others don't duplicate debugging. Share frequent updates on what's done so far, and make sure to celebrate milestones publicly. This not only motivates (progress is visible) but also keeps everyone informed. Often, you become the voice of the project in broader forums: giving status to directors, highlighting risks, etc. That is leadership: representing an effort and driving it to success.

Handle conflict or misalignment diplomatically.
If Team X is behind or Team Y built something not per the agreed specifications, approach it via problem solving, not blame. "I see we're behind here—how can we adjust? Do you need help or can another milestone move?" or "This component ended up different from what API spec said; let's reconcile—maybe the spec was incomplete? Let's figure it out." Large projects have issues; the leader sets a collaborative tone for fixing them rather than finger-pointing. This keeps morale and trust high, which is crucial over long efforts.

Give credit, take responsibility.
When reporting on the successes, acknowledge the teams: "Team A and B did an awesome job hitting their targets." When reporting problems, own them collectively or as a leader: "We underestimated the effort here—that's on me; we have a plan to get back on track." This protective stance endears you to teams (they know you won't throw them under the bus) and impresses higher-ups (you show leadership maturity).

AI for Project Management and Status Reporting

Leading a large, cross-team initiative involves significant coordination and communication overhead. AI can act as a project management assistant to handle routine tracking and reporting.

By connecting an AI to your team's project management tools (like Jira or Asana) and communication channels (like Slack), you can automate status updates:

Prompt: *Review the progress on the "Q3-Cloud-Migration" epic. Summarize the completion status for each team's sub-tasks, identify any tickets that are blocked or behind schedule, and draft a one-paragraph weekly status update for stakeholders.*

This frees the technical lead from the manual toil of chasing down updates and compiling reports. Instead of spending their time on administrative tasks, they can focus on the high-leverage leadership work: solving technical roadblocks, aligning teams on architecture, and making strategic decisions.

Leading big initiatives as an IC is challenging but can be a pinnacle of IC career achievement. You orchestrate a symphony of efforts, making sure the final outcome is harmonious. Many staff/principal engineers find this aspect—making something big happen across an org—immensely rewarding, rivaling or exceeding the gratification from writing code individually.

Successfully driving a big cross-team project is often what distinguishes a staff engineer from a senior engineer in promotion calibrations. It shows you can operate at an org level. It's also, not incidentally, a skill that transfers to management roles if you ever choose that route.

This is engineering leadership in the pure IC form.

Mentorship and Sponsorship: Lift Others as You Climb

I've mentioned mentorship several times. By senior levels, not only should you be mentoring others, but intentionally sponsoring promising talent too. This is a form of leadership that ensures the next generation grows, and it's often expected at high IC levels (many career ladders have criteria like "actively mentors others" for seniors and "develops other technical leaders" for principals). As a reminder:

- A *mentor* gives advice, answers questions, and provides feedback to help someone grow.
- A *sponsor* uses their influence to advocate for someone, recommending them for a key project or promotion.

Here are a few ideas for how to mentor effectively as a senior IC:

- Take on at least one regular mentee (often a new hire or junior). Set up a weekly or biweekly chat. Help them solve problems rather than giving direct answers. Ask guiding questions, share similar experiences.
- In code reviews, don't just fix issues, explain patterns and reasoning. For example, "I refactored this because our convention is X, which helps because Y. Keep it in mind next time."
- Encourage them to take on some stretch tasks and be their safety net. "Why don't you lead the implementation of this feature? I'll support you and review your design." They learn by doing, but know you have their back. This is huge for building their confidence and skills.
- Protect time for mentorship despite being busy. It's easy to deprioritize because it isn't "urgent." But remember, part of your job at senior levels is team growth (usually reflected in performance reviews).
- You also learn by mentoring; you solidify your own knowledge and gain perspective on how others approach things.

And you can take this a bit further with sponsorship as an IC leader:

- Identify junior/mid-level engineers who have potential. If you see someone doing great work quietly, draw attention to it. For example, tell your manager "Hey, I think Maria is doing senior-level work on that module—maybe consider her for promotion if she keeps it up." Sometimes managers aren't in the weeds to see it; your voice can highlight deserving folks.
- Nominate others for opportunities. If a new project needs a lead and you could do it but so could your colleague who's trying to grow, support them taking the lead (with you advising). Leadership isn't hoarding the best tasks; it's growing more leaders.
- Invite a less-experienced teammate to co-present with you at an internal tech talk, giving them visibility.
- If you have a seat at calibration meetings (some companies involve staff engineers in promotion committees), speak up for those you think meet the bar.

- Essentially, be the senior engineer you wish you had support from earlier in your career. That culture will pay back—people you sponsor might become your strongest collaborators.

You may be wondering why mentoring and sponsorship matter so much in the discussion of how to be an effective engineer. Here are a few things to recognize about the benefits of helping your colleagues:

- They multiply the capability of the team (so more gets done with quality).
- They become allies—engineers you've helped will trust and support you on initiatives, giving you more informal influence.
- It's deeply fulfilling—you get to take pride in others' success, which is a hallmark of great leaders.
- Company leadership notices those who raise others up; it's typically part of criteria for principal levels. It shows you're operating with the org's long-term health in mind, not just individual contribution.

It's also great for company culture. If every senior engineer mentors one or two others, knowledge flows and culture propagates healthily. It avoids silos and hero dependency. It also makes onboarding smoother and retention better (because people feel invested in). So, part of being an IC leader is fostering that culture. You can organize a mentorship program or simply lead by example, showing that mentoring is valued, not a chore.

In sum, leadership as an IC comes in many forms: guiding projects, influencing decisions, mentoring people, and spearheading improvements. It's often subtle—no formal authority, yet real impact. Embrace these roles:

- Step up to coordinate when leadership is needed.
- Persuade and communicate to align everyone toward common goals.
- Nurture the growth of your colleagues.

These are the contributions that make you not just a good engineer, but a force multiplier in your organization. As we move into thinking strategically in Chapter 8, these leadership skills will combine with seeing the bigger picture to make you an all-around effective senior technical leader.

Ethical Considerations and Taking Responsibility

As engineers gain more influence and leadership capabilities, they also bear greater responsibility for the ethical implications of their work. Effective engineers don't just build what they're asked to build—they think critically about potential negative impacts on users and society.

FORESEEING AND ADDRESSING USER RISKS

Throughout this book, we've discussed understanding user needs and delivering value. But effectiveness also means considering potential harms. When working on a feature or system, ask yourself the following questions:

- Could this negatively impact certain user groups disproportionately?
- Are there privacy implications we haven't adequately addressed?
- Could this feature be misused in ways that harm users?
- Are we collecting or using data in ways that respect user trust?

If you foresee risks, you have a responsibility to raise them. This can be uncomfortable, especially if you're early in your career or if the team is under pressure to ship. But ethical concerns are precisely the kind of issue where engineers need to speak up. Frame your concerns constructively:

Present specific scenarios.
"If we implement this feature as designed, users with slower connections will have a significantly degraded experience, potentially excluding users in developing countries."

Propose alternatives.
"What if we add a confirmation step that makes the implications clear to users before they proceed?"

Escalate if necessary.
If your concerns are dismissed without adequate consideration, escalate to your manager or appropriate channels. Most companies have ethics boards or processes for raising concerns.

HANDLING MISTAKES AND INCIDENTS

Making mistakes is inevitable in any engineering career—from small bugs to major incidents that impact users. What distinguishes effective engineers is how they handle these situations.

When you make a mistake that causes problems, follow these principles:

Take ownership immediately.
Don't hide it, minimize it, or blame others. Alert your team and relevant stakeholders quickly. Example: "I deployed a change that's causing checkout failures. I'm rolling it back now and will investigate the root cause."

Focus on resolution first, root cause second.
Your immediate priority is minimizing user impact. Once the situation is stable, then investigate what went wrong.

Conduct a blameless post-mortem.
After major incidents, write up what happened, why, and how to prevent it in the future. The focus should be on improving systems and processes, not punishing individuals. Good organizations recognize that most failures are due to systemic issues, not individual incompetence.

Share learnings broadly.
Turn your mistake into an opportunity for the team to learn. If you discovered that a particular testing gap led to the issue, propose improvements to your testing practices.

Forgive yourself and move forward.
Everyone makes mistakes. Dwelling on them doesn't help anyone. Learn what you can, make amends where appropriate, and move on with the knowledge that you'll handle similar situations better next time.

Build resilience into systems.
Beyond individual incidents, think about how to make systems more forgiving of human error. Can you add better monitoring, validation, or rollback capabilities? Making it harder to make catastrophic mistakes benefits everyone.

Taking responsibility for mistakes and considering ethical implications aren't just about avoiding negative outcomes—they're about building trust with your team, your users, and yourself. They're essential components of engineering effectiveness that extend beyond technical skills.

These leadership skills are most effective when applied to high-impact work. Chapter 8 will explore strategic thinking for engineers, helping you identify and align your efforts with what truly matters to the business.

| 8

Strategic Thinking for Engineers

Up to now, I've covered how to execute well and lead at the team level. As you become a senior/staff engineer, you increasingly need to think about doing the right work, not just doing the work right. This means identifying high-impact projects, aligning technical efforts with business goals, balancing long-term tech vision with immediate deliverables, and using data to drive decisions. In short, developing *strategic thinking* skills.

A common challenge is finding the time for this kind of high-level thinking amidst daily coding and meetings. A powerful technique is to proactively block out strategy time on your calendar—perhaps one or two hours at the beginning of the week. Treat this appointment with yourself as seriously as any other meeting. Use this time to zoom out, review your team's metrics and goals, think about the engineering vision for your area, or work on one of the high-impact identification strategies mentioned in this chapter. Without dedicated time, it's easy for strategic thinking to be perpetually pushed aside by urgent but less important tasks.

Identifying High-Impact Work

Not everything on the to-do list has equal value. Effective engineers learn to focus on what's going to move the needle for the business or team metrics. This is especially important as you gain autonomy over what to work on.

These practices will help you identify the most important things to focus on:

Focus on outcomes (reprise).

Recall the section "Outcomes Versus Outputs: Solve the Right Problem" on page 2 from Chapter 1. Always ask: "If we do this, what is the outcome and is it significant?" For example:

- Shipping a minor UI tweak that affects 0.1% of users versus tackling a performance issue affecting every page load. The latter likely has a higher impact.

- Automating a process that saves engineers five minutes a day versus building a feature that could attract new customers. The latter likely aligns more with business growth.

This doesn't mean ignoring all small tasks (some low-hanging fruit can be quick wins). But have a sense of proportion and priority.

Ask why.

When given a project, ask "What goal does this serve?" If it's not clearly tied to a goal, dig deeper. Maybe the requirement is outdated or misprioritized. You might discover a more impactful problem to solve instead. For example, a PM might ask for an analytics report feature. By asking why, you find it's to understand user drop-off. Perhaps an alternative solution is to improve the drop-off rate instead of just reporting on it. That might be more effective.

Use an effort versus impact matrix.

A common strategic tool is to list potential tasks and estimate their impact (e.g., low/medium/high effect on revenue, user satisfaction, or efficiency) and the effort required to complete them (low/med/high time cost). Try to do the high-impact, low-effort items first (quick wins). High-impact, high-effort ones might become projects to plan. Low-impact, high-effort tasks likely should be dropped or deprioritized (those are classic busy-work candidates).

Be willing to challenge assignments.

This can be touchy, but if you suspect a project is a lot of work for little gain, politely raise the concern. Use data if possible: "This feature is projected to be used by less than 2% of users—meanwhile, 30% of users are complaining about load times. Perhaps we shift some focus to performance, which could benefit all users." Managers/PMs might resist, but a good org will listen if you present a case well. Even if they don't pivot now, they'll consider it in future planning. This shows you're thinking about ROI, not just blindly coding, which marks you as a strategic asset.

Stay informed about business priorities.
Read the product strategy docs, attend product review meetings if invited, and understand how the company makes money or what usage metrics matter. Then align your suggestions and work with those. For instance, if the business is focusing on user retention this quarter, think about what engineering work could boost retention (maybe reliability improvements, faster load times, or adding a feature that brings users back). Propose those or prioritize them in your own task list. Work on things the company cares about and you'll multiply your impact (and your work is more likely to get noticed).

Consider the 80/20 rule.
The 80/20 rule, also known as the Pareto principle (*https://en.wikipedia.org/wiki/Pareto_principle*), states that for many outcomes, roughly 80% of consequences come from 20% of the causes. Identify what those key features or components are in your product. Ensure those are robust and evolving well. Spending days perfecting an admin panel that almost no one uses instead of enhancing the core feature everyone uses is misallocation. Strategic thinking is recognizing where the leverage is.

AI-Powered Work Prioritization

An IC's effectiveness hinges on working on the right things, but it can be difficult to connect a backlog of technical tasks to real-world user pain. AI can act as a data-driven assistant to help surface high-impact opportunities. By integrating with multiple data sources, an AI tool could provide some key insights:

Identify common user problems.
> An AI can ingest thousands of customer support tickets, use sentiment analysis to identify the most frustrating user problems, and then map those problems to related tickets in the engineering backlog.

Connect work to business goals.
> An AI could analyze the company's objectives and key results (OKRs) and cross-reference them with the product backlog to highlight features that directly contribute to a key result.
>
> By automating the routine work of data aggregation and correlation, AI gives engineers the evidence needed to advocate for high-impact tasks, ensuring their effort is spent where it matters most.

Next, let's discuss what it means to align your work more explicitly with the goals of the business you're working at.

Aligning Engineering with Business Goals

To be truly effective, engineering effort must serve the broader company mission. That means understanding business goals and translating them into engineering plans. There are a few ways to ensure your efforts are aligned with the overall goals of your organization:

Choose projects with strategic value.
> As a senior IC, you often have some choice in what to work on (or how to approach a goal). Tilt toward efforts that align with company strategy:
> - If the strategy is expanding to new markets, perhaps focus on making the product easily localizable or scalable internationally.
> - If cost reduction is a major goal, maybe that optimization project that saves on cloud costs should be prioritized over a slightly nicer UI feature.
> - If data privacy is now crucial due to regulations, focusing on compliance engineering has high business importance, even if it's not "cool" technically.
>
> This doesn't mean dropping all other work, but keeping an eye on "what does the company need most from engineering now?" and contributing there. It will maximize your perceived value as well as actual company success.

Be solution-oriented to business problems.

Sometimes the business will express a problem without a clear engineering ask. Effective senior ICs will try to solve it, even if it's not a purely technical problem. Consider this example: customer support says many users complain they don't know how to use feature X (a business problem: low feature adoption). Perhaps the solution is an in-app tutorial (so a bit of design, a bit of engineering) or adjusting the UX flow. Bringing a proposal to tackle that user problem even though it didn't come as an engineering ticket shows strategic initiative. It's bridging the gap between business need and tech execution—which is what staff engineers are often expected to do.

Establish guardrails.

Sometimes alignment means pushing back on something that will technically undermine long-term business ability. For example: product wants to rush a feature that hacks something insecure. A strategic IC communicates the risk: "If we launch this way, we risk a security breach that could cost us users and compliance fines. How about we take two extra weeks to do it safely?" You're aligning with the fundamental business goal of preserving trust and avoiding legal trouble, even if the immediate feature goal says, "Launch ASAP." This is thinking one step ahead about consequences—a very strategic trait.

Speak business language.

When communicating with non-engineers, frame your ideas by how they support business objectives. Chapter 4 mentioned this in the context of influencing PMs. Company leadership especially responds well when outcomes are included: revenue, cost, user growth, risk mitigation. So if you're advocating for technical work (like rearchitecting a service or paying down debt), articulate the business benefit. Here are a few examples:

- "This will let us handle holiday traffic spikes without downtime, protecting revenue."

- "Improving site speed has proven to increase conversion; this could realistically add $X in sales."

- "Refactoring this module will reduce maintenance time, freeing approximately 20% of engineering capacity for new features."

Balancing Vision with Execution

Technical vision is your idea of an ideal future state (architecture, capabilities). *Execution* is what you deliver incrementally now. Strategically, you must balance dreaming big with delivering value regularly.

Avoid spending months building the "perfect" system while delaying deliverables indefinitely. Instead, keep a long-term plan in mind, while connecting it to immediate actions:

Have a vision.
As a senior IC, you should have some sort of technical vision for your area. For example, "In a year, I think we should move toward a microservices architecture with well-defined APIs so each team can deploy independently." Or, "Our vision is to have zero downtime deployments and A/B testing on every feature." Vision provides direction; it's the North Star for technical decisions. Without it, you might make short-term choices that conflict in the long run.

But don't get lost in it.
Vision that isn't tied to current execution can become pie-in-the-sky. Instead, do the following:
- *Break the vision into phases:* Identify steps that incrementally move toward the vision, each providing some tangible benefit. For example, Phase 1: extract service A from monolith (improves one bottleneck, sets pattern); Phase 2: create common auth service (removes duplicate effort); Phase 3: ...etc. This way, you're shipping pieces and learning as you go.
- *Validate as you go:* Maybe your vision includes a new tech stack. Test it on a small scale (maybe one microservice or one part of the app) as a pilot. If it proves positive, that fuels further execution. If it shows unexpected problems, adjust the vision. Strategically, don't bet everything on unproven ideas—experiment, then invest.

Communicate your vision.
Share your end-goal idea with the team and stakeholders so they understand the purpose behind intermediate steps. It's motivating and also gets buy-in: "We're doing these refactors not just 'because engineering wants to,' but to enable a future of faster, independent deployments, which means we can deliver features to you PMs more quickly down the line."

This frames execution tasks (which might slow some feature delivery now) as an investment for greater future output—speaking the language of ROI.

Be flexible on vision details.

New information should refine your vision. Maybe while executing Phase 1, you discover microservices cause heavier operational overhead for your small team. Perhaps full microservices (original vision) isn't optimal; maybe a modular monolith or grouped services approach is better. A strategic thinker is not stubborn. They will say, "Our ultimate goal is independent deployability and team decoupling—there are multiple ways to achieve that; let's adapt our approach." Keep the high-level vision (the outcome), but be willing to change the means.

Don't neglect short-term wins.

It's easy when enamored with a grand vision to undervalue small improvements today. But those small improvements keep users and management happy and build momentum and credibility that lets you pursue bigger changes. So maintain a balance: spend some cycles on vision-building changes, and some on immediate features or bug fixes. This is somewhat like Google's innovation versus maintenance time, or product versus engineering allocation. Strategically allot time for each. For instance: in a quarter, maybe propose that 70% of cycles go to product features, 20% to foundational refactors (vision steps), and 10% to maintenance/tech debt. This ensures execution on visible stuff while still progressing toward the vision.

Amazon provides a case study of the balance between vision and execution. It famously has the mottos "Deliver results" and "Think big" as separate leadership principles. A strategic engineer does both: think big (visionary ideas) and deliver results (actually implement iteratively). For example, Amazon might have envisioned the idea of Amazon Web Services (AWS) long before it was fully built (think big), but it rolled it out service by service (delivering results at each step with S3, EC2, etc.). The idea of balancing visionary leaps and iterative delivery is how AWS effectively replaced much of on-prem computing. AWS didn't appear overnight fully formed—Amazon had a vision ("utility computing for all") and executed it gradually.

Using Metrics and Data in Decisions

We touched on data-driven decisions in the chapter on collaboration (Chapter 4) and earlier here and there, but this section will emphasize how crucial it is in strategic thinking. As systems grow and stakes get higher, intuition alone can mislead. Metrics add objectivity. They also help persuade others, as discussions become less contentious when supported by data.

Here's a guide for defining metrics and using them to inform your decisions:

Establish key metrics.
> For whatever you're working on, define success metrics (key performance indicators [KPIs]). For a performance refactor, this might look like "Requests per second, 99th percentile latency, error rate." If it's a new feature: "Daily active users of feature, conversion rate from use to purchase." Having metrics focuses efforts and allows you to know if the strategy is working.

Measure and adjust.
> Monitor these numbers continuously to inform your next steps:
> - If a metric isn't moving despite effort, re-evaluate your approach (maybe the problem wasn't where you thought). Perhaps you optimized the backend, but load times didn't improve much because the frontend was the bottleneck—data (like browser performance logs) could reveal that, informing you that you need to pivot your focus.
> - If metrics show improvement, communicate that widely (this proves the value of the engineering investment).
> - If metrics unexpectedly worsen (maybe a refactor made average speed better but tail latency worse), investigate and address. Data catches these trade-offs.

Use A/B tests or experiments.
> For strategic product decisions, propose experiments to gather data. *A/B testing* (also called *split testing*) is a method where you show different versions of a feature to different user groups and measure which version performs better. Instead of endless debate about whether redesigning onboarding will help retention, run an experiment on 10% of new users. As an IC, you can advocate for and even implement the test infrastructure if needed. This is strategically pushing for evidence-based decision making.

Benchmark and simulate.
   For technical strategies (like "will architecture X scale better?"), gather data by benchmarking. Maybe build a test harness to simulate load on a prototype of architecture X versus the current system. Data from that can justify the big architectural pivot (or warn against it).

Include data in technical discussions.
   When communicating with PMs or managers, bringing data gives you credibility. Instead of "I feel we have too much tech debt," say "We spent 40% of last sprint fixing bugs from system Y, which indicates significant maintenance drag." Hard data can compel action where a gut feeling might not.

Beware vanity metrics and test biases.
   A strategist uses meaningful data, not just any data. Ensure the metrics tie to real outcomes (like user success or team efficiency), not just numbers that go up but don't matter (like "number of deployments"—more deployments aren't inherently good or bad). Also be open to data that contradicts your initial assumptions (that proves its value!). If your favored approach doesn't show benefits in terms of data, be ready to adapt.

Promote data culture.
   You can lead by example, encouraging others to gather and share metrics. Maybe you create a monitoring dashboard for key team metrics and review it weekly with the team. Over time, the team starts thinking of success in terms of those graphs too, which aligns everyone on concrete goals.

Quantify engineering value.
   There's often a struggle to quantify engineering improvement work (like reducing tech debt or adding tests). But you can often find proxies or anecdotes: e.g., "Before, each release candidate had about 15 bugs found in QA; after our refactor, the last release had 5 bugs in QA—a 3x quality improvement." Or "Our on-call load dropped from five incidents per week to one per week after we overhauled logging—this frees roughly X hours for feature work and reduces burnout risk." Tying engineering work to tangible results makes it easier to justify and continue. If you can't tie work to tangible results, it's worth questioning whether that work delivers real value.

In conclusion, as you advance, you shift from focusing solely on "How do I implement this?" to also asking "What should we implement, and why?" You're engaging in some key practices:

- Prioritizing high-value work and ensuring alignment with business objectives
- Balancing long-term improvements with short-term deliverables
- Using data to choose paths and prove success

Strategic thinking elevates your role from code executor to a key decision maker in the product's direction. It's a hallmark of senior technical leaders. Combine this with the execution, collaboration, and leadership skills from earlier chapters, and you become a formidable engineer: one who not only builds things right, but also builds the right things and steers the team and product to greater success.

Strategic thinking and high-impact work are essential for advancing as a senior IC, but they come with an inherent risk: the more responsibility you take on and the more you care about outcomes, the easier it becomes to overextend yourself. The drive to identify and execute high-value projects, align with business goals, and maintain technical vision can paradoxically lead to an effectiveness-killing burnout that derails some promising careers.

As you develop these strategic capabilities, you must simultaneously develop the discipline to sustain them. Chapter 9 focuses on protecting your most important asset—yourself—so that your growing influence and impact can be maintained over the long term rather than burning bright and flaming out.

Avoiding Burnout and Sustaining Long-Term Success

Software engineering can be demanding. Without careful management of your time, energy, and boundaries, it's easy to burn out—losing effectiveness or even leaving the industry prematurely. The tech industry is known for high pressure, a rapid pace, and sometimes demanding workloads, with surveys finding that 73% of developers (https://oreil.ly/oEyV8) have felt burned out in their career and 83% have suffered work-related burnout (https://oreil.ly/Hq4_U).

Truly effective engineers sustain high performance over years while maintaining a healthy relationship with work. This chapter covers strategies to avoid burnout and keep yourself productive and fulfilled in the long run.

Recognizing Burnout and Stress

Before diving into prevention strategies, it's crucial to recognize the warning signs. Burnout is more than just a tough day; it's a state of chronic exhaustion (emotional, mental, physical), cynicism or detachment from work, and reduced effectiveness. Some warning signs are physical and emotional, and others show up in the work environment.

Physical and emotional warning signs include the following:

Exhaustion
> Feeling tired and drained most of the time, even after rest. You dread starting work in the morning.

Physical symptoms
> Headaches, stomach issues, or sleep problems that are stress-induced. Maybe you can't fall asleep because your mind is racing about work issues.

Emotionally flat or irritable
> You might feel numb about success (nothing is satisfying), or little frustrations set you off more than they should.

Work-related symptoms include the following:

Loss of motivation
> Tasks that used to excite you now feel like a slog. It's hard to muster enthusiasm or creativity.

Reduced performance
> You find it harder to concentrate and solve problems, or you notice an increase in mistakes. Work that used to be easy is now difficult.

Depersonalization or cynicism
> You might feel disconnected from your work or colleagues, or develop a negative, overly critical outlook. For example, thinking things like "nothing we do here matters" or "our code is all garbage anyway."

An effective engineer pays attention to these signs in themselves and teammates. Ignoring these warning signs leads to declining performance, strained relationships, and potentially severe burnout requiring extended recovery time.

If you're already experiencing burnout, the prevention strategies that follow are helpful, but more immediate action is needed. Consider taking time off to recover—even a week can help. Seek professional support through therapy or counseling. Have an honest conversation with your manager about workload and expectations. Sometimes a role change, project switch, or even a career break is necessary. Recovery from burnout takes time; be patient with yourself and prioritize your health over work deliverables.

Prevention is key. Far better than recovering from burnout is preventing it through proactive well-being management. The following strategies help maintain consistent, sustainable performance and job satisfaction.

Manage Your Energy, Not Just Your Time

We often talk about time management, but *energy management* is equally important. You might have 8 to 10 hours a day to work, but for how many of those are you mentally fresh? Back-to-back meetings, for instance, can be particularly draining, leaving little energy for focused technical work. Here are techniques for effectively managing your energy in a sustainable way:

Work in sustainable cycles.

If you try to code intensely 12 hours a day, day after day, quality and creativity will drop. Many developers find that they only have a few peak hours of flow for tough problem solving each day. Allow yourself breaks. The Pomodoro technique (25 minutes of focus followed by a 5-minute break) works for some, while others prefer 90-minute focus blocks followed by a longer break. Find what keeps you from mentally fatiguing. When you notice diminishing returns (staring blankly at code, making silly mistakes), it's often more effective to step away and recharge than to keep pushing.

Take regular breaks (micro and macro).

Use the Pomodoro technique or at least follow the rule of thumb to take a 5- to 10-minute break every hour or so. Micro-breaks help reset your focus (and give your eyes and wrists a rest, preventing repetitive strain injuries). Step away from the screen—get a coffee, stretch, look outside a window to relax your eyes.

For macro-breaks, use your vacation days and weekends. Avoid the trap of thinking, "If I just push a bit more, I can finish this, then I'll rest." There's always another task after. Rest is part of work, not the opposite of it. Also, consider occasional mental health days if you feel burnout creeping in. One day off to decompress can recharge you enough to prevent needing a month off later.

Take breaks and vacations without guilt.

A *10x engineer* is a mythical developer who is believed to be 10 times more productive or impactful than their average peer. In reality, even the best engineers need rest. Breaks, both short (like a walk around the office) and long (like multi-day vacations) improve your output. You've probably experienced coming back to a hard bug after a good night's sleep and solving it in five minutes. The brain needs time to process subconsciously.

A *burnout anti-pattern* is taking a vacation but still working or staying mentally attached to work. Truly disconnect during off time—your brain needs that recovery. If your workplace pressures constant overtime, try to discuss workload or expectations with your manager (or HR if needed). It's in the company's interest for you not to burn out (turnover is expensive).

Prioritize physical health.
Mind and body are linked. Regular exercise, even something as simple as daily walks or stretching, can drastically reduce stress and improve mood. Schedule it like a meeting if you must. Good sleep is not optional—it's foundational. Lack of sleep impacts cognitive function and emotional regulation, making you less effective and more prone to anxiety. Aim for a consistent sleep schedule. Also be mindful of diet and substances: too much caffeine can heighten anxiety and disturb sleep, fueling a burnout cycle.

Cultivate interests outside coding.
These practices have real benefits. Hobbies, exercise, and social activities all help reduce stress and prevent your identity from being 100% tied to work success. If your whole identity and happiness is tied to coding or your current job, any failure or stress at work hits much harder. Having interests outside work gives you perspective and alternate sources of fulfillment—when work is tough, you still have other areas of life providing joy or balance. Skills from other activities (teamwork skills from sports, musical discipline, etc.) can cross-pollinate, making you a more rounded developer.

Use company resources.
Many companies have mental health resources (counseling, stress management workshops), wellness days, subscriptions to meditation apps, and gym reimbursements, or encourage "no meeting days." Take advantage of these. They exist because employee burnout is a known issue in tech, and smart companies want to mitigate it. Using these resources demonstrates self-awareness and a commitment to sustainable performance.

Reducing Cognitive Load with AI-Powered Summaries

A significant source of mental drain for engineers is the need to stay on top of a constant stream of information in long email threads and busy Slack channels. Missing a key decision can be costly, but reading everything is exhausting. AI can act as a filter to reduce this cognitive load.

Tools are emerging that can integrate with your communication platforms to provide on-demand summaries. Instead of scrolling through 200 messages in a channel you were away from, you can prompt the AI with something like this: "Summarize the key decisions and action items from the #project-alpha channel from the last 24 hours." This allows you to quickly catch up on what's important while ignoring the noise, preserving your mental energy for deep work and preventing the fear of missing out that contributes to burnout.

Busting the 10x Myth—Focus on Team Effectiveness

The 10x engineer is not just rare, but is not always a healthy goal for every person of your team. In terms of long-term success, chasing that myth can absolutely lead to burnout. For example:

- People try to work 10x hours—burnout.
- People put the weight of 10 engineers on themselves—stress and burnout.
- It fosters isolation and lack of asking for help—leading to burnout or failure.

Instead, focus on being part of a 10x team. Even as a senior IC without formal reports, you can influence your team's culture and processes in the following ways:

Delegate and trust
> Keeps you from burnout from overwork and also encourages a culture where everyone contributes their share (as we discussed in Chapter 5).

Improve processes
> Fix the root causes that force heroics; 10x work often comes from 10x frustration due to poor tools. Solve those problems, and the whole team's efficiency rises as there's less need for any one person to be a hero.

Cross-train
> Tough tasks can be rotated. If one person handles all on-call pages, they'll fry. Train more people to handle issues so it spreads out. The team collectively can sustain a load that would burn out an individual.

Prioritize ruthlessly
> A team that tries to do everything will burn out. As a senior IC, help your team say "no" or "not now" to low-priority asks. It's better to do a few things well (and sanely) than to do everything poorly under stress.

Let's look at an example: a startup team I was on had crunch after crunch. People were exhausted. We sat down and realized we were treating everything as top priority. We got better at saying no to some feature requests, even if from the CEO, explaining we had to focus on stability and core features. After one particularly intense development cycle, we instituted recovery sprints, where every fourth sprint focused on low-stress cleanup and personal learning. Productivity in the other sprints actually *increased* because we weren't constantly red-lining. It's counterintuitive, but giving slack prevents burnout and improves output quality.

Setting Boundaries and Saying No

We covered delegation in Chapter 5 and managing up in Chapter 4, both of which involve sometimes pushing back. This section emphasizes how saying "no" (politely) is crucial to sustaining your workload and preventing overcommitment—a frequent cause of burnout.

BOUNDARIES TO PROTECT PERSONAL TIME

Decide your cut-off time and try to stick to it (with rare exceptions). For example, "I do not check email after 7 p.m." Communicate that to your team ("I'll be offline in evenings—if something urgent comes up, call my cell"). As touched on in "Remote Work Strategies: Thriving in a Distributed Environment" on page 151, it's critical to have clear boundaries between work and personal time. Avoid checking work emails or Slack late at night or on weekends (unless you are explicitly on call). If you often work from home, consider separating your work environment (e.g., shut the office door at night or put away your work laptop).

Weekends and vacations are yours, unless you choose to work or there's an absolute emergency. If your team routinely pings you on weekends for nonurgent stuff, gently push back: "Let's sync on this Monday; it's important

I recharge so I can tackle this at my best." And don't be the person creating a culture of "always on" by sending code or emails at midnight—use delayed send or draft it and send it the next morning if you get a burst of inspiration off-hours.

BOUNDARIES AT WORK TOO

It's OK to say, "I cannot attend that meeting because I need to finish debugging this critical issue by today. Please send me notes." You can't do everything at once. People often overload calendars, but as long as someone from engineering is there, it might not have to be you. Protect your deep work time by scheduling focus blocks and defending them.

When tempted to just keep working to finish "one more thing," recall that in tech, there's always another bug or another feature. You'll rarely feel finished. Set stopping points and accept them. A fresh you tomorrow will likely finish faster than a burned-out you tonight. As the fable teaches, steady and sustainable wins over fast and erratic.

SAYING "NO" TO TASKS AND MANAGING PERFECTIONISM

When product or management asks for something extra and you truly don't have capacity, it's more professional to say no upfront than to say yes and fail or kill yourself trying. A desire to please or prove oneself can lead engineers to take on too much. When saying no, when possible, provide an alternative: "We likely can't deliver Feature X in this quarter along with our other commitments. We could push it to next quarter, or drop Feature Y to make room for X now—how would you like to adjust?" This shows you're solution-oriented, not just obstinate.

Also, watch out for perfectionism. Many engineers have a perfectionist streak (it's part of what drives quality). But perfectionism can also cause unnecessary stress and burnout. If you feel nothing is ever good enough, you might be working significantly more hours than needed, polishing code or adding features that weren't requested. Learn to recognize diminishing returns: if the code meets the requirements and is decently clean, maybe it's OK to mark it done rather than refining it endlessly. Sometimes "good enough" is exactly what's needed, especially if it means delivering on time and moving to the next priority.

TRAIN YOUR CULTURE AND LEVERAGE SUPPORT

If one person always says yes and works late, management might (unfairly) start expecting it of everyone. By collectively standing firm on some boundaries, the culture becomes healthier. Senior ICs can lead here by example. When I became a tech lead, I made sure to explicitly say to teammates, "Make sure to take your vacation time, we'll handle things." Sometimes people need permission. As a senior IC, you can similarly encourage peers or juniors: "Hey, you haven't taken a day off in months, maybe do so? I'll cover anything urgent."

Be sure to connect with peers or mentors. Talking to others in the industry can normalize what you're feeling, and you can offer one another support. Perhaps join a community or Slack group where engineers talk about burnout or work-life balance. If your company has an employee assistance program (EAP) or counseling services, consider using them if you're struggling. Many people hesitate because of stigma, but mental health professionals can provide tools to manage stress, anxiety, or depression.

Cultivating a Sustainable Career

Sustaining a long and fulfilling career in tech isn't just about avoiding burnout; it's about proactively cultivating habits that support growth, learning, and well-being over decades. This means pacing your learning, remembering that your career is a long journey, and choosing environments that align with your values.

LIFELONG LEARNING WITHOUT BURNOUT

Tech changes rapidly. That can stress people out ("I must learn X, Y, Z or become obsolete!"). Pace yourself. Choose relevant things to learn, one at a time. It's great to do side projects or read books in your own time, but also maintain balance. For example, set a modest goal like "I'll spend two hours each week learning a new technology." That keeps you current but is bounded. Burnout can come from pressure to constantly be "on" even outside work. Focus on fundamentals (which endure) and selectively on new skills that align with your interests or job needs.

CAREERS ARE MARATHONS, NOT SPRINTS

If you burn out and quit for a year, that slows you more than if you had just worked at a reasonable pace consistently. I've seen brilliant engineers flame out by 30 due to brutal stints at companies. I've also seen steady, healthy engineers still coding strong and loving it at 50. Those who last treat their mental health and personal life as first-class priorities, not as afterthoughts to work. They still deliver great work (arguably more consistently), but they didn't sacrifice everything else for it.

Remember, you are your most important tool. As an engineer, you maintain servers, update software libraries, and refactor code for efficiency. Similarly, you must maintain yourself—your mind and body—because that's the engine that produces all your great work. Skipping maintenance leads to breakdowns. Taking care of your mental health isn't a luxury; it's part of being an effective professional.

PICK THE RIGHT ENVIRONMENT AND DE-STIGMATIZE MENTAL HEALTH

Part of sustaining success is working at places that support sustainability. Some companies have healthy cultures, some have sweatshop vibes. An effective engineer also knows when their environment is toxic and can't be fixed by individual effort. If you've tried setting boundaries and the org routinely violates them, or you see widespread burnout, there's no shame in planning an exit to a healthier company.

The culture around mental health in tech is improving. Many prominent voices have spoken about burnout and the need for balance. If you feel burned out, know you are not alone. Seeking help or adjusting work conditions is a sign of wisdom, not weakness. Companies are realizing burnout leads to attrition and mistakes, and are increasingly supportive of wellness initiatives.

Fictional Example: From the Edge of Burnout to Balanced Success

Priya was a talented engineer who often worked 10 to 12-hour days and weekends to keep up with her startup's demands. She began to dread going to work and felt exhausted, and her coding creativity suffered. After a big release, she realized she was burned out—even trivial tasks felt overwhelming, and she felt detached from the project she used to love.

She decided to speak to her engineering manager about it, who was supportive and helped redistribute some of her workload temporarily. Priya took a week off to recharge, during which she barely checked email (with her manager's encouragement). When she returned, she started implementing boundaries—no work after 7 p.m.; she reinstated her habit of jogging each morning; and she began delegating some responsibilities to a junior developer she had been mentoring.

Over the next couple months, her energy returned, and she actually became more productive than when she was pushing herself to the brink. The code she wrote was with a fresher mind, and she was happier at work. The team still met its goals—her constant overtime earlier hadn't been as necessary as she imagined. By speaking up about burnout, she opened a dialogue in the team, leading to better policies around after-hours communication and weekend work.

Avoiding burnout isn't just about feeling better—it's about maintaining your effectiveness. A burned-out engineer makes mistakes, loses creativity, and often becomes much less productive than a well-rested, motivated one. By managing workload, debunking harmful myths, setting clear boundaries, and ensuring you recharge, you actually perform better and for longer. Remember: *consistency beats intensity*. It's better to be a solid performer year after year than a superstar who fizzles out.

The strategies in this chapter—managing your energy, setting boundaries, and building sustainable practices—form the foundation for long-term effectiveness in software engineering. However, even well-intentioned engineers can fall into behavioral patterns that undermine both their own sustainability and their team's success. These patterns often emerge from the same drive to excel that makes engineers effective, but when taken too far, they become counterproductive anti-patterns. In Chapter 10, we'll examine common team-level effectiveness anti-patterns that can sabotage your efforts to maintain the healthy, productive career you've been building. Recognizing these patterns early is crucial—they're often the hidden culprits behind the very burnout and frustration that this chapter's strategies are designed to prevent.

| 10

Team-Level Effectiveness Anti-Patterns

While Chapter 5 focused on anti-patterns at the individual level, a team's effectiveness is also shaped by its collective habits and processes. *Team-level anti-patterns* are dysfunctional group dynamics that can stifle productivity, lower quality, and create friction, even when individual engineers are highly skilled. These issues are often systemic and require a coordinated team effort to resolve. This chapter explores common pitfalls that plague engineering teams, from knowledge bottlenecks to flawed product alignment, and provides strategies to build a more resilient, collaborative, and high-functioning team.

Knowledge Silos: The Dangers of Having Domain Bottlenecks

We've touched on the dangers of knowledge silos, but here we will explore it as a systemic, team-level anti-pattern. While an individual might create a silo, the persistence of that silo is a team or organizational failure that introduces significant risk and inefficiency.

A *knowledge silo* exists when critical information or expertise is concentrated in one person or a small subset of the team, instead of being shared. In such cases, certain team members become the sole go-to authorities for specific domains or components (e.g., "Only Alice understands the payment system" or "Bob is the database guy; no one else touches it"). While specialization is natural, extreme silos create a dangerous dependency: if those individuals are unavailable (or leave the company), the team might be unable to function effectively in those areas. This anti-pattern can severely limit a team's agility and pose serious continuity risks.

Having work bottlenecked through specific people also slows the team. Others might avoid code areas they aren't familiar with, meaning tasks queue behind the one expert. And if that expert is overloaded, tasks in their domain become slow or neglected. Moreover, it can lead to frustration both for the expert (who feels everything depends on them) and for other team members (who feel they can't contribute broadly).

WHY SILOS FORM

Silos often start innocently. Perhaps one engineer wrote a complex part of the system and, due to time pressure or convenience, they remain the only one who really understands it. Or teams divide work by component, and each engineer deep-dives into their piece without cross-training. Over time, each person accumulates deep knowledge of their area and others don't engage with it. There may also be an element of gatekeeping at times—intentionally or unintentionally, the expert might not disseminate their knowledge (maybe thinking it's faster if they just handle it, or job security fears may even play a role in toxic cultures). Organizational structure can also contribute: if teams are very siloed by function or microservice, knowledge might not flow between them.

THE DANGERS OF KNOWLEDGE SILOS

The following list highlights the key risks that arise when knowledge isn't shared across a team:

Single point of failure
: If the sole expert on a subsystem falls sick, goes on vacation, or quits, that subsystem becomes a closed box. Work on it may stall, and fixing bugs or outages becomes slow or impossible. For example, if only one engineer knows how the deployment pipeline works and they suddenly leave, the team might be unable to release new code until someone figures it out—possibly causing delays and mistakes.

Team bottleneck
: Others must frequently wait for the siloed expert to do reviews or answer questions since no one else can. This can create a queue on that person's time, limiting throughput. For instance, if only one person knows the analytics code and every change in that area needs their review or input, their bandwidth defines the pace of changes in analytics. In an extreme case, if that person has five projects waiting for their guidance, those projects stall.

Stagnation of knowledge and innovation
> When knowledge isn't spread, fewer people can contribute ideas or improvements to that component. The expert might have blind spots or be used to the status quo, whereas a fresh perspective could bring innovation. But if others feel "that's not my area," they won't chime in or suggest changes. Also, if the expert leaves and knowledge transfer fails, the remaining team might opt to rewrite the component because they don't understand it—potentially a huge setback.

Morale and workload issues
> If team members feel they are pigeonholed and not allowed to learn beyond their silo, it can hurt morale. Engineers often like learning new things; silos can make work feel narrow or repetitive. The siloed person might feel pressure and stress from being the only one carrying certain knowledge ("I can't ever be unavailable, everything will break!"). That can lead to burnout.

Quality and oversight problems
> When code ownership is siloed to a single person, reviews often become superficial because peers either implicitly trust the author or feel unqualified to critique the work. This lack of scrutiny allows issues to go unnoticed. A similar pattern emerges in small, insular teams; the Appfire report on review dynamics (*https://oreil.ly/U9iJB*) found that when the same small, exclusive group of engineers reviews each other's code, feedback quality degrades over time—potentially due to eroding trust. Whether it is a silo of one or a few, the lack of outside perspective can quickly turn a codebase into a "bug factory."

Ultimately, these dangers all point to a fragile and inefficient team where collaboration is stifled and risk is concentrated in a few key individuals.

SIGNS OF KNOWLEDGE SILOS

Recognizing the early warning signs of knowledge silos is crucial for maintaining team agility and resilience. Here are common indicators that knowledge is overly concentrated among a few individuals, potentially hindering collaboration and increasing organizational risk:

- Team members say things like, "Oh, that module...only Carol works on that, I have no clue how it works."

- When a particular system goes down, everyone immediately calls the same person to fix it.

- In code review or design meetings, certain areas have no discussion because only the expert has context and others don't engage.

- Vacation planning causes anxiety: "If Devendra is out, we should probably not release anything that week because he's the only one who knows the release process."

- When onboarding a new engineer, you realize there are entire subsystems that no one on the current team can explain well because the original authors left.

HOW TO BREAK DOWN SILOS

The following strategies offer practical ways to break down these silos by encouraging shared ownership, improving documentation, fostering mentorship, and aligning team structures to support broader knowledge distribution:

Spread code ownership.
> Encourage collective code ownership where feasible. This might mean rotating people into different areas of the codebase periodically. Pair programming is invaluable: pair the expert with other team members on tasks in the siloed area so the others learn. For example, if only Alice knows the payment system internals, assign Bob to work with Alice on the next payment-related feature. Bob doesn't just assist; he actively implements parts with Alice's guidance. Next time a payment bug comes, Bob might try to fix it (with Alice advising). Over time, Bob becomes comfortable in that area too.

Document and share knowledge.
> The simplest step is to document what the expert knows. It doesn't substitute fully for hands-on experience, but it mitigates the "if they disappear, knowledge is gone" issue. Have the expert write architecture overviews, or run knowledge transfer sessions or lunch-and-learns. Even recording a meeting where the expert explains the system's internals can be helpful for others later. A knowledge silo is evident when someone asks, "Is this documented anywhere?" and the answer is no. Strive to make that answer yes. For critical processes (deployment, setup, troubleshooting), write step-by-step guides and store them in an accessible location (wiki, repo, etc.).

Encourage questions and mentorship.
Create a culture where it's expected that knowledge is shared and asking questions is safe. The expert should mentor others proactively. For instance, during code reviews, the expert can leave informative comments to educate others on why something is done a certain way (not just what to change). Or they can host a short workshop. ("Let me show everyone how to debug an issue in the data pipeline.") Even casual practices like "Friday knowledge share: every Friday, someone spends 15 minutes showing something they learned" help erode silos. When juniors ask questions, the expert can answer in group channels (so everyone sees the Q&A, not just privately), multiplying the reach of that knowledge.

Cross-train and assign backups.
Intentionally assign backup owners. Perhaps officially designate that each critical component has at least two people who can handle it. If one person is primary for the caching system, choose a secondary who participates in all caching-related work. This could mean the secondary reviews every caching pull request (PR), or occasionally implements a change themselves with primary guidance. Rotate being on-call for that component between both of them, so each gains operational knowledge. Some teams maintain a *skills matrix*—list team members versus systems/skills, and ensure no system has only one check mark. Use pairing or training to fill the gaps.

Avoid hero culture and gatekeeping.
Sometimes an expert might be unconsciously (or consciously) gatekeeping—always swooping in to handle their area or not involving others because "it's easier if I do it" or they're proud of that domain. This relates to the hero complex and inability-to-delegate anti-patterns discussed in Chapter 5. Solving it requires the expert to let go a bit and trust colleagues, and the team/management to support that by not always turning to the expert first. Make it clear that success is when many people understand the system, not just one superhero. If the expert is swamped, leadership can step in and say, "We can't have only Jamie doing all cloud infra tasks. Let's have someone else shadow Jamie and take on some tasks." Recognize and reward experts for teaching, not just fixing everything themselves.

Restructure teams if necessary.
In some cases, silos are fostered by team organization. If one team owns the whole frontend and another owns the whole backend, people might

not learn the other side. If silos are hurting delivery, consider a more cross-functional team structure where knowledge areas overlap by design (e.g., each team has some frontend and backend expertise). Similarly, if one person has become the bottleneck for a critical path, adding another person to that area or splitting responsibilities can help (e.g., if there's only one database expert, consider hiring another or training an existing dev to also become a database specialist). At times, temporarily shifting an engineer into another team or project specifically to absorb knowledge can work—like an exchange program within the company.

Use the bus factor as a metric.
Some teams explicitly talk about the bus factor mentioned in Chapter 5 (or its analogue, risk). If any critical area has a bus factor of 1 (only one person is truly knowledgeable), treat that as a risk to mitigate. Management can include it in risk logs or OKRs: e.g., "Increase bus factor of payment service from 1 to 3 by Q4." While it's a somewhat cheeky metric, framing it this way helps communicate to stakeholders why time is being spent on documentation or cross-training (it's risk reduction). Some version control or contribution data can quantify knowledge concentration (e.g., if 90% of commits to a subsystem are by one person, that's a red flag). Aim to reduce that percentage over time by involving more contributors.

This proactive approach transformed a high-risk dependency into a shared team capability, making the entire team stronger and more resilient.

FICTIONAL EXAMPLE: THE ONE-PERSON SHOW

Company Alpha has a microservice architecture. Over time, one of the microservices, which handles notifications, has been solely maintained by an engineer named Ravi. Whenever something about notifications comes up—new feature, bug, deployment issue—everyone goes straight to Ravi. He built it from scratch and loves working on it, but now he's moved to another project. Still, the team pings him for notification problems because no one else knows it well. This becomes a serious issue when a major bug appears in notifications while Ravi is on a two-week vacation. The rest of the team scrambles; they read through code they've never touched, missing context. A simple fix that Ravi could have done in an hour takes two days and imposes a lot of stress on the on-call engineer who has to figure it out by trial and error. After this incident, the team lead acknowledges the silo problem. The resolution: Ravi conducts a thorough walkthrough of the notification service once he's back and writes an internal wiki page about its design and quirks, and two other engineers pair with Ravi on upcoming notification features. Within a couple of months, those engineers feel comfortable handling basic notification issues, and the documentation allows others to tackle simpler problems. The bus factor for the notifications service effectively went from 1 to 3. Next time Ravi is out, the team is confident they can manage notifications without him.

BEYOND INDIVIDUALS—SILOED TEAMS

Knowledge silos can also exist at a broader level: e.g., only Team A knows how the legacy billing system works, and they never talk to Team B. In large organizations, this can hinder collaboration. The remedies are similar: cross-team workshops, documentation, rotation of personnel between teams, or reorganizing teams to encourage knowledge flow. Modern DevOps and "you build it, you run it" approaches try to eliminate silos between development and operations, because traditional silos in those areas caused slowdowns and finger-pointing. The principle of DevOps was partly to increase shared ownership of delivery, avoiding the "dev throws code to ops and ops, has to run it" silos. So, on a team level, find ways to break barriers—maybe have feature teams rather than strictly component teams, or do regular syncs where teams present to each other what they're working on.

CULTIVATING A LEARNING CULTURE

Ultimately, avoiding knowledge silos comes down to culture. Teams should value collective code ownership, continuous learning, and teaching. If someone becomes a silo, it should be seen not as their job security but as a risk that the team needs to mitigate. Leadership can encourage this by recognizing and rewarding those who share knowledge (for instance, praise someone for writing a great onboarding guide or mentoring others, not just for coding solo). Engineers should also take initiative to learn outside their specialty when possible—read code in other modules, attend design discussions even if it's not your feature (you might learn something new).

By breaking down silos, the team becomes more resilient and flexible. Work can continue smoothly even if someone is out. People can take vacations (and sleep at night) without worry, and the overall bus factor increases. Plus, individuals grow in their capabilities, making the work environment more enriching. This aligns directly with being an effective engineering team—success and knowledge are shared, not bottled up. In the long run, teams with high knowledge sharing are more adaptive, faster, and less prone to catastrophic failures than those reliant on a few linchpins.

Rubber Stamping: Superficial Approvals That Degrade Quality

Rubber stamping in a software team context means giving routine, thoughtless approval to changes—essentially stamping "Approved" on code reviews without actually reviewing the code in depth. It's a code review anti-pattern where the reviewer provides little to no feedback and might not even fully read the code. They treat the review as an annoying formality or bureaucratic hurdle, rather than an opportunity to ensure quality. This can happen for various reasons: the reviewer is too busy, too trusting of the author, or too disengaged to do a proper review. Unfortunately, when code review becomes a rubber-stamp exercise, its effectiveness plummets.

Rubber-stamp reviews might look like this: Suppose Alice opens a pull request with 500 lines of changes. Bob is the assigned reviewer. Within five minutes, Bob clicks Approve with a comment "Looks good"—no questions, no suggestions. Maybe Bob only glanced at a couple of files, or just trusts that Alice is competent. Alternatively, Bob might always approve automatically because he assumes others will catch issues or because he doesn't want to appear nitpicky or slow things down. In some teams, there's an unspoken agreement to go easy on reviews—"I approve your stuff, you approve mine"—to avoid delays or interpersonal friction. In all these cases, the pull request (PR) gets merged without substantive scrutiny.

WHY IS THIS A PROBLEM?

Code review serves multiple purposes: catching bugs or design flaws, maintaining code standards, and sharing knowledge among the team. Rubber stamping short-circuits all of these:

Bugs and flaws slip through.
> The reviewer might have spotted something if they looked carefully, but they didn't, so issues go unnoticed until later (perhaps in testing or production). Maybe Alice's 500-line change had a security oversight or a performance issue that Bob glossed over. Now that becomes tech debt or a bug for the future.

Standards and consistency suffer.
A diligent review would flag deviations from best practices or style guidelines. A rubber stamp won't, so those inconsistencies accumulate. For example, if Alice introduced a different naming convention or didn't write unit tests, Bob might not bother to point it out—leading to a less uniform codebase.

Knowledge isn't transferred.
One big benefit of reviews is that at least one other person learns about the code change. If Bob barely reads it, he doesn't actually absorb what was done. So only Alice fully understands that piece of code. The team loses the chance to spread knowledge (which is the opposite of what we want, as discussed in the section "Knowledge Silos: The Dangers of Having Domain Bottlenecks" on page 117). If Alice is out later and something goes wrong with that code, Bob might be as clueless, as if he'd never seen it.

Review culture erodes.
If everyone knows reviews are superficial, developers may put less effort into preparing their code (why write thorough tests or docs if no one looks at them?) or be less careful when reading others' code. It becomes a check-the-box exercise rather than a valuable process. New team members will follow suit if they see that's the norm.

Rubber stamping is particularly risky if combined with knowledge silos—e.g., if only Alice understands that code area, Bob might feel unqualified to review it deeply and just approve it without really reading it. But that's exactly when a careful review or additional reviewer is most needed (or at least a conversation to educate Bob so he *can* review meaningfully).

WHY DOES RUBBER STAMPING HAPPEN?

Often it's time pressure or overload. If reviewers have many PRs to get through or heavy feature work of their own, they may skim and approve just to unblock the queue. In some cases, it's social discomfort: the reviewer might be junior to the author or afraid to critique a strong personality, so they just approve to avoid conflict or looking dumb. There's also team culture: if the norm is to "not waste time" on reviews and just trust each other, new members will follow suit and rubber stamp to fit in. And sometimes, frankly, laziness or apathy—a reviewer might not want to do the tedious work of reviewing a large diff, so they give it a cursory glance and click Approve.

A subtle form of rubber stamping can happen when two developers always review each other's code and develop too much mutual trust. The Appfire report on code reviews (*https://oreil.ly/URABC*) warned of pairs or cliques who review each other's work leniently. Because they trust that the other writes good code, their reviews become perfunctory. Over time, this insular approach can let errors slip in or result in divergence from wider team standards (because no outside perspective checks the code).

CONSEQUENCES ON QUALITY

Imagine a scenario where over a few months, most reviews have been rubber stamps. The codebase could accumulate various problems, such as the following:

- More bugs make it to testing or production because fewer were caught at review. Perhaps there are security oversights or edge cases missed.
- Code becomes inconsistent—different modules follow different styles or patterns because no one is enforcing consistency.
- Technical debt grows unchecked. Maybe a developer introduced a quick hack in one PR; a diligent review might have suggested a better design up front, but a rubber stamp let the hack merge. Multiply that by dozens of merges, and you have quite some debt. It's hard to quantify exactly, but teams often notice eventually if they have a rubber-stamp culture: features might require more rework later, or new team members find the code lacks cohesion or clarity, making onboarding harder.

In short, a culture of rubber stamping systematically dismantles the very quality gates that code reviews are meant to provide, leading to a slow but certain decline in codebase health.

HOW TO ADDRESS RUBBER STAMPING

Addressing rubber stamping in code reviews requires both cultural and procedural shifts within a team. Here are several practical strategies to encourage more thoughtful, thorough, and collaborative review practices that improve code quality and strengthen team knowledge:

Set review expectations explicitly.
> The team should agree on what a good review entails. For example, reviewers should at least read through all changes, run the code or tests if applicable, and provide constructive feedback or questions. If a PR is too

large to review well, that should be noted (and ideally that's a prompt to break it into smaller PRs next time). By openly stating that rubber-stamp approvals are not acceptable, you create a baseline. Some teams even have a checklist for reviewers (like "verify all new functions have unit tests; check for obvious error handling; ensure documentation is updated; consider performance implications;" etc.) to encourage thoroughness. The goal isn't to make code review bureaucratic, but to remind people of what to look for beyond "looks fine to me."

Adjust workload or process to allow time for reviews.
If people are rubber stamping due to lack of time, consider limiting how many active PRs a person can have assigned for review at once or lighten other duties to free up time for proper reviews. It might also mean encouraging smaller PRs, as noted—it's unfair to expect meticulous review of a 5k-line change on a tight schedule. Perhaps use pair programming or design discussions before coding to reduce the review burden later (because major points were sorted out already). If the issue is that senior devs are overloaded with reviews, train more people to be able to review (e.g., involve intermediate devs in reviewing complex code with a senior co-reviewing to build their skills).

Use multiple reviewers or gating for critical code.
For crucial changes or when a less experienced person reviews a tricky area, have a second reviewer glance at it, as well. DZone's Refcard on code review patterns (*https://oreil.ly/tnn8f*) advocates having at least two pairs of eyes on complex changes. Many teams require two approvals for high-risk code (like changes to authentication, security-critical sections, etc.). This reduces the chance of one person's rubber stamp letting through a serious issue. It also shares knowledge further. However, requiring multiple reviewers for every single change can slow down velocity, so use this judiciously (balance risk and speed).

Encourage a questioning and learning mindset.
If reviewers see their role as just an approver, review becomes rubber stamping. Instead, encourage them to see it as learning and quality assurance. They should feel it's acceptable to ask the author, "Can you explain why we're using approach X here?" or say, "I'm not familiar with this library you added—could you briefly outline how it works?" These don't have to be criticisms; they can be genuine queries. This not only improves

the code by prompting clarification (maybe a comment in code to explain something nonobvious) but also ensures the reviewer understands it. Create an atmosphere where team members don't take questions or suggestions personally. Code review isn't an evaluation of the person; it's a team process to improve code and share knowledge.

Make reviews a two-way dialogue.
Authors can play a part by inviting feedback: include context in the PR description ("This change does X; here's why and alternatives considered"). Reviewers then have more to chew on. Authors can also explicitly say, "I'd especially like eyes on the concurrency logic in `foo()`; not entirely confident there." That signals to the reviewer to focus there rather than gloss over it. When authors show openness to critique, reviewers are more likely to actually review and offer feedback instead of rubber stamping.

Hold reviewers accountable.
One tactic is to have the reviewer share responsibility for the code quality once they approve. For example, at some companies, if a severe bug is discovered from code that was approved, the reviewer is also involved in the post-mortem. The idea isn't to blame, but to reinforce that review is an active responsibility. When reviewers know their approval is not just a rubber stamp but a real endorsement ("I am vouching that this code is OK"), they might take it more seriously. Some teams even keep track of review metrics (e.g., if a lot of bugs escape from a particular reviewer's approved changes, that might indicate a need for that reviewer to be more thorough or get training).

Provide training on how to review.
Not everyone knows how to perform a good code review, especially less experienced devs. Conduct a short workshop or share articles on code review best practices. Topics could include looking for correctness, readability, maintainability, adherence to style, testing completeness, and potential impacts on security/performance. Giving reviewers a mental checklist or examples of good review comments can improve their effectiveness. Sometimes rubber stamping happens because the reviewer didn't understand the code well and felt embarrassed to admit it; training can increase their confidence to identify issues.

Leverage tools to reduce trivial review burden.
Use linters, formatters, and automated tests in CI to catch the easy stuff. If trivial style issues or obvious bugs are caught by tools, reviewers can focus on the logic and design. This also makes reviews less tedious (people might rubber stamp if they think the only feedback they have is nitpicks—remove the nitpicks via automation). Some platforms also have change suggestion features where the reviewer can propose a code edit that the author can accept with a click—this lowers the barrier to making minor improvements instead of ignoring them.

The key to eliminating rubber stamping is creating a culture where code review is seen as collaborative quality assurance, not a bureaucratic checkpoint. When teams combine clear expectations, adequate time allocation, and proper training with the mindset that reviewers share responsibility for code quality, reviews transform from perfunctory approvals into meaningful dialogue that strengthens both the code and the team's collective knowledge.

FICTIONAL EXAMPLE: THE QUICK OK

Team Beta is in a period where PRs are almost always approved with one-word comments or emojis. Developer Sarah merges a change that swaps out an authentication mechanism. Reviewer Tom gives it an LGTM (looks good to me) in under five minutes. Post-merge, it turns out the change inadvertently removed a crucial authorization check, introducing a security hole. In the post-mortem, it's clear Tom didn't notice the missing check in review—likely because he didn't actually review that part carefully. The team realizes they've been rubber stamping too often. As a corrective measure, they decide that any security or auth-related code changes must be reviewed by at least one person with back-end/security expertise (no matter who the author is), and Tom admits he rushed and commits to being more careful. The team also introduces a rule that reviewers should leave at least one substantive comment or question with an approval (even if minor), to prove they looked—not a perfect solution, but a way to slow down the instant-approve reflex. Over the next sprints, they see an increase in review discussion and a corresponding decrease in issues slipping through.

BALANCING EFFICIENCY AND DILIGENCE

It's understandable that not every code review will be deeply involved; minor changes might legitimately be fine with a quick skim. The key is ensuring that quick approvals are given when appropriate (truly simple, low-risk changes), not by default for everything. For more complex work, investing time in review actually saves time later by catching issues early. If the team is concerned about speed, consider *time-boxing* reviews (e.g., aim to review within one working day of PR submission) but not skipping them. Also, combine small changes—maybe batch trivial fixes in one PR so you don't have to review 10 tiny PRs separately (thus reducing overhead while still having oversight).

If a reviewer often finds nothing to comment on, maybe the code is indeed excellent—or maybe the reviewer isn't looking hard enough. One way to ensure engagement is to ask reviewers to summarize the change back to the author ("So this function will do X to handle Y, right?"). If they can't summarize it, they likely didn't grok it. This technique forces some level of understanding.

ENCOURAGE LEARNING THROUGH REVIEWS

Frame code reviews as learning opportunities both for the author (to get feedback) and for reviewers (to see how something was implemented). Celebrating instances where a reviewer's comment improved the code can reinforce the value of non-rubber-stamp reviews. Perhaps offer a highlight in the retrospective, like, "Hey, thanks to John's thorough review, we avoided a concurrency issue in the new scheduler code." This shows the team that careful reviews directly contribute to success, encouraging that behavior.

In summary, rubber stamping is the antithesis of a healthy code review culture. It provides a false sense of security. By fostering a culture of thoughtful review—where approvals are earned by virtue of code quality and adherence to standards, and where reviewers take pride in catching things or improving code—a team can significantly improve its software's robustness. Remember, the goal isn't to nitpick every line or make reviews adversarial; it's to make sure that when code is merged, at least one other qualified person has truly understood and vetted it. That raises the quality bar for everyone.

Flaky Product Ownership and "Just One More Thing": Engineering and Product Misalignment

Engineering teams don't work in a vacuum; they build software to meet product goals and user needs. When there's strong alignment between product management and engineering—clear priorities, stable requirements, and mutual understanding—teams can execute effectively. However, a common anti-pattern is *flaky product ownership*, where product direction is inconsistent or chaotic, often leading to the infamous "just one more thing" syndrome. This refers to the habit of injecting new features or changes late in the game, repeatedly, disrupting engineering plans and sprints. While this is related to the scope creep anti-pattern discussed in Chapter 5, the focus here is on the root cause being driven by inconsistent product direction rather than organic project expansion.

Flaky product ownership may manifest as the following:

Constantly changing requirements or priorities
> For example, one week the team is told Feature A is top priority; the next week it's dropped or replaced by Feature B without clear reasoning. Or each new stakeholder meeting yields a different set of marching orders.

Last-minute additions to a release
> For example, "We must also include this minor feature—just one more thing—before we launch." Each time the team thinks scope is set, something new is tacked on. There's always another must-have coming in at the 11th hour.

Poor backlog grooming or sprint commitment
> Things get added mid-sprint or pulled out unexpectedly. The product owner might agree on a sprint plan, then midway say, "Actually, pivot to this other task," repeatedly. This leaves the team chasing a moving target.

Lack of clarity or decision making
> Engineers might build something, then the product owner says, "This isn't what I wanted," because the vision wasn't clearly communicated or it changed mid-implementation. Or product management might be indecisive ("maybe do it this way...no wait, let's try that way"), causing thrash.

Over-promising to external stakeholders
> A product owner might keep saying yes to customer or leadership requests and pushing them to engineering without filtering or scheduling properly, causing overload and unrealistic deadlines.

This flaky approach leads to misalignment—engineers feel they're aiming at a moving target and can't catch up. It's demoralizing and inefficient. Here, the emphasis is on the product-management side fueling that scope creep or volatility.

WHY IS THIS A PROBLEM?

Flaky or inconsistent product ownership can have significant negative effects on the engineering team. When priorities shift frequently or decisions lack follow-through, it disrupts not only what teams build, but also how they feel about their work. Here are some key ways this instability impacts engineering execution and culture:

Context switching and waste

If engineers frequently have to drop what they're doing to accommodate a new request or change direction, time is wasted on partially done work and ramping up on new work. For instance, they might have built half of Feature A, only to hear it's no longer needed. That work might never be used (classic waste) or will have to be picked up later and recontextualized. It's like constantly planting seeds and then digging them up before they grow.

Quality suffers

"Just one more thing" often comes at the end of a sprint or release cycle, forcing engineers to rush or hack something in to meet a deadline. Technical debt can pile up from all these last-minute changes that weren't planned or designed properly. Testing might be cut short due to time crunch, introducing bugs. Late additions lead to lower quality; flaky product management institutionalizes that problem by making late additions the norm.

Team morale suffers

It's frustrating for engineers to feel like their careful planning or architecture is thrown out on a whim. They might start believing that planning is futile. ("Why bother designing robustly when the requirements will change anyway?") Burnout can creep in due to constant fire drills and a lack of a feeling of accomplishment (since priorities shift before finishing things). The team can become cynical about management and disengage—doing just what they're told at the last minute, rather than proactively thinking about the best solution.

Trust erosion

The relationship between engineering and product can become strained. Engineers might start viewing product managers as capricious or unreliable. ("They never stick to a plan.") Meanwhile, product managers might see engineers as resisting changes or being too slow—not realizing the churn they cause. Misalignment means they aren't working as a unit; instead, it can create a blame game, or at least a lack of mutual understanding.

Ultimately, flaky product ownership creates a cascade of dysfunction that transforms engineering from a craft focused on building excellent solutions into a reactive scramble to accommodate ever-shifting demands. The cost isn't just delayed features or technical debt—it's the erosion of the collaborative partnership between product and engineering that's essential for sustainable success.

WHY PRODUCT OWNERSHIP CAN BE FLAKY

Sometimes product ownership can be flaky due to external pressure—maybe sales or executives are demanding new features or changes frequently, and the product owner feels they have to accommodate them. Sometimes the product owner lacks experience or authority to stick to a decision and gets easily swayed by the latest feedback. It could also be a sign of not having a clear product strategy, so the product direction is reactionary rather than planned. Startup environments often change course as they seek product-market fit, but even then, there are ways to manage change without chaos (e.g., short iterative cycles with clear goals, rather than mid-iteration thrash).

HOW TO REALIGN AND ADDRESS THIS ANTI-PATTERN

Addressing the anti-pattern of flaky or inconsistent product ownership requires a proactive and structured approach to planning, communication, and accountability. The following strategies provide practical ways to restore alignment between product and engineering teams, reduce mid-sprint disruptions, and foster a more predictable and collaborative development environment.

Establish clear priorities and avoid mid-sprint scope changes

One remedy is to have a rule that once a sprint or development cycle has started, the committed work shouldn't be changed unless absolutely necessary (a true emergency or critical bug). Agile methodologies allow for flexibility between sprints, but not constant change within them. Product owners should respect the sprint commitment. If something truly critical emerges mid-sprint, swapping it in should involve removing or reprioritizing something else of equivalent effort (a trade-off), not just adding it. By instituting a scope freeze for the duration of an iteration (except emergencies), you limit chaos. This means product needs to do due diligence before the sprint—grooming and prioritizing effectively. Some scrum teams formalize this: once sprint planning is done, any new requirement goes to the next sprint's backlog unless the team agrees it's urgent and swaps something out.

Improve communication and planning processes

Often, flaky ownership is a communication issue. Regular meetings between product and engineering to clarify the roadmap can help. If engineers know the broader roadmap and the rationale behind it, small changes are easier to accommodate in context (and they might foresee needs earlier). Conversely, product should understand the engineering plan (and the cost of changes). Techniques like *sprint goals* can be useful—if the team has a specific goal (e.g., "Improve onboarding flow conversion by 10% this sprint"), then any last-minute request that doesn't serve that goal can be more easily identified as out of scope. Incorporating design and requirement reviews before sprints start can reduce mid-sprint surprises—e.g., have product walk through upcoming user stories with engineering so misunderstandings or missing pieces are caught and added to the plan *before* coding starts.

Enforce a review of late changes (change control)

If product does propose a late addition or pivot, pause to explicitly assess the impact. For example, do a quick team huddle: "If we add Feature Y now, it will push out our timeline by X days or reduce the quality of Z." Make that trade-off visible to all stakeholders (including whoever is pressuring the product owner). As mentioned, consider the project management triangle: scope, time, and resources. If one changes, at least one of the others must change. Often, once the cost is clear, stakeholders might decide the change can wait or isn't worth it. If they still want it, at least engineering can adjust expectations or get extra help. The key is to handle it as a conscious decision with input from engineering, rather than an edict that engineering silently absorbs.

Maintain a backlog for next time

Product owners can manage the urge for "just one more thing" by putting it into the backlog for the next release or sprint. Train the mindset that *iteration* is fine: it's better to deliver what's ready and then do the next increment, rather than cram and risk delivering nothing or a broken something. For example, if, near code freeze, a PM says "Users might also want to sort this table by date," instead of derailing the release, log it for the next iteration. Knowing it's captured and will be addressed soon can satisfy stakeholders. This is fundamental to Agile methodology, but under pressure, people forget and try to jam features in at the last minute. A strong product owner will manage internal expectations: "That will be in our next sprint, which starts Monday, not in this release going out tomorrow."

Strengthen the product-engineering relationship

Ideally, product and engineering operate as partners with mutual respect. If a product manager is inexperienced, a senior engineer or tech lead might help educate them on the development lifecycle and consequences of changes. Sometimes doing a retrospective specifically on requirement changes can highlight issues: e.g., "We changed course three times last month; how did that impact us? How can we handle it better?" If both sides talk openly, product might say, "I changed things because I got late feedback from user testing," and engineering might say, "If we'd known user testing was still going on, we could have anticipated changes." Then they could plan differently (perhaps schedule coding to start after getting that feedback, or plan a spike to accommodate possible outcomes). Joint retrospectives or blameless post-mortems can reveal misalignments in process and allow fixing them collaboratively. Also, involve product in sprint retrospectives regularly so they hear engineer concerns in a structured way rather than as pushback in the heat of the moment.

Agree on definitions of done and acceptance criteria upfront

One cause of last-minute tweaks is when the product owner only realizes what's missing when they see the nearly finished product. To combat this, invest time in clearly defining requirements and acceptance criteria for each story/feature during planning. If "user uploads profile picture" was the feature, acceptance criteria might include "User can crop the photo to a square." If cropping is considered from the start, it can be built in rather than bolted on. It requires product to think through user needs in detail ahead of time, which can be hard but is part of effective product ownership. Using concrete user stories ("As a user, I want to crop my profile photo to fit the circle avatar display") can prompt those extra requirements early. This reduces the "Oh, we forgot cropping, quick, add it" scenario because cropping would have been part of the original definition of done if it was truly needed for a good feature.

Adopt Agile ceremonies earnestly

Flaky product ownership often means sprint planning and retrospectives aren't being used properly. In sprint planning, ensure product is present and making prioritization decisions clearly. Once priorities are set, treat them as commitments. In the retrospective (retro), if scope change was an issue, bring it up and let product hear the impact from engineers. The product owner should also feel like a member of the team and be accountable for improvement. If they realize that they provided confusing priorities, they can commit to fix that.

It's not about blame, but about adjusting the process. Many Agile teams drift into pseudo-scrum, where they do stand-ups and demos but not real planning or retros—re-embracing those ceremonies can realign product and engineering. Planning gives a forum to agree on what will (and won't) be done; retros give a forum to discuss the process, including requirement volatility.

FICTIONAL EXAMPLE: THE EVER-CHANGING ROADMAP

A development team at a mid-size company struggles because their product manager, Carol, keeps shifting focus. They'll be midway through building a new dashboard when Carol hears feedback from a sales demo that a different feature is key, and she abruptly redirects the team to start on that, leaving the dashboard half-done. Later, the CEO mentions an idea to Carol, and she again tells the team to drop what they're doing. Engineers feel whiplash; nothing gets finished. Deadlines slip, and the CEO is unhappy at the lack of deliverables. In a joint retro, the engineering lead explains how much time was lost to context switching and partially done work. Carol acknowledges she didn't realize the full impact of these pivots. They agree to implement a simple change: any major change in priority must be discussed in a quick meeting with tech leads, and mid-sprint changes will be avoided. Instead, Carol will maintain a backlog of new ideas and at the end of each sprint, they will reprioritize for the next sprint. Over the next quarter, Carol still updates priorities often (market realities demand it), but now changes are slotted into the next sprint instead of derailing the current one. The team finishes the dashboard (which turns out useful for customers), and then the next sprint tackles the CEO's idea. The CEO sees more consistent delivery, and Carol finds that even with a small delay in implementing feedback, the outcomes are better and the team's morale has improved. Essentially, they moved from a chaotic reactive mode to a controlled iterative mode.

ENGINEERING-PRODUCT ALIGNMENT

The antidote to flaky product ownership is strong alignment and trust. Engineering needs to trust that product will provide clear and relatively stable goals, and product needs to trust that engineering will execute those goals efficiently and with quality. Both sides need to remain flexible but disciplined. When change is needed, they coordinate rather than unilaterally impose it. Over time, this alignment leads to a much more effective organization: product can anticipate how to work with engineering (e.g., bundling changes into sprint boundaries), and engineering has confidence in the direction it's building toward.

In short, avoid being "flaky" by being communicative and intentional. Embrace agility (respond to change), but not at the expense of stability (have structure in how changes are introduced). The "just one more thing" urge should be tempered by asking: what is the cost, and can it wait? If it truly can't wait, then what are we willing to sacrifice or change to accommodate it? Making those decisions jointly keeps both product and engineering accountable and in sync, thus preventing misalignment and the frustration it brings.

Low Bus Factor: The Risk of Team Dependencies

In Chapter 5, we discussed knowledge silos and the risks of having only one person know critical parts of the system. The bus factor directly relates to that. Recall that the bus factor is the minimum number of team members who would have to be hit by a bus (i.e., leave or be incapacitated) before the project is in serious trouble. A *low bus factor* (like 1 or 2) means the team has a high dependency on specific individuals—if they disappear, the project stalls. A *high bus factor* means knowledge and responsibilities are spread out such that losing any one person would not cripple the project.

Having a high bus factor is desirable because it equates to resilience. It ensures that no single absence (due to vacation, illness, or departure) can derail delivery or maintenance. In contrast, teams with a bus factor of 1 for key components operate under constant risk.

Ensuring a high bus factor is essentially ensuring that the team doesn't have heroes or silos that everything depends on. It's about building backups and overlap in skills and knowledge.

SIGNS OF A LOW BUS FACTOR

A low bus factor indicates that a project or team is overly reliant on one or a few individuals, putting progress at risk if those people become unavailable. Here are some common warning signs that suggest critical knowledge or responsibilities aren't being adequately shared across the team:

- Team members fear or avoid taking time off because they worry progress will halt in their absence. Conversely, when a certain person is on leave, a whole area of work pauses. ("We can't make database changes until Sam is back, because none of us fully understands it.")
- Key decisions or approvals always route to the same individual—e.g., architecture decisions can't be made unless the chief architect is in the meeting.

- New hires find that certain systems have no mentors available except one guru who's perpetually overloaded.
- People jokingly (or seriously) say things like, "We need to bubble-wrap Priya; if we lose her, this project is done for." This joke indicates that everyone knows Priya is a single point of failure.
- Knowledge-sharing meetings or documentation are nonexistent—institutional knowledge is held in certain heads, and others constantly ping them for help.

WHY LOW BUS FACTORS PERSIST

Sometimes low bus factors persist simply because they're historical—say a founding engineer built many systems and remains the oracle for them. Sometimes it's a trust or delegation issue—senior people not delegating, either due to control or lack of confidence in others. Company culture might unintentionally reward indispensability (praising those who seem irreplaceable), so people cling to knowledge. Or in very small teams, it's just not enough people to share all areas (though even then, proactively sharing context is possible).

It can also persist if managers don't recognize the risk, or if short-term deadlines always take precedence over cross-training and documentation. When the team is in perpetual crunch, they might say, "We don't have time to have Bob learn this; it's faster if Jane just does it"—which keeps Bob in the dark and Jane as the sole expert.

STRATEGIES TO INCREASE THE BUS FACTOR

Building a resilient team involves spreading critical knowledge to avoid dangerous single points of failure. This section outlines practical, team-level strategies to raise your bus factor before your project grinds to a halt. From rotating responsibilities to strengthening documentation and encouraging cross-ownership, these tactics help ensure that systems—and teams—can thrive even amidst unexpected changes:

Redundancy in knowledge

This echoes my advice from "Knowledge Silos: The Dangers of Having Domain Bottlenecks" on page 117—ensure at least two people know each significant component. Use pair programming, code reviews, and cross-training as key tools. If only one dev knows the build pipeline, have them teach another and co-own that domain. If one engineer has all customer context, bring a second engineer into customer meetings or requirement discussions. Approach it like backup systems in engineering: any critical function has a secondary one. On the human side, that means planning who could cover for whom in various areas. You can even ask questions like, "What if X got sick for a month—who could do X's duties?" If the answer is "no one" for something important, you have a bus factor problem to fix.

Rotation of roles and tasks

Some teams practice rotating on-call duty, component ownership, or technical leadership on a project basis. By rotating roles, more people get exposure. For example, if only one person usually releases the software, try rotating release captain responsibility each sprint—soon multiple people learn the ropes. Or rotate module ownership every quarter so knowledge spreads (one quarter Alice leads module A development with Bob assisting, and the next quarter Bob leads it and Alice moves to another). Rotation must be done carefully to avoid losing depth entirely, but done right it gradually raises everyone's familiarity.

Shared documentation and institutional memory

It's worth repeating: maintain updated documentation for critical systems. Make sure if someone left, another person could use docs to figure out how things work. Document not just how but why decisions were made—that context often lives only with individuals. Using a wiki or repository for design docs, architecture decision records (ADRs), etc., means the team's knowledge persists beyond individuals. Encourage engineers, when solving a tricky problem, to document it (like "Runbook: How to recover when cache cluster goes down"). Documentation increases the bus factor because someone else can follow the steps if needed instead of having to call the one person who remembers.

Automate knowledge out of heads

Automating processes can reduce reliance on memory or personal skill. For example, if the environment setup is complex and only one person knows all the steps, automate it with scripts—then others can run the script, and the knowledge is encoded in code. If server deployment is manual and only one person is practiced at it, invest in continuous deployment. Now anyone can push a button to deploy (or it happens automatically), not just the one deployment guru. This reduces the special status of that knowledge and frees that person to work on other things (and if they leave, deployment isn't blocked).

Mentorship and pairing as policy

Establish a practice that critical tasks are done in pairs or groups, not alone. For instance, code reviews ensure at least two people see every change. *Mob programming* (where the whole team codes together on one thing) can, when used occasionally, spread knowledge quickly (all participants see how a part of the system works). When planning work, avoid assigning all tasks in a given domain to the same person—mix it up so people have to dabble outside their usual zone. Senior folks should be evaluated partly on how well they enable others on the team, not just on their solo output—this incentivizes them to share knowledge rather than hoard it.

Encourage collective code ownership culture

Shift the mindset from "that's my code" or "that's your component" to "it's *our* codebase." This doesn't mean no expertise (people will still have strong areas), but it means anyone can, in theory, work on any part given enough time. You can encourage this by sometimes deliberately assigning bugs or features to someone other than the usual owner, just to broaden familiarity (with support from the expert). It might take a bit longer, but it's an investment in resilience. Celebrating instances of team members jumping into new areas helps reinforce that culture. For example, if a frontend dev fixed a backend bug while the usual backend dev was out, commend that and the help provided by others to make it possible.

Monitor and discuss risk openly

If you have risk management meetings or even just retros, talk about bus factor risks openly. Sometimes listing key-person risks in a retro (in a blameless way) can prompt the team to decide on actions. For example, "We identified that only Jamie understands the legacy authorization module. Action item: Jamie will conduct a training session on it and pair with Alex on the next ticket in that area." When the team treats this as normal ("Of course we shouldn't have single points of failure"), then addressing it becomes part of regular planning.

Leadership support

Often, increasing the bus factor requires spending some team time on cross-training or documentation, which might seem to reduce immediate velocity. Management needs to understand and support that this is valuable work—like an investment in risk reduction and future velocity. A good engineering manager will push back if higher-ups always want new features at the expense of team resilience. If you are an IC and feel siloed, bring data or examples to your manager: "If I get hit by a bus, we have a problem with X—I'd like to spend a bit of time to ensure Y and Z are up to speed on it." Likely the manager will agree that's prudent. It's much cheaper to transfer knowledge than to hire a replacement in a crisis.

FICTIONAL EXAMPLE: INCREASING THE BUS FACTOR

Team Gamma realized that their bus factor for the critical analytics pipeline was 1: only Ming fully understood it end-to-end. When Ming had a family emergency and was away for two weeks, the team had a scare when the pipeline broke, and no one else knew how to fix a particular data parsing bug quickly. They managed a workaround, but it was a close call.

After this, management and the team made it a priority to broaden knowledge. Over the next quarter, they took deliberate actions: Ming ran a series of internal workshops explaining the pipeline's design. Two other engineers shadowed Ming in tackling a couple of backlog improvements on the pipeline, learning the code by doing. They also jointly wrote a troubleshooting guide. By quarter's end, those two engineers felt comfortable handling typical issues, and the documentation allowed others to resolve simpler problems.

The bus factor for the analytics pipeline effectively went from 1 to 3. Ming could finally take a real vacation without the laptop, and the next incident that happened was handled by one of the others with only minor consultation. In fact, the incident response was faster since someone else was on call and didn't have to wake Ming at 2 a.m.; they could read the runbook and solve it. The team celebrated this as a big achievement in their retro, noting how much stress was reduced.

Now the team can distribute work more evenly. They don't panic over one person's departure or unavailability. It also opens opportunities—someone besides Ming can now propose improvements to the analytics pipeline because they understand it. The knowledge cross-pollination often leads to fresh ideas (e.g., one of the other engineers had a background in a different tool and saw a way to simplify a part of the pipeline that Ming hadn't considered). High-bus-factor teams tend to be more innovative because knowledge isn't bottled up.

BEWARE OF OVER-SPECIALIZATION

Specialization is natural and fine—someone will always be *the* expert in a given area. The goal isn't to make everyone equal experts in everything (impossible and inefficient), but to avoid single-expert fragility. You want overlapping expertise—like a Venn diagram with overlapping circles. Any critical area should have overlap between at least two team members. That way, if one circle is removed, the area is still covered by another.

Think of it like pair programming over the long term: at least two people should be able to discuss or modify any important piece of the system intelligently. If you achieve that, not only is the team safer from disruption, but working on the system becomes more fun—you can bounce ideas off someone who understands the context, rather than one person carrying it alone.

RESILIENCE AS A TEAM VALUE

Part of being an effective team is building resilience—including to personnel changes. This often resonates with management too: a high bus factor reduces risk for the business. (Sometimes a leader might worry, "If we lose so-and-so, we're doomed"; increasing the bus factor mitigates that worry.) It also improves flexibility: if more people know an area, you can reallocate people as needs change without massive relearning.

From an IC perspective, don't fear sharing knowledge, thinking it makes you less indispensable. In fact, engineers who uplift their team's skills are often more valued (they are seen as leaders). Also, when you share responsibility, you free yourself to learn new things and not be stuck maintaining the same legacy code forever because no one else can.

In conclusion, striving for a high bus factor is about building a strong bench—a team where multiple members can step up when needed. It turns individual knowledge into collective power. It might feel counterintuitive for individuals to make their own roles less unique, but ultimately it leads to more freedom (no one is chained to a subsystem or can't take a day off) and more team success. Effective software engineering teams ensure that success and knowledge are not dependent on single points of failure. By proactively sharing knowledge and responsibilities, you convert personal brilliance into collective capability. That is a hallmark of an effective, resilient engineering team.

Ineffective Sprint Retrospectives: When Reflection Fails to Drive Action

Agile teams commonly hold *retrospectives* (retros) at the end of each sprint or milestone to reflect on what went well and what didn't, and to decide how to improve. When done right, retros are a powerful tool for continuous improvement. However, an anti-pattern emerges when retros become routine discussions that don't lead to real change. Teams might identify issues sprint after sprint but take no concrete action to address them, effectively spinning their wheels. The result is that problems persist, and team members become cynical about the value of retros.

Symptoms of ineffective retros include the following:

- The same issues keep coming up repeatedly. ("We're still having outages due to configuration errors, like we talked about last time...and the time before...")
- Action items are discussed or written on a board, but never tracked or followed through. Perhaps they're not assigned to an owner, or everyone forgets them as soon as the meeting ends.
- Retros devolve into venting sessions or blame games, rather than constructive problem solving. People might focus on complaining about things outside their control (e.g., "Marketing always gives us last-minute requests!") without formulating a plan to mitigate that.
- Some teams even start skipping retros entirely because they feel it's a waste of time. ("We talk and talk, but nothing changes.") This is a tragic outcome, as it indicates a lost feedback loop.
- The retro meeting feels perfunctory—people give generic feedback ("communication could be better"), and then everyone goes back to work with no specific plan. There's low engagement; it's seen as just another ceremony to tick off.

Automating Retrospective Analysis to Find Deeper Insights

A common failure for retros is collecting feedback without identifying the most critical patterns. AI can serve as a powerful assistant here. By feeding anonymized retrospective notes into an AI, teams can automate thematic analysis to group related comments, identify recurring keywords, and even gauge team sentiment over time.

The goal isn't to replace human conversation but to augment it. An AI can handle the routine task of sorting the raw data, presenting the team with a summary of key themes. This frees the team to focus on the more important work: discussing *why* these patterns are emerging and deciding on meaningful, actionable solutions.

Often, ineffective retros occur due to a lack of ownership and follow-through. The meeting happens, and people nod in agreement on issues, but then no one is explicitly responsible for improvement actions. There might also be too many action items, making it unrealistic to tackle all, leading to inaction due to overwhelm. ("We identified 10 things to fix, but we can't do 10 things at once, so we did none.") In some cases, the team might feel powerless to change certain issues (like something dependent on another department), so they bring it up repeatedly but don't escalate or find creative solutions, resulting in a kind of learned helplessness.

Another reason is that retros sometimes focus only on discussion, not decisions. It's easy to run out of time after everyone voices thoughts, leaving no time to agree on what to do. Without a clear plan, even well-identified problems linger. Facilitators might also avoid assigning owners to actions in a mistaken effort to be democratic (hoping volunteers will step up later), but that often means nothing gets done.

TURNING REFLECTION INTO ACTION

A productive retro ends with clear, actionable steps that drive continuous improvement. This section outlines how to turn insights into impact by identifying concrete actions, assigning ownership, and ensuring accountability in future sprints:

Always derive a few concrete action items.
A retro should end with a short list of improvements the team *will implement*. An action item could be as simple as "Action: Pair a junior and

senior for code reviews to spread knowledge (assigned to Alice, to arrange this week)" or "Action: Try using a dedicated Slack channel for urgent issues to reduce distraction (team agrees to pilot this next sprint)." The key is that these are specific and testable. Avoid vague goals like "Communicate better"—instead, define how ("Set up a 15-minute daily sync between frontend and backend teams to share progress"). Think in terms of experiments the team will run next sprint to see if it improves things.

Limit and prioritize those actions.
It's tempting to fix everything at once, but that's likely to fail. Pick the top one to three things that will make the biggest impact or are most feasible. Scrum.org (*https://oreil.ly/_9DkB*) suggests focusing on one to two improvements each sprint. If you have a laundry list, prioritize it and accept that you'll only be able to tackle some of the issues at a time. This ensures the team isn't overwhelmed and can commit to making real progress on a couple of changes. It's better to fully solve one problem than half-solve five problems. Also, the psychological boost of actually fixing something is huge—it builds confidence in the retro process.

Assign ownership and deadlines.
Every action item should have an owner or owners and, ideally, a timeframe. For example, "Bob will create a wiki page for deployment steps by next retro" or "Team will adopt code formatting tool X starting this sprint—Jane will integrate it into our CI by Friday." Owners drive the task to completion. Without owners, it's unclear who should do it, and it's likely to fall through the cracks. If an action is owned by the whole team (like "Everyone remember to do X"), it helps to still have someone check up or facilitate that change (e.g., scrum master or tech lead reminds everyone mid-sprint to follow the new process, etc.). Essentially, ensure there's accountability.

Review previous retro's actions at the start of the next retro.
This is crucial. Begin each retro by checking the status of the last retro's action items. Did we do them? If not, why not? Are they in progress, or were they forgotten? This practice closes the feedback loop and creates gentle pressure to actually do what was agreed on. If an action wasn't done, discuss whether to carry it forward or drop it (maybe it turned out not to be so important, or circumstances changed). Scrum guidelines (*https://oreil.ly/Yoj1v*) indeed recommend starting by reviewing past improvements

to see if they were enacted, and if so, if they were helpful. This also allows celebrating successful improvements ("We instituted code review checklists and our bug rate went down—great!") or learning from failures ("We planned to have fewer meetings, but we didn't really manage that—what blocked it?").

Make the improvements visible.
Sometimes action items fade from memory because they're not visible day-to-day. Consider putting them on the team's task board or somewhere prominent. Some teams add them as sprint backlog items or create a dedicated Trello or Jira ticket for the improvement (so it gets tracked like any other work). If, for example, the action is "Reduce PR review time—aim for less than 24 hours," maybe put a visible graph in the team area or channel showing PR turnaround times each week to keep focus on it. For process changes like "Use new testing framework," have a checklist or reminder where code is reviewed. The idea is not to forget the action item until the next retro—instead, integrate it into the team's workflow or tracking.

Facilitate to avoid rabbit holes and blame.
A good retro stays solution-oriented and inclusive. Ensure the retro has a facilitator (often the scrum master or an unbiased team member) who can keep things on track. They should allocate time properly—e.g., time-box the "what went well/what didn't" discussion so that there is time to discuss action items. They should also cut off unconstructive negativity: if conversation devolves into "Department X screwed us again," refocus by asking "What can *we* do to mitigate that next time? Should we involve someone from Department X earlier or adjust our own planning?" That turns the gripe into a potential action (like "Action: Product owner will meet with Department X monthly to align roadmaps.").

Also, facilitators can use techniques to draw out quieter team members and ensure actions have buy-in. If blame arises ("The testers didn't find that bug!"), guide it toward process ("How can we improve our testing or collaboration so that bugs are caught?") and maybe an action ("Dev and QA will jointly create test cases for tricky features moving forward").

Vary the format if things get stale.
If the team seems bored or disengaged in retros, change how you run them. Use different formats or questions to spark insight. For instance, try *Start, Stop, Continue* (list things to start doing, stop doing, and continue

doing) instead of the usual "what went well/poorly." Or do an anonymous survey before the meeting to surface issues people might be shy to mention. Another approach is to focus the retro on a specific area if general retros are yielding little; e.g., "Let's specifically examine our last release process—what can we improve there?" Changing it up can break monotony and surface new perspectives. However, always end with action items regardless of format.

Address higher-level or external issues appropriately.
Sometimes a team identifies an issue beyond their direct control (say, "Unrealistic deadlines imposed by leadership"). It's important not to just shrug and continue suffering. The action might be to escalate or raise the concern with those who can address it. For example, "Action: Engineering manager will bring up deadline-setting issues in the managers' meeting and propose incorporating team estimates." Or, if something is company-wide, maybe the team can experiment within their sphere. ("We will pad our estimates by 20% to account for integration overhead that upper management doesn't realize.") If the team feels heard and has a plan to at least attempt improvement or communicate upward, it keeps morale up. Thus, even if an item is largely outside the team's power, formulating an action like "PM will communicate to sales that last-minute changes have X cost, to negotiate better timelines" is better than just lamenting.

Celebrate improvements in subsequent retros.
When an action item results in positive change, acknowledge it. For example, if, in the last retro, you decided to implement pair programming on complex tickets, and in this retro, you note "fewer bugs in module X," connect the dots and recognize that the improvement came from the action. This validates the retro process and motivates the team to continue participating earnestly. It shows that the time spent reflecting leads to concrete benefits.

The retro process works only when teams commit to implementing their insights. Without clear ownership, deadlines, and follow-through, even the most thoughtful discussions become empty rituals. The measure of a successful retrospective isn't the quality of the conversation, but whether the team actually changes how they work based on what they learned.

FICTIONAL EXAMPLE: TALK-BUT-NO-ACTION RETROS

A team used to have retros where they would list many grievances: testing took too long, stories were too large, deployments were problematic. They'd talk in circles and nod, but when the next sprint came, the same issues happened. Nothing was being done differently. Recognizing this, the scrum master rebooted their retro approach.

In one session, they concentrated on just one issue: slow code reviews. They discovered developers were overbooked and some PRs sat idle. They made a concrete plan: "Next sprint, assign a rotating review buddy each week whose primary job is to review PRs within a few hours. Mark is up first." They wrote it down. In the next retro, they checked: PR turnaround improved. The team felt a boost—a problem was identified and fixed. The following retro, they tackled the deployment process: they decided to automate a step that caused delays, and assigned two people to script it.

Over a few sprints, the team built a habit: identify one to two key pain points, address them, check for improvement, and repeat. Issues like "stories too large" were solved by an action: "Split stories in planning if they seem bigger than three days of work." One by one, many recurring complaints disappeared from the retro board, and new ones were more nuanced. The team now looks forward to retros as a time where they gain control over their process.

RETROSPECTIVES AS AN ENGINE FOR CONTINUOUS IMPROVEMENT

Scrum and Agile methodologies emphasize adapting processes. The retro is the tool to do that. But it only works if adaptation actually occurs. As one Agile principle states, teams should regularly reflect, and *tune and adjust* their behavior accordingly. The retrospective must produce that adjustment.

To ensure retrospectives result in action, some teams incorporate the improvements into their definition-of-done or team-working agreements. For example, if a retro action was "Each PR must have at least one automated test," the team can add that to their definition-of-done checklist. This ensures the action persists beyond one sprint and becomes part of normal practice.

In conclusion, treat the retrospective not just as a cathartic conversation but as a planning meeting for improving your process. Approach it with the same seriousness as sprint planning for product work. If something was painful this sprint, the retrospective is where you figure out a remedy and plan it. By diligently doing this sprint over sprint, a mediocre team can become a high-performing team. You'll tackle root causes of issues instead of firefighting symptoms endlessly. The team will feel more in control of their destiny, which boosts morale. And most importantly, it creates a culture of continuous improvement—a hallmark of effective engineering teams. Over time, you'll likely find fewer drastic problems to fix and more fine-tuning to do, which is a good place to be. That's when you know your retrospective practice has turned reflection into meaningful action.

By actively addressing these team-level anti-patterns, you shift the group's culture from one of recurring friction and risk to one of resilience, shared ownership, and continuous improvement. This creates a much more effective—and enjoyable—work environment. Just as important as the team's internal dynamics is how it adapts to the broader context of the modern workplace. In Chapter 11, we'll explore strategies for thriving in today's work environments, including remote work, and maintaining long-term well-being.

11

Thriving in Modern Work Environments

The nature of software engineering work is constantly changing, shaped by new technologies, evolving team structures, and shifting cultural norms. To remain effective, engineers must adapt not only their technical skills but also their work habits.

This chapter focuses on thriving in the modern tech landscape. We'll cover practical strategies for succeeding in distributed and remote teams, methods for protecting your mental health to ensure a sustainable career, and the growing importance of communication skills for technical influence.

Remote Work Strategies: Thriving in a Distributed Environment

Remote and distributed work has become increasingly common in software engineering, offering flexibility and access to global talent. However, working remotely introduces unique challenges that can become anti-patterns if not addressed: communication gaps, feelings of isolation, blurred work-life boundaries, and coordination difficulties across time zones. Effective software engineers adapt their strategies to thrive in a distributed environment, turning potential pitfalls into productivity and collaboration advantages.

Some common challenges in remote work include the following:

Communication breakdowns
> Without face-to-face interactions, it's easy for information to silo or for misunderstandings to occur. Nuances can be lost in text, and remote teams might suffer from a lack of spontaneous knowledge sharing (no hallway conversations or overhearing teammate discussions).

Isolation and reduced team cohesion
> Remote engineers might feel less connected to colleagues. Social bonding and team culture require deliberate effort when you're not co-located. People can start to feel like lone operators rather than part of a team if there's no social interaction.

Blurred boundaries and overwork
> Working from home can lead to working longer hours, as there's no clear "leaving the office" event. Some remote workers struggle to switch off, ending up always on. Studies have shown (*https://oreil.ly/R2BEZ*) that remote employees can find it difficult to disconnect, leading to longer working days and potential burnout. Conversely, others might have the opposite boundary issue: too many home distractions making them under-productive. Both are boundary problems.

Time zone differences
> In distributed teams across regions, synchronous collaboration is hard. One person's working hours might be another's night. If not managed, some team members might feel perpetually out of the loop or forced to attend meetings at odd hours.

Technological or logistical issues
> Poor internet, an inadequate workspace, or a lack of proper equipment can hamper remote productivity. Additionally, not everyone is adept at using remote collaboration tools effectively—some may feel shy on video or not speak up on conference calls, leading to imbalances in contribution.

Despite these challenges, remote work can be extremely productive and satisfying with the right strategies.

KEY STRATEGIES TO THRIVE REMOTELY

Thriving in a remote work environment requires more than just strong technical skills—it calls for intentional communication, disciplined routines, and the ability to collaborate across both time zones and toolsets. The strategies in this section are designed to help you stay connected, productive, and balanced while working from anywhere.

Over-communicate, but effectively

In a remote setup, it's better to err on the side of sharing too much information (within reason) than too little. This doesn't mean writing verbose emails no one reads; it means proactively updating stakeholders, clarifying expectations in writing, and making your work visible. For example, use project management tools or daily stand-up messages to post status updates ("Finished API integration, starting on UI now"). If something is stuck, say so explicitly in chat or a stand-up. In an office, a manager might see you struggling or looking frustrated; remotely, they won't unless you tell them. Also, document decisions and discussions so people who weren't there can catch up. Many successful remote teams follow the mantra of *default to transparency*: meeting notes, design docs, etc., are shared broadly by default.

Use multiple communication channels for different purposes

Leverage the right tool for the right message. For quick questions or casual check-ins, chat (like Slack or Teams) works well. For more complex discussions or sensitive topics, a video call may be better to avoid misinterpretation and to read body language and tone. Important decisions or information should be documented in a persistent form (email summary or wiki) so it doesn't get lost in chat history. Some remote teams adopt an *open channel* policy where project discussions happen in public channels rather than private messages, so everyone can learn and chime in. Additionally, schedule regular check-ins, like a weekly team video call to sync on the big picture, which can reduce flurries of confusion the rest of the time. Essentially, be deliberate: e.g., engineering design discussions on Zoom (with notes captured), day-to-day minor Q&As on Slack, team announcements via email/slides, etc.

Establish routines and boundaries

To avoid burnout and also avoid slacking, set a routine similar to if you were in an office. Have a start time, take a lunch break, and have a clear end-of-day shutdown ritual. Communicate your working hours to your team and use status indicators (like calendar or chat status) to signal availability. When your workday ends, actually disconnect—close work apps, maybe even shut down your work laptop. Many remote workers find that having a separate workspace (even a specific desk or room) that they leave at day's end helps mentally switch off. If you work with colleagues in other time zones, it's OK that you're not constantly reachable—just let them know your overlap hours. Protecting personal time is vital; studies have found (*https://oreil.ly/R1fdy*) that remote employees often work more hours due to boundary creep. On the flip side, if you struggle to focus at home, setting stricter "office hours" for yourself and dressing up as if going to work can put you in work mode.

Foster human connection intentionally

Remote doesn't mean purely transactional relationships. Take time for nonwork conversations, as you would in an office. This could be as simple as a watercooler Slack channel for sharing weekend stories or hobbies, or scheduling virtual coffee breaks or team games occasionally. In team meetings, spare a few minutes for personal catch-up ("How was your weekend?" or a quick round of personal updates). Some teams do fun Slack threads (like sharing pet photos in a channel or a daily music share) to build camaraderie. If possible, plan periodic offsites or in-person meetups for the team or company—even once or twice a year can significantly strengthen bonds, which then make remote collaboration smoother. If in-person isn't feasible, even a longer video social event (like a remote team lunch or online game session) can help. The key is to create shared experiences beyond just work tasks.

Excel at asynchronous communication

Embrace asynchronous (async) work as a strength, not a hurdle. This means people don't all have to be online at the same time to make progress. Write things down in detail so others can respond when they see it. For instance, instead of waiting for a meeting to outline a design idea, write a design proposal in a shared doc and ask for comments by a certain date. This allows thoughtful input from people in different time zones.

Async communication also means being patient for responses—don't expect an immediate reply at odd hours. Use techniques like *async stand-ups* (everyone posts what they did, will do, and blockers in chat each day; others check when they start their day). One can also record short demo videos or walkthroughs for colleagues to watch on their own time. Async does not mean never having real-time meetings, but it reduces their necessity. It also encourages more permanent records of decisions (because decisions might happen in a Slack thread or doc instead of a quickly forgotten meeting).

Tools like issue trackers, wikis, and version control comments become your communication media as much as meetings—treat them as such (e.g., write clear commit messages that explain why, not just what, since your colleagues might read that to understand changes).

Creating Better Async Artifacts with AI Meeting Summaries

In a distributed team, the most valuable meetings are those that create a clear, documented outcome for teammates in other time zones. AI-powered meeting assistants can automatically transcribe, summarize, and identify action items from any video call. This ensures that a decision made in a synchronous meeting doesn't get lost. The generated summary and action items can be automatically posted to a Slack channel or Confluence page, providing a perfect async artifact for the rest of the team. This automates the tedious task of note-taking and allows all participants to be fully present in the conversation.

Set up a productive workspace

On a personal level, thriving remotely means having an environment conducive to work. If possible, designate a specific area in your home for work—this helps psychologically separate work from personal life. Ensure you have a comfortable, ergonomic chair, good internet, and necessary peripherals (quality headset, maybe an external monitor to replicate a good office setup). Many companies offer stipends for home office equipment—use those to optimize your setup (like a better router or an ergonomic keyboard). A good workspace reduces distractions and physical discomfort, letting you focus and work effectively. If home is too noisy or cramped, consider coworking spaces or even a library as alternatives (some companies will cover coworking membership). The key is to find a place where you can concentrate and also step away when work is done.

Practice self-discipline and structure

Remote work gives flexibility, but with that comes the responsibility to manage your own time. Some people find it helpful to adhere to a fixed schedule to stay disciplined (like 9 to 5, with lunch at 12:30). Others take advantage of flexibility (maybe doing a split shift, such as working 7 to 11 a.m., taking a long afternoon break for personal activities, then working 4 to 8 p.m.). Find what yields your best work and aligns with team needs. Use calendars and task lists to plan your day, because no one else will do that planning for you in a remote setting. Also communicate any deviations—e.g., "I'll be offline this afternoon for personal reasons, but I'll catch up tonight." In a co-located office, someone might notice you stepping out; remotely, they only know if you tell them.

Be mindful of tone and assume good intent

Without body language, text communication can be easily misinterpreted. Remote workers should develop emotional intelligence in writing—use clear language, and sometimes add an emoji to convey tone if appropriate (to show something is meant in good humor, etc.). Conversely, when reading others' messages, give the benefit of the doubt if something comes across as curt—maybe they were busy or are not a native speaker of your shared language. If conflict arises, hop on a video call to sort it out rather than having a Slack war. It's easy for minor issues to escalate due to poor communication in remote settings, so address them promptly with real conversation.

Invest in your communication skills

As remote work relies heavily on writing and video calls, improving these skills is key. Take time to craft well-thought-out messages. Read them over to ensure clarity before sending. For important messages, consider the medium: an announcement might be best via email so it doesn't get lost in chat. On video calls, practice speaking clearly and listening actively (don't multitask excessively during meetings—it's noticeable and leads to disengagement). Remember that in remote work, your communication is your presence—how you write and speak is how colleagues experience you. Effective remote engineers often become excellent communicators by necessity, and that skill pays dividends in all aspects of their career (see "Public Speaking and Communication Skills for Engineers: Becoming an Influential Technical Communicator" on page 157).

FICTIONAL EXAMPLE: REMOTE REBOOT

A software team went fully remote over the past year. Initially, they struggled—messages were missed, tasks slipped through cracks, and some devs felt lonely and out of sync. Recognizing these pain points, the team implemented some changes: they instituted a morning ritual of each member posting a short message about what they're tackling (simulating the daily stand-up asynchronously in their chat channel). They set core hours (e.g., 10 a.m.-to-2 p.m. overlap time) for any live discussions and kept the rest flexible for deep work. They created a rotating "virtual coffee" pair—each week, an app randomly paired team members for a 15-minute nonwork chat, which greatly improved team camaraderie. The team also made a rule that no one should be expected to respond to nonurgent messages outside their normal working hours (to fight the tendency of always being online).

Over a few months, these strategies significantly improved their cohesion and output. Team members reported feeling more connected and less stressed. Work got done more smoothly because expectations around communication were clear and consistent. They turned what was a chaotic remote experiment into a well-functioning distributed team.

Remote work is here to stay, and it can be a double-edged sword. To avoid the anti-patterns of remote work (miscommunication, isolation, burnout), you must intentionally cultivate good habits and team agreements. The best remote engineers are proactive communicators, self-disciplined, and empathetic collaborators. They ensure they're not just coding in a silo at home, but remain an integral, visible part of the team. By setting clear boundaries, they protect their mental health and prevent burnout (tightly related to Chapter 9). By sharpening written and async collaboration skills, they often find they can get more done with fewer interruptions. And by nurturing team relationships virtually, they turn a distributed group of individuals into a unified force. In essence, they take control of their environment and tools, rather than letting remote challenges control them.

With thoughtful strategies, remote work can lead to excellent effectiveness—you can have increased focus, access to a broader range of colleagues, and enjoy better work-life harmony. Many highly effective engineers operate remotely by following these principles, demonstrating that distance is not a barrier to success when approached correctly.

Public Speaking and Communication Skills for Engineers: Becoming an Influential Technical Communicator

Being an effective software engineer isn't just about writing code—it's also about communicating ideas and influencing others. Whether it's explaining your design to the team, advocating for a new technology to management, or sharing knowledge with the broader community, communication skills amplify your impact. Public speaking and effective writing can transform an engineer from a solid contributor into a true technical leader. Conversely, lacking these skills can become an anti-pattern where brilliant ideas stay buried or miscommunication causes projects to falter.

Communication skills are vital for ICs because of several factors:

- You often need to convince others—perhaps you see a better architecture, but you must present it compellingly to get buy-in.

- You share knowledge and mentor—your expertise helps the team only if you can transfer it, which requires clear explanation.
- You represent your work—in meetings with stakeholders or at conferences, how you articulate technical concepts can determine whether they're understood and adopted.
- Communication gaps can lead to engineering rework or wasted effort—e.g., misinterpreting requirements or not alerting others to a risk in time.
- Career progression for senior ICs (staff, principal levels) heavily involves influence, which comes through communication. As Fran Soto put it (*https://oreil.ly/ZjigP*), "We often assume our work will speak for itself, but that's rarely true. Communication and visibility are just as essential to career growth as technical ability."

Public speaking, specifically—giving talks, presentations, or even leading meetings—is a form of high-leverage communication. It can be intimidating (fear of public speaking is common), but it offers many benefits:

It increases your visibility and credibility.
When you present on a topic, people see you as knowledgeable in that area. A well-delivered talk at a meeting or external conference showcases your expertise. Fran Soto also noted, "Public speaking opportunities are a free ticket to being seen by your company's leaders. They don't have time to dive into our pull requests, but a well-delivered talk can showcase your technical insights and grab attention, positioning you as someone worth listening to." This can open career opportunities (e.g., being consulted for other projects or being considered for technical leadership roles).

It forces you to deepen your understanding.
Teaching or presenting requires organizing your thoughts and anticipating questions. In preparing, you often fill gaps in your knowledge, which makes you a better engineer. Explaining a concept helps you understand it.

It improves team communication.
If you can speak clearly to a room of people, you'll also be clearer one-on-one or in design documents. Public speaking builds confidence in all forms of expression. You become known as someone who can articulate ideas—so teammates will loop you into discussions, knowing you can clarify complex issues.

It multiplies your impact.
> Instead of explaining something individually multiple times, you give one presentation to the group. For example, presenting a new coding standard to the team ensures everyone hears the rationale together, avoiding piecemeal adoption. If you speak at a conference or write a blog (a form of public communication), you could influence engineers far beyond your company, spreading good ideas or best practices in the industry.

It enhances leadership presence.
> Even as an IC, if you can effectively communicate to upper management or cross-functional groups, you often become the de facto leader in those situations because you can represent the team's technical perspective well. Many staff engineers cite communication as a key skill that allowed them to drive large initiatives—they could align different stakeholders via persuasive communication, not just technical correctness.

In essence, strong communication skills transform your technical expertise from a solo instrument into an orchestral force, capable of leading and aligning the entire team.

COMMON OBSTACLES FOR ENGINEERS AND HOW TO OVERCOME THEM

Engineers often face unique challenges when it comes to developing strong communication skills, especially in high-stakes or unfamiliar settings. Recognizing these common obstacles—and knowing how to navigate them—can empower engineers to become more confident, influential, and effective communicators. Let's discuss some of these obstacles.

Stage fright or anxiety

This is natural. Even experienced speakers get nervous. The key is preparation and practice. Start small: present to your team (a supportive audience) on a topic you know well. Practice your talk multiple times by yourself or with a friend. Familiarity with the material reduces fear of blanking out. Use notes initially if needed. Remember that the audience is generally supportive—colleagues want you to succeed and share knowledge. Some nervousness actually helps you perform with energy. With each presentation, it will lessen. Consider joining a group like Toastmasters to practice in a low-stakes environment.

Also, in tech presentations, the audience cares more about content than polish—you don't need to be a TED-style orator. If you communicate something useful, people appreciate it even if you say "um" or look at your slides a few times. So don't let the perfect be the enemy of the good. As you practice, consider recording yourself to identify and work on quirks (like speaking too fast, which is common when nervous). Breathing exercises before speaking and remembering to pause can steady you. Many engineers find that with time, they even enjoy public speaking (the adrenaline becomes excitement rather than fear).

Believing "I'm not a good speaker" or "I'm an introvert"

Communication is a skill, not an innate trait. Introverts can be excellent speakers—they often prepare well and deliver thoughtful content. If you think you're not good at it, treat it like learning a new technology. Do some training: plenty of books, online courses, or workshops exist for technical speaking and writing. Practice in safe settings and gradually scale up. Seek feedback from peers you trust. You can also leverage your strengths: for instance, if you're better at writing, script out more of what you want to say. If you're good one-on-one, imagine your talk as a series of points you're individually explaining to different people in the room. Remember that nearly every great speaker you see was once not-so-great but improved through iteration.

Not knowing how to simplify complex topics

Tailor depth to your audience. If speaking to nonengineers (like product managers or executives), focus on outcomes and metaphors rather than implementation details. If speaking to engineers, you can dive into detail, but still provide context. A tip: start high-level, then drill down. Even with a tech audience, frame the problem and why it matters before you dive into solution details. Use analogies or real-world examples to make abstract concepts relatable (e.g., describing a load balancer as a "traffic cop for network requests" can cement the concept). When writing or speaking, try to avoid excessive jargon, or explain it briefly if you must use it. Also, structure your content—maybe present three main points, or a before/after scenario—so listeners can follow the narrative. If you just throw a bunch of fine-grained info at them without structure, they'll tune out. Storytelling techniques can apply: present a problem scenario, walk through attempted solutions, describe a climactic success with the final solution, and finish with the resolution (benefits realized). This keeps people engaged.

Time constraints/not prioritizing communication

In a busy engineering schedule, preparing a presentation or writing a blog can seem low priority. But consider it an investment in your influence and effectiveness. Perhaps integrate it with work—e.g., volunteer to present the results of a project you did. That both disseminates knowledge and gives you practice. Block a small amount of time regularly (like one hour a week to work on a tech talk or writing an internal newsletter). Small, consistent effort prepares you better than a last-minute rush. Also remember the point from the introduction: communication amplifies your impact. So spending time on it can be as valuable as coding, if not more, for certain career goals. If your environment truly doesn't value engineers' communication (which is rare nowadays), you can still practice externally (write on Medium, speak at local meetups on your own time). That can even open doors to jobs that do value those skills.

Thinking that communication is for managers

Certainly, engineering managers communicate a lot, but senior ICs do, too. If you want to remain technical but still advance and drive big decisions, you must articulate ideas clearly to people who aren't in the code daily. For instance, a staff engineer often writes proposals for architecture changes or gives presentations to align multiple teams on a technology direction. Those are essentially acts of technical leadership through communication. Many companies have an IC track that's parallel to the management one, with those skills expected at higher levels. If you remain silent or ineffective at communication, you might get stuck at mid-level despite great coding skills, simply because bigger-scope roles demand collaboration and influence, which require communication.

Underestimating the benefits

Perhaps you think, "I'm doing fine, why bother with talks or writing?" But consider this: effective communication can make your day-to-day easier (fewer misunderstandings, better teamwork), and it can boost your career (someone who can explain something complex in simple terms is often seen as more senior). Moreover, sharing knowledge is a way to give back and improve your team and community—which can be intrinsically rewarding. Some engineers find that mentoring or speaking rekindles their own passion when pure coding is starting to feel rote.

BUILDING COMMUNICATION SKILLS BEYOND SPEAKING

When people think of "communication skills," they often picture public speaking or confident presentations. However, for a senior individual contributor, their effectiveness relies just as heavily on the quieter, daily interactions that keep a team aligned. Whether it is writing a persuasive design document, active listening during a heated debate, or translating technical complexity for a nontechnical audience, these skills determine whether your engineering solutions are understood and adopted. This section explores how to cultivate these essential, often overlooked, modes of communication.

Writing well

Much of engineering communication is written—design docs, technical specs, emails, commit messages. Aim for clear, concise writing. Structure documents with headings so they're easy to scan. Use diagrams or bullet points to break up dense text. A well-written design doc can save hours of meetings. One strategy is to have a peer review your important documents like you would with code—they can point out if something is unclear or too verbose. Pay attention to grammar and tone, especially when communicating with nonengineers or external parties; professionalism in writing builds trust. Over time, becoming known as someone who writes clear documentation or proposals will make colleagues more inclined to read and support your ideas (whereas if docs are confusing, they might be ignored).

Active listening

Communication isn't just broadcasting; it's also listening and engaging. In meetings, practice active listening—truly focus on whoever is speaking; don't plan what you'll say while they're talking. Reflect on what you heard before speaking. If you're thinking of how to respond while they talk, you might miss nuance. Ask clarifying questions—it shows you care to understand.

Speaking up in discussions

However, if you have something to say, don't hold back out of shyness—find a polite way to interject or wait for a pause, and then speak. It can help to jot a quick note while you listen so you remember your point when it's your turn. Many brilliant engineers stay quiet in meetings and later see a decision go differently than they'd like. Learning to contribute your thoughts in the moment is key. If direct speaking is hard, communicate through the chat of a video call or follow up with an email—but make sure your perspective is heard at some point.

Adapting to different audiences

Tailor your message to who you're speaking to. We touched on this in Chapter 4: for management, focus on the "so what"—how does this technical issue affect timelines, costs, user experience? For junior devs, you might go slower and explain basic concepts; for senior devs, you can use shorthand and dive into details. For cross-functional calls (like with sales or clients), minimize technical jargon or explain it analogically. Being able to shift your communication style makes you effective in diverse situations. If you're not sure how technical your audience is, ask them directly or gauge their reactions and adjust. Over time, you develop intuition (e.g., knowing that the VP doesn't care about the algorithm details, just the outcome and risk). Adaptation also includes modality: maybe a stakeholder never responds to emails but will answer a quick chat question—adjust your approach to what works for them.

Tailoring Technical Documentation for Nontechnical Audiences

A frequent challenge for engineers is translating complex technical work into summaries that nontechnical stakeholders can understand. An effective IC can use an LLM to handle this routine translation.

> Prompt: *Act as a product manager. Take the following technical update and rewrite it into a three-bullet-point summary for an executive. Focus on the user benefit and business impact.*

This technique saves valuable time and ensures clear, impactful communication across the organization, helping you build influence without getting bogged down in writing and rewriting updates for different audiences.

Narrative and storytelling

We are wired to remember stories more than raw facts. Try to frame your communications with a narrative arc where possible. For instance, when writing a post-mortem, instead of just listing data, tell the story of the outage. ("At 2 a.m., our pagers went off—the database had hit connection limits. We discovered that a code change earlier that day caused a connection leak. We rolled it back and service returned. Here's what we learned...") This makes the content more engaging and the lessons more memorable. In presentations, start with a relatable problem scenario. ("Users were abandoning checkout—we didn't know why.") That hooks the audience. Then explain how you investigated and solved it, and conclude with the payoff (improved metric, etc.). Even in daily communication, framing your suggestion as a story ("We saw this error. It reminded me of an issue last year—we tried X, which didn't work, then Y, which did. I propose we do Y again here because...") can be more convincing than a flat statement. It shows reasoning and experience.

BENEFITS OF STRONG COMMUNICATION

Strong communication is a cornerstone of effective engineering work, extending far beyond just speaking clearly in meetings. Building skills in writing, listening, adapting to different audiences, and using storytelling techniques can dramatically improve how ideas are shared, understood, and acted upon within technical teams and across an organization. The benefits include the following:

Broader influence

> You can rally people around your ideas. For example, maybe you believe the team should adopt a new testing framework. If you can present a compelling case (say through a doc and a short talk), you're much more likely to get everyone on board. Otherwise, the idea might die in a side conversation or not be understood.

Better teamwork

> Clear communication reduces friction. Misunderstandings cause conflicts or duplication of work. If everyone practices good communication, the team coordinates more smoothly (see how this ties to retrospectives and remote work—it's all interconnected).

Personal career growth

> Those who communicate well are often seen as leaders or go-to people. They get opportunities to represent the team, interface with other departments, or speak at conferences—all of which can accelerate a career. Even for promotions, managers will note things like "presented architecture vision to execs effectively" as evidence of impact at higher levels.

Sharing knowledge widely

> By speaking or writing publicly, you contribute to the community and also put your name out there as an expert. This can lead to networking opportunities, offers, or simply personal fulfillment. Many effective engineers in the industry dedicate time to blogging or open source efforts partly to sharpen their communication skills and give back knowledge, which also ends up opening doors (like being invited to speak at events, etc.). It's not required, but it can amplify your positive impact beyond your company.

FICTIONAL EXAMPLE: THE SOFT-SPOKEN ARCHITECT

Ryan was a brilliant software architect who often had the best ideas in design meetings but struggled to get them across. He was soft-spoken, and his explanations often got lost in details. As a result, some of his proposals were overlooked until problems arose later and people realized his idea would have helped. Recognizing this, Ryan's manager suggested he work on his communication skills. Ryan took this to heart. He started by studying well-written design documents from other senior engineers and used them as templates to make his own writing clearer, incorporating more headings and diagrams. To tackle his fear of speaking, he joined a local Toastmasters club to practice in a friendly, low-stakes environment.

Over a year, his coworkers noticed a difference—Ryan's presentations in design reviews became more structured. He would start with a clear outline and problem statement, speak up a bit more confidently, and directly address concerns others raised. In one critical project, he gave an internal tech talk comparing two approaches, laying out the pros and cons systematically. His recommendation prevailed, and the successful project that followed made leadership take note of Ryan's impact. Ryan himself felt more fulfilled—instead of silently thinking "my idea is better, why don't they listen," he was able to convey *why* it was better and win support. He joked that he "refactored his speaking like refactoring code—making it cleaner and more efficient." This shift elevated him from just the guy with good ideas to the technical influencer who guided the team's direction.

THE VALUE OF GOOD COMMUNICATION

In summary, cultivating communication skills and embracing opportunities to speak or write about your work can dramatically extend your influence as an engineer. You don't have to become a keynote speaker overnight; you can do so step by step—write that design doc and solicit feedback, speak up in the next meeting with a well-thought-out point, or volunteer to demo your feature at the company meeting. Over time, as your comfort grows, consider presenting at a meetup or conference, or writing a blog post about a tricky problem you solved. Each effort not only helps others understand and appreciate your work, but also reinforces your own understanding and signals your leadership capabilities.

Remember, engineering is a team sport. Those who can clearly articulate ideas, knowledge, and vision enable their entire team to align and excel. As you hone these skills, you evolve from being an excellent IC to being an excellent communicator and leader, all while staying on the IC path if you choose. Your code may be the engine, but communication is the drive belt that connects it to the wheels of progress. With both running smoothly, you become an engine of effectiveness in your organization.

The strategies we've covered—excelling in remote environments and developing strong communication skills—equip you to thrive in today's tech landscape. But as we look ahead, the role of the individual contributor continues to evolve at an unprecedented pace.

AI is reshaping how we write code, new hybrid roles are blurring traditional boundaries, and the very definition of what makes an engineer effective is expanding. In the upcoming chapters, we'll explore how to position yourself not just for success today, but for a thriving decades-long career as the industry transforms around us.

12

The Future of Individual Contributors

The tech industry is constantly evolving, and so is the role of the IC. In this chapter, let's gaze forward. How will being an IC change in the coming years? We'll consider trends like AI and automation, the increasing need for interdisciplinary skills, and emerging hybrid roles that blur the line between IC and management or other fields. The goal is to think about how you, as an IC, can stay effective and relevant in the face of these changes.

Embracing AI as Your New Collaborator (Not Your Replacement)

Perhaps the biggest shift on the horizon (or already upon us) is the advent of powerful AI tools in software development. We have code assistants (GitHub Copilot, etc.) that can generate code from comments, AI-driven testing, and systems that may eventually handle some programming tasks autonomously.

You may constantly be wondering: will AI replace developers? Probably not entirely, and certainly not those who adapt. Instead, AI will augment developers:

- It will handle a lot of boilerplate and repetitive coding. (Copilot already helps fill in lots of routine code.)
- It might find bugs or suggest optimizations automatically (acting as an AI pair programming partner).
- It can generate multiple solution approaches (e.g., "give me three different implementations of this function" as a creativity boost).

Instead, your role will shift:

Problem definition and system design
   AI is not great at knowing what problem needs solving or how to break down a complex system. Humans will likely still decide the architecture and high-level approach.

Verification and guidance
   AI can write code, but you will verify it's correct, efficient, secure, etc. Much like code review, but you're reviewing AI output. You will need a strong grasp of fundamentals to catch AI's mistakes or weird edge cases.

Training and customizing AI tools
   Engineers increasingly need to tailor AI integration with specific codebases and contexts via agentic engineering, feeding models rich project history, examples, skills, MCPs, or dynamic inputs so the outputs stay reliable and relevant. Skills once labeled "prompt engineering" are now part of a broader practice that blends intelligent querying with context engineering and workflow orchestration. Being able to ask the right questions of an AI and provide it with appropriate surrounding context isn't just useful, it's a core part of building and maintaining AI-augmented development environments.

More focus on integration and high-level logic
   If AI handles micro-level coding (like writing out a class implementation), you might spend more time ensuring different components (possibly coded by different AIs or teams) work together correctly since integration issues and subtle system behaviors are tricky for AI to anticipate without global context.

The Emerging Frontier: AI for Simulating System Behavior

Looking ahead, one of the most powerful applications of AI for senior ICs will be in system design and validation. Before writing a single line of production code, engineers may be able to use AI to simulate the behavior of a proposed architecture under various conditions.

For instance, an engineer could describe a microservices architecture and ask an AI to model its performance:

> **Prompt:** *Given a system with a user service, an order service, and a payment service with these latency characteristics, simulate the system's behavior under a Black Friday traffic spike of 10,000 requests per second. Identify potential bottlenecks and single points of failure.*
>
> The AI could run a simulation and predict that the payment service's database connection pool would be exhausted, allowing the engineer to address the bottleneck in the design phase. This would shift a significant amount of performance and reliability testing from a reactive, post-implementation activity to a proactive, pre-code strategic exercise.

We should consider this an opportunity. Offloading grunt work to AI can free you to tackle more complex challenges or consider more creative approaches. You might deliver features faster because AI wrote 30% of the trivial code. That could let you add an extra polish, test, or think of a better algorithm with the time saved.

It will be important to stay up-to-date with AI tools. Already, some job descriptions mention familiarity with AI dev tools. Embrace them early. Use Copilot or others in your personal projects to learn how to work with them. Find their strengths and blind spots. For example, many find Copilot is great for suggesting code based on similar code in the repository, but sometimes it confidently writes something subtly wrong. Learning to catch that is key.

Historically, new tools (like compilers and integrated development environments [IDEs]) raised abstraction and made developers more productive, but didn't eliminate the job; it just changed what you focus on. The same is likely with AI. Those who leverage it will outpace those who don't, similar to how developers who used Stack Overflow effectively got answers faster than those who refused to look things up. It's an evolution of the skill set.

Note

Could entry-level jobs be fewer because AI handles simpler coding? Possibly, which means that growth paths might be different (maybe new engineers focus more on integration/testing initially rather than writing simple code because AI can do that part). It's something to watch. But likely, new types of tasks will emerge.

I also recommend that you keep learning fundamentals. AI might only be able to handle syntax and boilerplate, making conceptual understanding even more valuable. AI can write code following patterns, but if the pattern itself or architecture is wrong for the problem, only a human can usually tell. So understanding data structures, complexity, system design principles, etc., remains crucial.

The Hybrid Individual Contributor

As technology evolves and AI continues to reshape the engineering landscape, the traditional boundaries of individual contributor roles are shifting. In the future, successful ICs may embrace more hybrid skill sets—blending technical expertise with management, product, design, operations, and security knowledge to remain effective and adaptable in multidisciplinary teams. Hybrid roles may look like the following:

IC/manager hybrid
Many companies now have roles like "tech lead" where you're still an IC (coding, designing) but also do some management tasks (planning, mentoring team members). "Staff engineer" roles are another example; they involve significant cross-team coordination (which is somewhat managerial in influence). Even if you remain technically focused, developing some management and people skills broadens what you can do (and makes transitions easier, as discussed in Chapter 6).

IC/product hybrid
There's a trend of engineers thinking more like product people (some companies call certain engineers "product engineers"). In the future, with AI doing some coding, ICs might spend more time on product decisions, user experience considerations, and experimentation. You could be writing code one day, analyzing user data the next, and brainstorming features the third. It pays to build some product sense. At minimum, learning how to conduct an A/B test or how to interpret user analytics will make you much more effective in a modern, data-driven product team.

IC/designer hybrid
With technologies like low-code development or with AI smoothing UI implementation, engineers may engage more directly in UX decisions. Frontend engineers of the future might drag-and-drop interface components (with AI generating the underlying code) and thus focus more on layout and user flow—which crosses into design territory. Having an eye

for design or at least an understanding of design principles (color theory, spacing, accessibility) can set you apart.

DevOps and SRE skills for all

The line between software engineer and DevOps engineer has been blurring with DevOps culture (you build it, you run it). In the future, virtually all ICs may need to be comfortable with deployment pipelines, infra-as-code, monitoring, etc. Tools keep improving to offload heavy lifting, but being able to own your code from development to production makes you extremely effective (and is often expected in smaller teams).

Security and privacy

As data regulations tighten and threats increase, future ICs will likely need more built-in security knowledge. Some roles may combine development and security (DevSecOps). It's wise to add basic AppSec (application security) to your skillset—e.g., know the Open Worldwide Application Security Project (OWASP) top 10, threat modeling, and encryption basics. That way, you can design systems that are secure by default rather than always needing a separate security review team to fix issues. It might become a standard part of senior IC competencies.

T-SHAPED SKILLS REVISITED

In "The Importance of Breadth: Being Versatile" on page 31, we mentioned being T-shaped with your skills (deep in one, broad in many). This will be even more important in a hybrid role. Depth might be in a technical domain (say you are a performance guru), but breadth will include understanding of cloud DevOps, some ML (if applicable to your domain, since ML is creeping into many products), some basic design/product sense, etc. Future engineering problems often require knowledge beyond coding (like the ethical implications of AI features, or understanding the user's context in the Internet of Things [IoT]). So continuing to learn adjacent fields is good.

AVOID SHALLOW IN EVERYTHING, DEEP IN NOTHING

There's a risk of trying to learn *everything* and becoming a jack of all trades, but master of none. The future likely still values specialists—there will always be a need for someone who truly knows database internals or is a whiz at iOS performance or has PhD-level ML knowledge. Being hybrid doesn't mean giving up your specialty; it means complementing it with enough understanding of related areas to collaborate intelligently and make holistic decisions.

EXAMPLE FUTURE ROLE

Consider the "full-stack ML engineer" roles popping up: someone who can develop an ML model (usually a data scientist's job), *and* deploy it as a scalable API (backend eng job), *and* perhaps integrate it into a product and monitor its performance (DevOps and product analytics). That's a very interdisciplinary IC role. If you can fill such shoes, you have immense value. We already see this in smaller companies, where one engineer might be doing all of that. The future might push more people to have that breadth, at least to some degree.

Continuous Learning and Adaptability

To remain effective as an IC over a decades-long career, the overarching meta-skill is learning how to learn and adapting to change.

We've touched on AI, new hybrid roles, etc. The specifics will continue to change. Maybe a new programming paradigm comes (quantum computing? who knows), or new processes (Agile replaced waterfall; something might replace Agile). The one constant is change. So:

Keep learning.

Not just specific frameworks (which come and go), but fundamental concepts and new concepts. Always have a learning goal—maybe one new language per year (even if you just use it for fun side projects) or one big tech conference/video series. It keeps your skills fresh and signals to employers you are growth-minded, which is highly valued.

Be adaptable.

Try to get out of your comfort zone periodically (take a task in an area you normally don't; work with a different team for a sprint). It trains adaptability. When new stuff comes along, you'll be less intimidated. The more you expose yourself to varying tech stacks or environments early in your career, the easier it is to drop into a new scenario later (say you switch jobs or your company pivots to a different product).

Maintain soft skills.

Technology may change, but skills like communication, leadership, critical thinking, problem decomposition—these will remain valuable and actually become differentiators as tech gets commoditized by AI or numerous libraries. Many future job descriptions might look for "strong communication skills, ability to work cross-functionally" even more than a specific language (maybe AI can help with language, but it can't talk to a stakeholder for you effectively).

Network and observe the industry.
Follow tech news (Hacker News, tech blogs, podcasts). Not obsessively, but enough to spot trends (like "hmm, many companies are adopting Rust for systems programming; maybe I should take a look" or "Everyone's moving to cloud native architecture; is our company behind? Should I propose something?"). A broad awareness helps you anticipate skills to learn or changes to advocate for.

The engineers who thrive across decades aren't those who excel in every new technology, but those who cultivate the meta-skills of continuous learning and adaptation while building deep expertise in timeless fundamentals. In a field where specific tools become obsolete but problem-solving abilities endure, your capacity to evolve becomes your most valuable asset.

BALANCE NEW AND OLD

There's a future-proofing aspect to skill development. Learning fundamental computer science (which doesn't change) is more important than learning a new framework (which likely will change). Do both: fundamentals give you base knowledge that outlasts any specific technology; new tech skills give you immediate relevance and the ability to contextualize fundamentals in modern practice. For example, understanding networking theory is fundamental; learning Kubernetes is current tech. With both, you're formidable.

LIFELONG INDIVIDUAL CONTRIBUTOR AS A VIABLE PATH

In the past, some thought you "had to go into management" after a certain point to advance or have influence, as I touch on in Chapter 6. The industry has opened up staff+ IC paths, where you can remain an IC and reach a level equivalent to senior management. The future likely holds even more technical leadership roles (like "distinguished engineer" or specialized principal roles). If you love coding and design, know that you can continue doing that deep into your career and still have advancement (especially at companies with technical ladders and with the increasing need for specialists in advanced tech).

Also, hybrid IC roles may allow you to do some management without fully leaving coding. Some orgs allow switching between manager and IC tracks (the pendulum, as we discuss in Chapter 6). The future might have more flexible career models, where you can manage a team for a project, then go back to IC work. Being open to fluid roles can provide the best of both worlds and reduce burnout (some enjoy a break from coding in a management stint, others enjoy a break from meetings by going IC again).

I believe the future IC is:

- Empowered by AI, focusing more on big-picture and creativity rather than grunt work.
- Likely working in multi-disciplinary ways, blending coding with product thinking and DevOps.
- Always learning and adapting as technologies emerge or fade.
- Possibly stepping in and out of quasi-management responsibilities as needed, but fundamentally leading through technical expertise.

If you cultivate the habits we've discussed throughout this book—focusing on impact, working well with others, writing clean code, continuously learning, and caring for your well-being—you'll not only be effective now but well-positioned to thrive in the evolving future of software engineering, whatever it brings.

The career of an IC can span decades and many technology cycles. By being adaptive, collaborative, strategic, and balanced, you can remain an effective software engineer throughout, delivering value in an ever-changing landscape.

| 13

Practical AI for Effective Software Engineers

Effective software engineering prioritizes high-leverage activities that amplify impact. AI has become a powerful amplifier for individual contributors, if used wisely. This chapter provides a pragmatic, tool-agnostic playbook for using AI day-to-day to ship better software more quickly and safely. We'll walk through where AI helps most, how to wire it into your daily workflow, how to measure its impact, and how to stay within essential security, privacy, and compliance guardrails. The goal isn't to turn you into an AI engineer, but to make you an engineer who gets more done with AI.

Before we dig into the details, I want to set the stage with some key points to remember:

AI can speed you up, but it won't replace your judgment.
> Modern AI coding assistants have demonstrated significant productivity boosts—for example, one controlled study found developers completed a task about 55% faster with an AI pair programmer's help (*https://oreil.ly/qLZSu*). However, faster doesn't automatically mean better. AI suggestions can be wrong or insecure. Research has shown that AI models can produce incorrect or misleading information in a significant percentage of cases (*https://oreil.ly/C6rRe*), so you must apply engineering judgment and oversight at every step. In practice, you'll still reject many AI-generated ideas, and you'll need to review the ones you accept just as critically as if a junior developer wrote them.

Treat AI like any other dependency: test and verify its outputs.
Don't blindly trust vendor hype about magical productivity gains. Instead, instrument your AI usage and gather your own data. For example, use your AI tool's built-in telemetry dashboard (if available), tag AI-assisted commits with a marker in commit messages, or track acceptance rates through IDE plugins. Measure things like how often you accept AI suggestions, how much of that code ends up in final commits, and the defect rates of AI-assisted code. Put guardrails around AI involvement in your workflow—for example, require tests for AI-generated code and run additional reviews or scans on it. Think of your AI assistant as a powerful library function: you wouldn't call an unknown library without unit tests and monitoring, and the same caution applies here.

Security and governance must be first-class concerns.
AI can and will introduce vulnerabilities or license compliance issues if you're not careful. Large-scale evaluations have shown that *nearly half* of AI-generated code samples contain security flaws (*https://oreil.ly/aaNtw*) or unsafe practices. To counter this, build security and responsible AI practices into your AI-augmented development process. This includes explicitly prompting for secure coding, using automated scanners on AI-written code, and enforcing policies (like banning certain unsafe APIs). Governance-wise, keep track of where your code is going. (Is the AI tool sending your code to a cloud service? Is it training on your proprietary code?) And control it just as you would any third-party service.

Stay ahead of the legal and compliance curve.
Regulations around AI are quickly becoming a reality. For example, the EU's AI Act entered into force in 2024 and has been phasing in new obligations since (some transparency and data requirements kicked in by 2025, with broader rules by 2026 (*https://oreil.ly/tzxlH*)). Even if you're not directly impacted yet, it's wise to align with emerging best practices like the National Institute of Standards and Technology (NIST)'s AI Risk Management Framework (*https://oreil.ly/ZbLVw*) (which encourages processes to govern, map, measure, and manage AI risks). In short: know the rules that might apply to your use of AI (privacy, licensing, safety), and err on the side of caution by implementing proactive policies *now*.

With those principles in mind, let's explore how you, as an IC, can harness AI in a practical, day-to-day way. We'll start with understanding what today's AI coding tools are (and aren't) good at.

Where AI Shines (and Where You Still Need a Human Touch)

AI coding assistants have matured into reliable partners for certain classes of tasks. They excel at well-defined, bounded problems where there's lots of prior example data to draw from and the stakes are relatively low. For instance, here are several things that an AI assistant can quickly produce:

Boilerplate and scaffolding
> Need a skeleton of a Representational State Transfer (REST) API endpoint or the boilerplate for a new React component? Give the AI a clear description, and it can crank out the tedious setup code in seconds. This is code you could write yourself (and have written a dozen times before), so delegating it to AI frees you up for more important work.

Test drafts
> You can ask an AI to generate an initial suite of unit tests or property-based tests for a given module. It often comes back with a decent first pass—covering obvious edge cases, checking error conditions, etc. These AI-generated tests might not be perfect, but they save you from staring at a blank test file and help ensure you cover the basics.

Summaries and explanations
> Struggling to understand an unfamiliar code snippet or a huge diff in a pull request? AI can summarize what a piece of code does or highlight the significant changes in a PR. It can also explain concepts in code (e.g., "Explain how this binary search works") in a human-like way. This is great for onboarding to a new codebase or reviewing contributions from others.

Migration scripts and repetitive edits
> If you need to migrate from one library to another across your codebase or apply a repetitive refactor in dozens of files, an AI script or agent can often do the mechanical work. You describe the transformation once, and the AI helps apply it everywhere consistently (we'll revisit AI agents in "AI Agents: What They Can Do and How to Keep Them Tamed" on page 202).

Structured documentation and search

> AI can turn structured data into human-readable docs (e.g., generating Markdown API docs from inline code comments). It also shines at semantic search: you can ask in natural language, "Where in our repo do we validate user emails?" and get a likely pointer to the code because the AI can connect your question with code context better than basic text search.

Crucially, these use cases work best when you provide a tight prompt with clear constraints. The more you can frame the task for the AI (including context from your codebase, specific requirements, etc.), the better the results. In fact, field studies often show significant time savings on programming tasks when using AI for things like boilerplate, tests, and documentation drafting. In enterprise settings, developers are already accepting a meaningful portion of AI suggestions—roughly 30% of suggestions on average (*https://oreil.ly/gXe-L*)—indicating that AI is contributing to real production code in a support role.

That said, there are plenty of areas where you, the human engineer, must remain firmly in the driver's seat. AI is not good at understanding the big picture or the unwritten requirements of your specific system. You should *always* be hands-on (or at least eyes-on) for tasks like the following:

Architecture and design decisions

> AI can suggest design ideas (and you'll see how to use it for brainstorming in the next section), but it doesn't truly understand your users, your business, or the long-term implications. Deciding on the right architecture, interfaces, or library dependencies requires human judgment. Use AI as a sounding board, not an architect.

Failure modes and critical logic

> If you're writing code for performance-sensitive components, security-critical paths (auth, crypto, payments), or anything with complex state like concurrency and distributed systems, don't trust AI to get it right on its own. AI doesn't reliably foresee race conditions or subtle memory issues. And if something must be absolutely correct (like a core algorithm), you need to carefully vet every line.

Anything without tests or monitoring

> A good rule of thumb is never accept AI-generated code for functionality that you can't immediately verify. If there's no test to confirm the code works or no way to observe it in action, you should be extremely cautious.

AI might churn out something that looks plausible but is subtly wrong. Until you have a safety net (tests, logging, etc.), treat AI suggestions in these areas as potentially hazardous.

In essence, use AI for the mundane and well-trodden tasks, the kind of code that's boring for you but plentiful in training data, and personally handle the novel, critical, or sensitive tasks. Studies in 2024 and 2025 back this up (*https://oreil.ly/WcO-o*): many AI-generated code submissions will compile and run, but a significant subset hide bugs or security vulnerabilities unless a human explicitly guides the AI to avoid these issues. For example, a 2025 analysis by Veracode (*https://oreil.ly/1BRTs*) found that 45% of code written by generative AI contained *OWASP-class security flaws* (things like SQL injection, cross-site scripting, or XSS), even though that code often appeared production-ready. The takeaway is that AI doesn't know what it doesn't know. It will cheerfully offer insecure or inefficient code unless you set the ground rules.

Note

Don't expect AI to write your whole codebase while you lounge on the beach. In practice, teams see suggestion acceptance rates around 20–35% in nontrivial codebases (*https://arxiv.org/html/2501.13282v1?*). Even power users who integrate AI deeply into their workflow aren't just hitting Accept on every suggestion. The majority of AI outputs get discarded or heavily modified.

As you and your team refine how you prompt and feed context to the AI, you might bump that acceptance rate up a bit. But the "everything is auto-written" fantasy remains just that—a fantasy. Effective engineers treat AI as a helpful assistant rather than an autonomous coder. For example, you shouldn't use AI for time-critical production hotfixes where deep system knowledge is essential, nor for highly regulated code like medical device firmware where every line requires formal verification. Measure its usefulness with real metrics (what percentage of the code is AI-generated or how many of those suggestions introduce bugs?) instead of relying on anecdotes or hype.

Now that we know where AI can help and where it can't, let's see how to integrate these strengths into your daily work. The next section walks through a day-in-the-life of an engineer who uses AI at each step of the development process, from planning to coding to deployment. This end-to-end view will show how individual techniques compound to yield big benefits.

An AI-Enhanced Daily Workflow (That Compounds over Time)

How can AI techniques become part of your routine in a sustainable, compounding way? Let's walk through a typical day for a software engineer—planning a new feature, writing and testing code, reviewing changes, and communicating updates—and see where AI can plug in. Each step on its own provides a boost; together, they reinforce each other, leading to outsized gains in productivity and effectiveness.

As you read through this workflow, imagine an engineer named Sam. We'll use Sam as a fictional example IC who leverages AI throughout their day. By following Sam's journey, you'll see not just isolated tricks, but how an effective engineer strings them together.

PLAN AND DESIGN WITH AI (BRAINSTORM, THEN DRAFT AN ARCHITECTURE DECISION RECORD)

Every good feature starts with a plan. In the morning, Sam begins by clarifying what needs to be built and how to approach it. Rather than staring at a blank document, Sam turns to an AI assistant for a brainstorming boost in crafting an ADR for a new feature. Note: some teams use requests for comments (RFCs) for open proposals and ADRs to capture final decisions; in this example, we're using ADR in the broader sense, to document both the exploration and the decision.

Generate a decision brief

Sam feeds the AI a prompt to summarize the problem and propose a few solution approaches. For example, a prompt might look like this:

> Summarize the problem we're trying to solve as a one-page decision brief for an ADR. Propose 3 to 5 candidate approaches to implement the feature and discuss the trade-offs of each—consider scalability, latency, security, data model complexity, and operability for each option. Include any relevant prior art (similar solutions we've used or seen elsewhere) and at least two real case studies of other companies or projects that took each approach.

After a few seconds, the AI returns a structured summary. It outlines, say, four possible approaches to the feature, each with bullets on pros and cons. It might note that Approach A is simplest but might not scale beyond 1,000 users, Approach B uses a more scalable architecture but introduces higher latency, etc. Crucially, it even cites a couple of external examples (with links)—perhaps a blog post or tech talk where another company implemented something similar. This gives Sam a head start on research. Rather than replacing Sam's thinking, the AI is augmenting Sam's exploration of the solution space. Sam now has a clearer picture of options to discuss with the team.

Pressure-test the requirements

Next, Sam wants to ensure the chosen design will hold up under real-world conditions. He asks the AI to act like a critical examiner and challenge the nonfunctional requirements (NFRs). The prompt could look like this:

> *Given the following service-level agreements and constraints (list your performance, availability, and other requirements), ask adversarial questions about potential failure modes. For example, what happens if we get sudden throughput spikes or a retry storm? Where could backpressure build up? What are resource limit bottlenecks? Propose some failure injection tests or worst-case scenarios for each.*

The AI (in this case, a conversational LLM like ChatGPT or Claude) responds with a series of pointed questions and scenarios. It might say, "Have you considered what happens if two of your dependent services are slow at the same time? How does your approach handle a sudden 10× traffic surge—will it drop messages or overload the queue? What about a scenario where your caching layer goes down—do you have a fallback?" For each, it suggests a potential test (like "simulate a spike of 1000 requests per second for 60 seconds and verify the system throttles gracefully"). This is incredibly useful because it helps Sam uncover edge cases early, during design, rather than during an incident in production. The AI basically acts as an NFR checklist, making sure Sam doesn't wear rose-colored glasses about the happy path.

Draft the architecture decision record

Armed with the AI's research and tough questions, Sam now feels ready to write the ADR. Here, again, the AI can help: Sam asks it to take the content so far (the summary of approaches, the chosen solution, the identified risks, and the open questions) and format it into the company's ADR template.

> #### Warning
> This step is crucial—capturing design decisions in a structured ADR ensures that future engineers understand not just *what* was built, but *why* it was built that way, including alternatives considered and trade-offs made.

The assistant produces a draft ADR document with sections like Context, Decision, Alternatives Considered, Risks, and Mitigations. It even includes the references to sources the AI mentioned (e.g., links to those case studies or any spec documents Sam provided). Sam knows better than to blindly accept everything in this draft; instead, this is a starting point. Sam will now review the draft carefully, verify any facts or links, and likely tweak the wording. As part of the review process, Sam double-checks any external facts the AI cited—if the AI says "Company X did Y in 2021," Sam clicks the link to ensure it's real. The AI's suggestions do *not* absolve an engineer from due diligence. The human is still accountable for the final design. But what used to be a three-hour slog of writing and research has been jump-started by AI into a 30-minute editing task. Sam has effectively outsourced the first-draft labor, not the thinking.

By late morning, Sam has a solid ADR draft for the new feature. The team can now discuss it, poke holes, and come to a decision faster than if Sam had done all this prep from scratch.

FROM REQUIREMENTS TO BACKLOG: TURNING PRODUCT REQUIREMENTS DOCUMENTS INTO WORK ITEMS

After the design discussion, suppose the team green-lights the approach. Now comes the project planning: breaking down the work. In many organizations, product managers supply a PRD, or there are research notes describing user needs. Sam's next move is to turn that high-level document into a concrete engineering backlog. This is another area where AI can save time.

Sam feeds the AI the PRD (or a lengthy design doc or even a bunch of Slack notes about the feature) and asks it to generate a structured list of epics and user stories. Specifically, Sam uses a prompt like this:

> *Take these requirements and draft an organized list: first, high-level epics, then under each epic list, user stories with acceptance criteria. Include notes on what telemetry/monitoring might be needed for each story, any test data or migration steps required, and a rough rollout plan. Essentially, turn this prose into a numbered backlog ready to put into Jira.*

The assistant processes the request and out comes a neat breakdown. For example, for a feature like "Allow users to upload profile pictures," it might output something like this:

- Epic 1: Profile Picture Upload Backend
- Story: *Implement image storage service integration*—Acceptance criteria: can upload image via API, image persists in storage, etc. Telemetry: count upload attempts, failures. Tests: need sample images of various sizes.
- Story: *Validate image format and size*—Acceptance criteria: reject non-JPEG/PNG, reject images >5MB, appropriate error messages... (and so on).
- Epic 2: Profile Picture in UI
- Story: *Frontend upload form*—Details...
- Story: *Display user's profile picture on dashboard*—Details...
- Epic 3: Rollout and Monitoring
- Story: *Feature flag and gradual rollout*—Details...
- Story: *Add profile pic upload to user metrics dashboard*—Details...

And so on.

Sam reviews this and finds it's a pretty good starting point. It mirrors the kind of breakdown Sam would do manually, but in a fraction of the time. Of course, Sam adjusts a few things (maybe combining or splitting some stories, or adding a missing edge case), but the heavy lifting of translating a big requirements doc into actionable tasks is largely handled.

This technique essentially connects the dots between planning and implementation. By having the AI generate the backlog from the PRD, this approach helps reduce translation errors—if the PRD mentioned a compliance requirement or a performance target, that likely appears in the acceptance criteria of a story because the AI caught it. It also increases the chances that even supporting tasks like adding telemetry or doing gradual rollout are captured, which junior planners might overlook.

By early afternoon, Sam has an ADR and a filled-out backlog. The team knows what to do. Now it's coding time, where AI will again play a major role.

IMPLEMENT WITH A "TESTS FIRST, THEN CODE" PATTERN

One of the most effective ways to use AI in coding is to work backward from tests. We often hear, "Write tests first," but in practice, many engineers still start with code. AI gives you an incentive to actually do tests first because it can generate them for you—and having those tests ready makes it much safer to let the AI suggest code.

Here's how Sam approaches implementation:

1. *Let AI draft the unit tests.* For each story or function Sam is about to implement, he first writes a short description of what it should do (essentially the acceptance criteria or behavior) and asks the AI to generate unit tests for it before any code exists. For example:

   Write unit tests for a function, processImageUpload(file), that should reject files over 5MB, reject non-image file types, and store valid images to the user's profile.

   The AI produces a suite of tests: it creates a dummy file over 5MB and expects an exception, tries an invalid file type, tries a small valid image and expects a success result, etc. It might even generate property-based tests or edge cases Sam hadn't explicitly mentioned (e.g., a zero-byte file).

   Sam reviews these AI-written tests. He ensures they make sense and cover the key cases (sometimes he might ask for more tests or remove redundant ones). Importantly, these tests currently fail because processImageUpload isn't implemented yet. That's fine—that's the point! The tests define what "done" looks like.

2. *Run the tests (and watch them fail).* Sam runs the test suite to see the failures. This verifies the tests are actually testing what we think (e.g., a failing test that says "Function not implemented" or "Expected X but got Y" is a good sign—it's catching the absence of functionality). This step prevents a scenario where the AI wrote tests that are themselves buggy or not actually asserting anything. Sam might catch, for example, that the AI's test for the success case expected a certain return value, and Sam knows the function should return something else. So he adjusts the test expectations now, before writing the code. By doing this, Sam ensures the target behavior is correctly specified.

3. *Have AI generate the scaffold or boilerplate code.* Now with failing tests in hand, Sam starts implementing. He could code it all manually, but he smartly uses AI to handle the mundane parts. Sam might prompt:

   Implement the processImageUpload (file) function to make these tests pass.

Since the AI has context (Sam likely gave it the test code or the requirements in the prompt), it produces a candidate implementation. For instance, it writes code that checks the file size and type, and either throws errors or stores the file via some API. Sometimes the AI gets it mostly right, and other times it might misidentify an API call or use a slightly different library than what the project uses. That's OK—Sam is reviewing the diff. The tests act as a safeguard: if the AI's code doesn't actually do the right thing, at least some of the tests will still fail. Sam can then iteratively refine the prompt or code until all tests pass.

4. *Use AI for explanations and examples.* During this coding phase, Sam encounters a part of the code that uses an unfamiliar library method, ImageCompressor.compress(). Instead of digging through docs for an hour, Sam asks the AI:

   Explain how ImageCompressor.compress() works and show an example of compressing a JPEG.

   The AI provides a quick explanation pulled from documentation (or its trained knowledge) and even gives a short code snippet using that method correctly. This helps Sam integrate the new piece without losing momentum. In general, whenever Sam's flow is about to break (because of a question or an unknown), AI is like an instant *rubber duck* (a debugging technique where explaining your problem out loud helps you solve it) and documentation search rolled into one.

5. *Keep changes small and commit often.* One trap to avoid with AI assistance is letting it generate huge swaths of code in one go. Sam is careful to break the work into small, reviewable chunks—implement one function or one logical piece at a time, run tests, commit, then move on. AI is best used as an accelerant for the boring bits (like creating boilerplate or repetitive code), not for creating the core critical logic all at once. By keeping changes small, Sam can pinpoint if something goes wrong, and the team's code reviews stay sane.

This tests-first approach not only yields more reliable code, it also turns coding into a more measured, high-confidence process. There's empirical evidence that this strategy works well: teams have found that using AI for the "boring parts" of coding (after defining the problem through tests or specs) can significantly speed up development without sacrificing quality, especially when coupled with small, frequent commits. In Sam's case, by mid-afternoon, most of the new feature's code is written and covered by tests. The AI didn't replace Sam—it paired with Sam to get the job done faster.

CODE REVIEW: AI AS AN AMPLIFIER, NOT A GATEKEEPER

The feature implementation is ready for review. Now imagine one of Sam's teammates, Jen, is the reviewer. Jen can also use AI to assist her code review process (and Sam could have done a pre-check using AI on his own diff as well). The key mindset is this: AI can flag issues and suggest improvements, but it does not approve code on its own.

Here's how AI can help a human reviewer like Jen:

Generate a review checklist for the PR.

Jen prompts the AI:

> Analyze this pull request. What are the key changes and potential risk areas I should pay attention to? Generate a checklist.

The AI goes through the diff and comes back with something like this:

1. *Security:* Check input validation on file upload (is it sufficient?).
2. *Performance:* The new image compression loop—any risk of slowing down the request?
3. *Style/Consistency:* New code uses library X, ensure this aligns with our existing usage.
4. *Testing:* Verify that tests cover error cases like invalid file types.

Essentially, the AI provides a to-do list for the reviewer, highlighting areas in the code that deserve scrutiny.

Highlight risky or non-obvious changes.

If the diff includes, say, changes in an authentication module or some configuration in infrastructure-as-code, the AI might highlight those as particularly sensitive. It might say,

> Lines 40–60 in File Y handle permission changes—double-check logic.

This is useful because in a large PR, it's easy for a human to miss something subtle; the AI is like an extra pair of eyes that never gets tired.

Draft review comments or suggestions.
Jen can even select a chunk of code and use this prompt:

> Does this follow our style and best practices? Suggest any improvements or point out issues.

For example, if Sam's code had a function 50 lines long (violating a style guide rule about small functions), the AI might draft a comment:

> Function `processImageUpload` seems a bit long—consider refactoring for clarity (our style guide recommends <30 lines)—for instance, extracting the validation into a helper.

It might cite the style guide section if that was provided. Or if there's a potential bug (maybe forgetting to close a file handle), the AI could point it out with a comment suggestion. Jen can then review those AI-suggested comments, edit or discard as needed, and post them as her own.

The critical point is that *Jen remains the decision maker*. The AI might suggest five comments; Jen might decide two of them are off-base and only send three to Sam. The AI might miss something that Jen, with her domain knowledge, catches—so Jen writes her own comment for that. Under no circumstance does Jen just let the AI auto-approve the PR. Code reviews involve architectural considerations, broader context, and sometimes project-specific judgment calls that AI isn't equipped to handle. For instance, AI can't truly know if a piece of code fits the intended feature or if it impacts a planned future refactor—that's human territory.

What this AI-assisted review does accomplish is speeding up the grunt work of reviewing. It's like having a tireless junior reviewer that points out the obvious things (style issues, certain bug patterns) so the human reviewer can focus on higher-level concerns. (Is this approach the right one? Are we handling the business requirements correctly?) It also can reduce human error—we've all done reviews where we missed an important detail because of fatigue or time pressure. The AI can serve as a safety net.

AI makes code reviews more about collaboration than gatekeeping. The AI is an amplifier for the reviewer's effectiveness: highlighting potential problems and even wording some feedback, but deferring to the human for the final judgment. This ensures that by the time code gets merged, it has been seen from multiple angles (human and AI) and nothing glaring slips through. Teams that adopt AI in reviews often find that while AI can't approve code, it can significantly reduce review turnaround time and improve code quality by catching low-level issues consistently.

AFTER THE CODE: DOCS, OBSERVABILITY, AND COMMUNICATION

Sam's feature gets approved and merged. Normally, at this point, many engineers would consider the job done—but effective engineers know that finishing a feature involves clean-up and communication: updating documentation, adding or adjusting dashboards and alerts, and informing stakeholders of the changes. These are tasks that are easy to neglect or rush, but AI can make them much less painful and faster, so there's no excuse to skip them.

Here's how Sam uses AI in the post-merge phase:

Update runbooks and documentation.

Sam asks the AI to draft updates to the user guide and the on-call runbook based on the changes. For example:

> Document the new profile picture upload feature: update the API documentation section and add a note in the on-call runbook about the new image service (including any new alerts or troubleshooting tips).

The AI, having context from the code or the PR description, generates paragraphs that describe how the new feature works, how to configure it, and what to do if it fails (maybe referencing the telemetry it knows was added). Sam will verify these, but it's much easier to edit an AI-written doc than to write one from scratch after you've mentally moved on to the next task.

Generate or update dashboards.

Suppose part of this feature was adding some new metrics (like number of profile uploads, or image processing time). Sam can use AI to quickly create queries or even code for a dashboard config. For instance:

> We added a metric for upload size and a counter for uploads—suggest a Grafana dashboard panel JSON for average upload size over time and total uploads per hour.

The AI can output a ready-to-use JSON or at least a template of it. Or if the ops tooling uses a domain-specific language (DSL) or Terraform (*https://terraform.io*), it could draft the config. Sam pastes that in, tweaks names or thresholds, and voilà—monitoring is set up with minimal fuss.

Draft the release notes or stakeholder email.

Finally, Sam needs to communicate the user-visible changes to nonengineering stakeholders (product managers, support, maybe customers if there's a changelog). Crafting a crisp summary in business-friendly language is something AI is quite good at. Sam might use a prompt like this:

> Summarize the impact of the profile picture feature in two to three sentences for the release notes, focusing on the value to users. Then draft a brief email update to the support team explaining the change, any limits (e.g., file size), and what to tell users who ask about it.

The AI produces a polished blurb:

> Release Notes: Users can now upload profile pictures to personalize their accounts. This feature supports JPEG/PNG images up to 5MB and will enhance user profiles with a visual identity.

And an email:

> Hi team, as of today, users can upload a profile picture. This is optional and images must be under 5MB. If users have trouble, common issues might be large file size or unsupported format.

And so on.

Sam reads it over, makes one or two wording changes, and sends it out. Task done in minutes.

These kinds of communication tasks often differentiate effective engineers from merely efficient ones. By ensuring everything around the code (the context in which the code lives) is updated and broadcast, Sam prevents a lot of future pain—fewer confused users, fewer on-call surprises, more transparency. AI here acts as a force multiplier for thoroughness. It's easier to be diligent when the busy work of diligence (writing docs, summarizing changes) is alleviated by an assistant. As a bonus, this ties back to advice in Chapter 4 about keeping stakeholders informed and in Chapter 2 about writing good documentation; AI helps you do those soft tasks more effectively, not just the hardcore coding.

At this point, Sam's day (or sprint) is complete: from planning to rollout, AI has been a helpful collaborator, and every step's output feeds the next. The planning outputs created the to-do list for coding; the tests made coding safer; the code and tests made review easier; the code and monitoring changes made documentation and comms straightforward. For an IC, AI shines through the steady accumulation of small assists, creating a compounding effect that allows the team to move significantly faster and with greater confidence.

FICTIONAL EXAMPLE: SAM'S AI-POWERED WORKDAY

Let's take a look a how all these pieces come together in a single (very productive) workday for Sam:

9:00 a.m.—planning

Sam starts the day with a feature idea and a vague requirement doc. By 9:30, with the AI's help, Sam has a one-page decision brief comparing four implementation approaches, complete with trade-offs and links to case studies. At 10:00, Sam uses the AI to poke holes in the preferred approach's scalability and failure modes, uncovering a potential performance bottleneck that wasn't obvious at first. By 10:30, Sam has drafted an architecture decision record that the team can review during the 11:00 design meeting.

11:00 a.m.—design review

In the team meeting, Sam presents the AI-assisted ADR draft. The team discusses it, and since the draft already included multiple options and risk analysis, they quickly converge on a decision, with minor tweaks. The meeting ends early. Sam takes 15 minutes to update the ADR with a couple of manual edits based on the feedback, then finalizes it.

12:00 p.m.—breaking down tasks

Right before lunch, Sam feeds the project PRD into the AI and gets a structured backlog out. After reviewing and adjusting it, Sam now has a full list of epics and stories in the tracker. The project suddenly feels organized and manageable, rather than a big fuzzy blob of work.

1:30 p.m.—coding (tests first)

After lunch, Sam picks the first story (backend API for image upload). Using AI, Sam generates a suite of unit tests describing the expected behavior. By 2:00, Sam is iterating on implementation. The first AI-suggested code fails one of the tests (it didn't handle a certain file type correctly), so Sam refines it, and soon all tests pass. Sam commits this chunk. The next story (frontend form) is tackled similarly: by 3:00, tests are written (the AI helped), code is implemented (the AI suggested most of it; Sam tweaked), and all tests are green. Sam commits again.

3:30 p.m.—self-code review

Before pushing the code for review, Sam uses the AI to double-check his own diff. The AI flags a possible improvement: "Hey, you're logging the image size in two different places, maybe consolidate or ensure the format is consistent." Sam realizes he did add redundant logging—a quick refactor fixes it. The AI also suggests adding a test for an empty image file scenario. Sam adds that test (it fails), then adjusts the code to handle it. By 4:00, the branch is in even better shape. Sam pushes the code.

4:15 p.m.—code review (peer and AI)

Jen, the reviewer, gets a ping. She opens the PR and runs her AI assistant on it to generate a review plan. By 4:30, Jen has left a few comments—two of which were formulated by AI (style nits), and one she wrote herself about a naming clarification. Sam quickly responds (the AI even helps draft a clarification comment for one of Jen's questions). By 4:45, Jen is satisfied and approves the PR.

5:00 p.m.—documentation and wrap-up

The code is merged. Sam spends the last part of the day on polish: using AI to update the user guide section for profile pictures, adding a note in the team's on-call playbook about the new service ("If the profile-pic service is down, users will see a default avatar"), and drafting a summary for the release notes and an internal email. All of these take maybe 15 to 20 minutes, with the AI doing the heavy lifting. Sam skims them, makes small edits, and sends them out.

5:30 p.m.—reflection

Sam looks back on the day: a design is decided on, tasks are defined, and code is written, tested, reviewed, merged, documented, and communicated—all in one day! It's a lot of forward progress, with high quality. Sam didn't skip tests or docs (common shortcuts under time pressure) because AI made those tasks almost effortless. There's also a sense of confidence knowing that tests cover the feature and monitoring is in place. Sam heads off knowing that if anything goes wrong with this deployment, the team is prepared—and if things go right, users will immediately see value, and everyone knows about it.

This fictional day might sound idealized, but it's increasingly attainable with the prudent use of AI tools. The point is not that Sam is some 10× hero (the tools did a lot of the grinding work)—the point is Sam invested time in leveraging AI to do things the right way (tests, docs, etc.), and as a result, both speed and quality were maximized. The workflow compounds: each step's output makes the next step easier, creating a positive feedback loop that boosts overall effectiveness.

Having seen this soup-to-nuts example, we can move on to more specific tips. The next sections will cover crucial considerations like providing the AI with the right context, baking in security from the start, handling legal/privacy concerns, using autonomous AI agents carefully, measuring the impact of all this work, and even some ready-made prompt templates you can use. These will enrich the basic workflow we've outlined with additional best practices and safeguards.

Feeding the AI Context: Getting Repository Awareness Right

One of the most important factors in getting useful, correct outputs from an AI assistant is *context*. An AI model is only as good as the information you give it (plus what it already "knows" from training). If you ask a generic AI about your specific codebase without providing context, you'll get generic answers. Effective engineers take control of the context fed to the AI.

Here are some ways to give your AI buddy the awareness it needs:

Connect it to your codebase and knowledge sources.
> The best AI coding tools at present integrate deeply with your development environment. This means the AI can "see" your repository (at least the parts of it relevant to your prompt), your API schemas, your database schemas, your service catalog, etc. If your tool supports it, ensure it's plugged into your IDE with repository indexing enabled. If not, you can manually copy-paste relevant code snippets or definitions into the prompt. For example, if you want the AI to help with a function in a particular file, it helps to also provide the content of said file (or at least the signature of the function and related data structures) in the prompt. The difference is night and day—an assistant with context can tailor suggestions to your actual code, whereas one without is guessing from general knowledge.

Use semantic search for deep references.

Modern AI tools often come with *semantic search* capabilities: you input a natural language query or a code snippet, and it finds semantically related code in your repo. This is incredibly useful for questions like "Do we have an example of using OAuth2 client credentials flow in our codebase?" or "Where is the X pattern implemented?" Instead of blindly grepping or searching manually, you ask the AI or search tool, and it will leverage vector embeddings to find relevant matches (like that one time Bob wrote a similar caching mechanism in a different service). You can then feed those code snippets back into the assistant when asking it to generate new code or explanations, ensuring it doesn't hallucinate something that doesn't fit your codebase. Essentially, think of semantic search as an extension of the AI's memory into your code repo.

Make prompts reproducible and shareable.

This is a pro tip that many teams learn over time: if you craft a good prompt for your AI assistant (e.g., a prompt that explains your project's coding style and asks the AI to always include certain comments or citations), save that prompt! You can put prompt templates or example conversations in your repository—some teams create a *prompts/* directory, or even embed key prompt instructions in the repository's README for AI tools that auto-load context. By keeping prompts versioned alongside code, everyone on the team can reuse and refine them. It also helps in onboarding new team members—they can see, "Oh, when we write tests with AI, we usually use this prompt structure." Treat prompt writing as a mini art/science and share successful patterns.

One effective prompting approach worth calling out is the *context sandwich* pattern. This isn't a formal term, but it's a handy mental model for structuring prompts to maximize quality.

When asking the AI for help coding, structure your prompt in four layers:

1. *Goal/outcome*

Start by clearly stating what you want to achieve. "I want to implement X functionality..." or "I need to understand Y..." Be specific about the desired outcome or answer.

2. Relevant context

Next, include the smallest set of snippets or information from your repo that are relevant. This could be function signatures, error messages, configuration excerpts, etc. More context is not always better—you want the key pieces without overwhelming or confusing the model. For each snippet, you might add a one-line comment explaining its relevance (e.g., "// this is the interface definition we have to implement").

3. Constraints/requirements

State any rules the solution must follow, or any assumptions. This can include performance constraints ("must run in O(n) time"), style preferences ("follow our internal style guide for naming"), or technological constraints ("we use library X version 3"). Also define what "done" looks like ("Solution must handle these five cases and pass these tests").

4. Request guidance

Finally, ask the AI for what you need, and if possible, request any supporting evidence or pointers. For instance:

> *Provide the implementation and explain any security considerations. If you use any significant formula or code from somewhere, cite the source or file path.*

> Or

> *Give me step-by-step reasoning along with the answer.*

This explicitly tells the AI how to format its output and encourages it to surface its reasoning or sources.

Using this sandwich structure, you're bracketing the AI with clarity: goal upfront, context in the middle, constraints next, and a guided ask. Engineers have found that this significantly improves the quality of AI output and reduces hallucinations or irrelevant tangents. It's like giving the AI a well-framed problem on a silver platter.

In practice, doing this manually for every prompt might sound tedious, but you can create prompt templates (as mentioned) or even scripts to automate some of it (some advanced teams integrate with their IDE so that you can select a piece of code and hit an Ask AI button that automatically fills in context around it).

Remember: context is king. An AI coding assistant with no awareness of your project is like a new hire who hasn't read the wiki or looked at the repo—they'll produce generic answers that might be totally off-base. But an AI with rich context is more like a team member who's been ramping up on your code and can give insights that actually make sense for your situation. Investing time in feeding the right context pays off in both the accuracy of AI outputs and the trust your team can place in them.

That trust, however, shouldn't lead to complacency. Even the most context-aware AI can generate code that looks correct but isn't safe. Which brings us to the next critical dimension of AI-assisted development: security.

Security First: Build AI into Your Secure Development Lifecycle

With great power (AI coding assistance) comes great responsibility (security!). One of the biggest pitfalls of using AI in software engineering is that it can lull you into a false sense of security. The code it produces often looks clean and correct at first glance. But security vulnerabilities can lurk beneath that veneer. As I noted at the beginning of this chapter, nearly half of AI-generated code samples in a recent study had security flaws. This isn't because the AI is malicious; it's because it doesn't inherently know what could go wrong—unless you explicitly tell it or have processes to catch issues.

The solution is to design security into your AI-augmented workflow from the start. Don't treat AI-written code any differently than code written by an intern when it comes to scrutiny. In fact, be even more vigilant initially, since AI can introduce subtle bugs you might not expect. Here's a checklist of practices to make sure you maintain a strong security posture while reaping AI's benefits:

Always prompt for security considerations.

When asking an AI to generate code, include security requirements in the prompt. For example:

> *Generate a scaffold for the new user signup form with proper input validation and output encoding. Avoid using any deprecated crypto or insecure random functions. Include logging of important events (without sensitive data) and comments on security assumptions.*

If you explicitly ask the AI to address security (and mention specific categories like OWASP top 10 issues relevant to your task), it's more likely to produce secure patterns. Think of it as priming the AI to be a security-conscious copilot.

Run automated security scans on AI-generated code.
Integrate static application security testing (SAST) (*https://oreil.ly/JD2DV*), software component analysis (SCA) (*https://oreil.ly/tNoy_*) (dependency vulnerability scanners), secret scanners, and other security tooling into your continuous integration pipeline—and flag it when they specifically catch something in AI-authored code. For instance, if the AI adds a new dependency, your SCA tool should immediately tell you if that library has known vulnerabilities. If the AI writes an SQL query, your SAST might catch that it's not parameterized (a SQL injection risk). Automate these checks for every pull request. This is something you should ideally do for all code, but make it a point to *always* do it for AI-assisted code because the AI might not have the same gut feeling for insecurity that an experienced developer might.

Enforce tests and reviews for AI contributions.
Consider setting up branch protections or CI rules: if a PR has more than a trivial amount of AI-generated code (some orgs tag or identify AI-generated commits), require that it has adequate test coverage before merging. Essentially, say, "If AI wrote it, we test it." Similarly, maybe require an extra human reviewer for AI-heavy changes or mandate code review checklists that include security items (which, as discussed in "Pressure-test the requirements" on page 181, AI itself can help generate!). The idea is to never let AI code slip through unexamined. Teams at companies like Microsoft and Google have internal policies where AI-written code must be reviewed with at least as much rigor as any other code—often more, since the AI might not follow all internal best practices unless guided.

Use policy-as-code to encode secure patterns.
If your company has specific banned functions or insecure patterns (e.g., using eval or direct SQL string concatenation), enforce these via linters or static analysis rules. That way, even if the AI suggests something discouraged, your automated tools will catch it. Some AI tools even allow custom rules that you can feed to the model (like "do not use function X"), but don't rely on that alone—back it up with actual scanning. Treat the AI assistant like a dependency that sometimes does the wrong thing, and have guardrails to catch known bad patterns.

Create a feedback loop for insecure AI outputs.
When (not if) a security issue is discovered in AI-written code, use it as a teaching moment for the AI and your team. For example, I've seen cases where an AI suggested using an outdated cryptographic hash function (MD5) instead of SHA-256, or generated SQL queries vulnerable to injection. In each case, we updated our prompt templates to explicitly forbid these patterns and added linter rules to catch them. For instance, suppose a pen test or later review finds that an AI-suggested regex for input validation was too permissive (letting through malicious input).

Take that example, abstract it into a prompt test case, and next time you or anyone on your team asks the AI for similar code, explicitly include a caution or pattern from the learned lesson. Some teams maintain an internal wiki or snippet repository of AI gotchas—code that the AI suggested that had a flaw and the corrected version. Over time, this becomes part of the prompting guidelines (e.g., "Always remind the AI to do X when asking for Y"). Additionally, if your AI tool has a way to be customized or fine-tuned, feeding these examples in can improve it. In short, treat it as an iterative process: the first time, the AI might introduce a bug; you catch it, fix it, and then adjust your usage to prevent that class of bug in the future.

Manage where AI can operate (and learn).
For compliance and risk management, you need to establish clear policies around AI usage and ensure your team follows them. If your organization doesn't yet have AI usage policies, work with your manager and security team to create them—this is not optional. Note that many large organizations now have dedicated AI governance and security functions that are specifically addressing AI-related risks, so check if your company has such resources available.

You may want to control which parts of your codebase AI suggestions can be applied to or derived from. Some organizations maintain an allowlist of repositories or projects where AI assistance is enabled (less sensitive apps or newer projects), and a blocklist for highly sensitive modules (like cryptography code or proprietary algorithms that are too sensitive to even expose to an AI service).

Similarly, consider whether you allow the AI provider to retain snippets of your code for training their models. Enterprise-focused AI tools often let you opt out of training and turn off data logging—these features are essential for proprietary code, not optional. If the AI isn't learning from your usage, that's fine—you can still benefit from its pre-training, and you avoid potential leaks of your internal code into the model's future outputs for others.

The overarching message is to bake security into the process, not retrofit it later. AI tools can absolutely be used in a secure way, but it requires discipline. By setting the expectation that every AI-generated line is treated with zero trust until proven otherwise, you'll naturally build workflows that include prompts for security, automated checks, and rigorous reviews. This way, you enjoy the productivity boost without opening yourself (and your users) up to risks.

Anti-Pattern: Vibe Coding

Vibe coding is a term that's emerged to describe a laid-back (and dangerous) approach where a developer just lets the AI generate code without a clear spec or rigorous tests, trusting that "if it runs, it's fine." It's coding by vibe: "This feels right, ship it."

This approach might produce a flurry of activity and even some working features quickly, giving the illusion of hyper-productivity. But the hidden costs pile up. Without concrete requirements, the AI might make assumptions that don't hold. Without tests, those assumptions aren't caught until production. Without security prompts, the AI may unknowingly introduce glaring vulnerabilities (e.g., using outdated crypto or mishandling user input). Studies and industry reports have noted that many insecure patterns slip in exactly in these scenarios—a developer was in a rush, relied on AI to fill in gaps, and didn't thoroughly validate the output. The result is often a fast, but insecure codebase that will require significant rework or, worse, will suffer an incident.

Don't vibe code. Always anchor AI usage in solid engineering practice: clear specifications, tests, and reviews. If you ever find yourself just hitting Tab on AI suggestions without fully understanding them because "it looks about right," take a step back. You don't want to be the person who introduced a SQL injection because the AI offered a convenient snippet and you didn't double-check it. The fastest way to lose organizational trust in these tools is a preventable security lapse. One of my other books, *Beyond Vibe Coding* (O'Reilly) (*http://beyond.addy.ie*), goes into this topic in more detail.

Privacy, Licensing, and Compliance: Guardrails You Can't Skip

Beyond security, there are other project health responsibilities that fall on an engineer's shoulders when using AI. These include protecting privacy and sensitive data, avoiding license or IP violations, and ensuring compliance with external regulations. Many companies already have established guidelines in these areas, particularly around intellectual property (IP) and licensing—concerns that often become critical during mergers, acquisitions, or initial public offerings. Check with your legal or compliance team about existing policies before adopting AI tools. Effective software engineers don't consider these as someone else's problem—they integrate these considerations into how they use AI day-to-day. Here's how you can do the same.

DON'T FEED THE AI SENSITIVE DATA

This might sound obvious, but in the flow of using a chatbot or coding assistant, it's easy to accidentally paste something sensitive—like a private key, a customer's personal data, or proprietary algorithm code—into a prompt. Remember that cloud-based AI services may log prompts (and even if they say they don't retain them long-term, breaches or mistakes can happen). Always err on the side of caution: never paste passwords, API keys, personally identifiable information (PII), or company-confidential info into an AI tool that isn't explicitly designed for the secure handling of such data.

If you need the AI to analyze a production log that contains user emails, for instance, redact or anonymize those details first (you can have a script replace real emails with fake ones, etc.). If you need to discuss a proprietary algorithm, abstract it—say, "a sorting algorithm," instead of the actual name if the name itself is sensitive. Some advanced tools let you run on-prem or have a local mode—use those for sensitive stuff if available. The rule of thumb: assume anything you send to an external AI service could be seen by a human or leak someday. So sanitize your inputs accordingly.

WATCH OUT FOR LICENSING AND ATTRIBUTION ISSUES

AI that generates code might regurgitate code patterns from its training data. In some cases, it could even output a verbatim snippet from an open source project. If that snippet is under a viral license (like GNU General Public Licenses) and you include it in your proprietary codebase without noticing, you could create a legal problem. Now, the extent to which AI output is considered a derived work is an evolving legal question, but you shouldn't ignore the risk. To be safe:

- Prefer AI tools or settings that provide citation or provenance hints. Some coding assistants can be configured to cite sources for larger code completions (e.g., "this chunk is similar to code on Stack Overflow or GitHub at URL X"). Use these features if available, and then manually verify whether you're allowed to use that code.
- Run a similarity check on significant AI-generated code. There are tools that can compare a block of code against a database of known open source code to see if it's likely copied. If your AI suggests a large chunk (say more than 50 characters of exact text) that is nontrivial, it's worth checking.
- When in doubt about a piece of code, *ask the AI directly:* "Did any of the code you just provided come from an identifiable source? If so, what license is it under?" It may or may not answer correctly, but it's a nudge. You can also prompt it to rephrase or rewrite in a more original way if you suspect it's too similar to something.
- Finally, document the use of AI. In the pull request or code comments, note that "this function was initially generated with the help of AI." Include any references the AI provided. This creates an audit trail. If, later, someone finds that the code resembles library X, you can show that the AI suggested it and you weren't intentionally copy-pasting without attribution.

In short, treat AI like an intern who might accidentally plagiarize—you, as the responsible engineer, must ensure all code you commit is safe to use license-wise and is attributed properly if needed. And while you're thinking about responsible use, it's equally important to stay aware of the broader rules shaping how AI can be used.

STAY AWARE OF AI-RELATED REGULATIONS WHERE YOU OPERATE

We touched on the EU AI Act at the beginning of this chapter. It's an example of a regulatory framework that could affect software teams. As an IC, you're not expected to be a lawyer, but it's part of being effective to be aware of the "rules of the road." If your software or your customers are in the EU, you should know that certain AI practices are restricted or require disclosures. For instance, using AI that might be considered high-risk (like something impacting people's legal rights or safety) comes with documentation and transparency requirements (*https://oreil.ly/tzxlH*).

Even if you're just using an AI coding assistant, your company might be considered an "AI provider" if, say, it fine-tunes models or offers AI-driven features in the product. The EU AI Act has a bunch of tiers and deadlines—it's worth coordinating with your legal/compliance folks to get a cheat sheet of what applies to you. Similarly, other jurisdictions might have rules about AI output (e.g., requiring user notification if a chatbot response was AI-generated, etc.). The takeaway is this: don't operate in a vacuum. If you're adopting AI heavily, engage with your leadership or counsel to ensure compliance. It's much easier to integrate compliance from the start than to retrofit your processes later under a time crunch.

ALIGN WITH RISK MANAGEMENT FRAMEWORKS (THEY'RE HELPFUL, REALLY!)

Frameworks like the NIST AI Risk Management Framework (RMF) provide a structured way to think about the risks of AI and how to mitigate them. As an engineer, the jargon might seem abstract, but you can extract practical checklists. NIST's framework breaks down into functions: govern, map, measure, and manage. In practice, this is how these domains might translate to questions:

Govern
> Does our team have guidelines for AI use? Is someone responsible for reviewing AI-related policies?

Map
> Have we identified where we're using AI and what the impact could be if it fails or misbehaves? (E.g., AI writing code—risk: bugs; AI suggesting test cases—risk: missing cases; AI in product feature—risk: biased outputs).

Measure
> Are we tracking the performance and outcomes of AI (like all the metrics we'll discuss in the upcoming section "Measuring Impact: How to Quantify AI's Effect Like an Engineer" on page 206)? Are we measuring error rates, security incidents, productivity changes?

Manage
> Do we have processes to respond if something goes wrong (like when AI-generated content causes an issue)? Are we continuously improving how we use AI based on what we measure?

It sounds like a lot, but these are basically the things we've been discussing, formulated generally. Many organizations might make this formal (e.g., an AI risk checklist every quarter). As an IC, your role is to be aware of these and contribute. If you notice something—like the AI is suggesting outdated code that could lead to a vulnerability—raise it and get it addressed as part of this risk management cycle.

In essence, using AI as an engineer isn't just a technical challenge, it's also an ethical and legal one. Privacy, IP, and compliance guardrails ensure that while you speed ahead with AI, you're not crossing lines that could harm users or get your team in trouble. Effective engineers internalize these guardrails as part of the definition of done. It's not done if you solved the technical problem but leaked data or violated a license in the process.

By keeping these considerations in mind and building habits (like always scrubbing sensitive data, double-checking licenses, staying educated on regulations, and following frameworks), you will use AI in a way that's responsible and professional. This not only protects you and your company, but it also builds trust—both with the public and within your team—that your company's AI usage isn't a Wild West, but a well-managed tool in your engineering toolbox.

As your organization matures in its AI adoption, the next challenge isn't just using AI responsibly—it's managing the growing autonomy of the tools themselves.

AI Agents: What They Can Do and How to Keep Them Tamed

We've mostly discussed scenarios where you are directly in the loop—prompting an AI, reviewing its outputs, and guiding it step by step. But another frontier of practical AI use is the rise of *autonomous* or *semi-autonomous AI agents* in software development. These are systems where you give a high-level goal (like "update all dependencies to the latest version and fix any build issues" or "try to resolve this GitHub issue automatically") and the AI agent will iteratively take actions: write code, run tests, maybe open pull requests, etc., with minimal further input.

It sounds almost like science fiction, but as of 2026, there have been demos and some real progress here. Tools and frameworks (some open source, some internal at big companies) can spin up such coding agents. For example, OpenAI's SWE-bench (*https://oreil.ly/zJi4E*) is a benchmark that tests how well AI agents can handle real-world coding tasks and issues from GitHub. The results (*https://oreil.ly/SG6ki*) have been promising—some agents can solve a majority of those tasks, even if not perfectly on the first try. However, the key word is *constrained* tasks. Agents are far from ready to build a complex feature from scratch reliably, but they can be very effective at mechanical, repetitive chores.

So where can these agents help you today, and how do you ensure they don't go off the rails? There are some great uses for coding agents right now:

Automated refactoring or cleanup across many files
> Suppose your project has to rename a widely used API or change a logging format across hundreds of files. This is grunt work that an agent can handle. You give it the instructions ("rename all usages of oldFunction to newFunction, and update import statements accordingly, ensure tests pass"), and let it iterate through the codebase. It might run tests as it goes, and maybe even split the changes into multiple commits or a PR. Essentially, think of it as a super-charged find-and-replace that actually understands code context.

Dependency upgrades and fixes
> Keeping dependencies up-to-date is important but tedious. An agent can be told, "Upgrade library X from v1 to v2, run the build and tests, and make any code changes needed for compatibility." It will bump the version, see where things break, and attempt fixes. For example, if a function moved to a new package, it can update the import. If an API changed, it can attempt to adjust the call. You might have seen Dependabot in GitHub—think of an AI agent as Dependabot on steroids: it doesn't just open a PR saying "update version"; it tries to actually make the updated code work too (maybe using changelog information or docs to guide it).

Writing tests for legacy code
> If you have older modules without tests (and you're afraid to touch them), you can unleash an agent with the task "generate thorough unit tests for module Y (without altering the module)." The agent will treat it like a puzzle: call every function with various inputs, etc.; and it might end up discovering edge cases or even bugs in the process. It won't be perfect, but it's a fast way to bolster your test coverage, especially for code that you don't fully understand but want to safeguard.

Reproducing and isolating bugs
> This one is a bit experimental, but some agents can take a bug report or failing test and try different things to pinpoint the issue or even create a minimal reproduction repository. For instance, given a flaky test, an

agent could try to rerun it under various conditions, add logs, bisect which commit introduced it, etc. It's like a junior developer who tirelessly tries dozens of debugging steps at 3 a.m. while you sleep, and in the morning you get a report of what it found.

Now, these agents are powerful but also potentially chaotic if left unchecked. They could make a huge mess (imagine an agent refactoring half your codebase incorrectly). So, it's essential to impose *safety rails* on them (constraints and controls that limit what the agent can do—similar to guardrails we discussed in "Code Review: AI as an Amplifier, Not a Gatekeeper" on page 186, but specifically focused on autonomous agent behavior).

Limit the scope and permissions.
When you run an agent, give it a narrow goal and strict boundaries. For example, run it in a sandbox branch, not directly on main. Set a time limit or step limit (like "if it hasn't finished after 30 minutes or 50 steps, stop it"). Limit the directories it can modify ("only work in /src and don't touch /docs or config files unless told"). If the agent uses tools (like running shell commands or tests), ensure it's not able to do destructive things outside its scope (you wouldn't want it deploying something or deleting data because it thought it was cleaning up). Some tech stacks let you specify which actions are permitted. This can include which files can be read or written to and whether you can push changes directly to the main branch without requiring review or approval.

Require human review of agent outputs.
A good practice is to have the agent open a pull request with its changes (or multiple PRs if it's a big change), and then a human reviews them just like any other code. The agent can even include a summary of what it did. For example: "Agent PR: Updated 20 files to remove deprecated API usage. All tests now pass locally." The human reviewer can scan through to ensure nothing crazy slipped in. You can treat agent contributions like those from a very fast but naive engineer—double-check them.

Integrate tests as guardrails.
I mentioned it implicitly: the agent should be running tests (and linters, type-checkers, etc.) as it works. Make that a hard requirement. If tests aren't green, the agent's job isn't done. Some agents will stop and report failure or ask for guidance if they can't get tests to pass. That's good—

better to have it stop than to introduce failures. You might even inject extra tests *before* running an agent to pin down things you're worried about. For instance, if you task an agent with optimizing a function, first add a few assertion tests about that function's output for known inputs to ensure the agent doesn't optimize by changing behavior.

Label and log everything.

Any changes made by an agent should be clearly labeled (in commit messages or PR descriptions). This is partly for transparency ("this was done by AI agent Alpha 1.2 on date X") and partly for auditing. You should keep the full transcript or log of what the agent did—the commands it ran, the intermediate decisions it made, etc.—as much as possible. This log is invaluable if something goes wrong. It's like a flight recorder. If the agent introduces a bug that slips through, being able to trace why it made a certain change will help you fix both the bug and improve the agent next time. Some agent frameworks automatically keep a history and even allow replaying steps.

Start with noncritical tasks to build trust.

Use agents on chores that, if messed up, won't be catastrophic. Maybe start with that internal tool code, a documentation site, or a small service, rather than your core payment processing service. Over a 90-day pilot (e.g., "Rolling AI Out to Your Team: A 90-Day Plan" on page 216), evaluate how often the agent's PRs are good versus how often they cause issues. If the agent works well, you can expand its usage gradually. If it's flaky, you constrain it further or hold off on using it for anything critical.

The state of agents in 2026 is somewhat like self-driving cars: they can handle the highway under good conditions, but you still want a driver ready to take the wheel if needed. They are assistive automation, not full autonomy in the general case. Use them to take on the tedious tasks you'd rather not do, but always keep an eye on them.

In practice, adding agents to your team's toolkit can yield nice efficiency gains. Engineers often have a backlog of "we should really update X" or "someday we must refactor Y" that they never get to. An agent gives you a way to tackle some of those in the background. Just maintain that healthy skepticism and control. If you treat an agent as a junior dev who works super fast but has no judgment, you'll set the right expectations and processes to supervise it.

Also, document what your agent does and how to run it, so others know and can benefit (or pause it) as needed. For example, if you have an agent script that auto-fixes lint issues every night, let the team know that it exists so someone doesn't duplicate effort or get surprised by nightly ghost commits.

To summarize, AI agents are here in early forms and can be very useful for scoped tasks. They extend the idea of AI assistance from reacting to your prompts to proactively taking initiative on structured tasks. This is an exciting area, and by experimenting carefully, you can be at the forefront of using these tools to eliminate drudgery from your team's workload. Just make sure the humans remain ultimately in charge of what goes into the codebase.

As these tools become part of everyday engineering, it's important to move from experimentation to evaluation—to ask not just what they can do, but what difference they actually make.

Measuring Impact: How to Quantify AI's Effect Like an Engineer

Up to now we've focused on *how* to use AI in your engineering practice. But how do you know if it's actually making you (and your team) more effective? As with any new tool or process, it's crucial to measure the impact. This isn't just to prove to your boss that the AI subscription is worth it (though that can be handy); it also provides information on your own iteration of AI use. As an engineer, you'll appreciate that gut feel and anecdotes aren't reliable—we need data.

Let's break down metrics you can track into a couple of categories.

ADOPTION AND BEHAVIOR METRICS

Adoption and behavior metrics tell you *how* the AI is being used by the team. Some useful metrics include the following:

Daily/weekly active users
　　How many engineers are actually using the AI assistant regularly? If you rolled out licenses to 50 devs but only 5 are using it weekly, that's a sign of either low usefulness or awareness. Track usage rates over time to see if adoption grows as people get comfortable. Maybe you set a goal like "80% of the team uses the assistant at least three times a week within two months of rollout" as a success criterion.

Suggestion acceptance rate
　　Out of all the code or suggestions the AI offers, what percentage do engineers accept into the codebase? This can often be measured via the

tool's telemetry or even by scanning commit diffs for AI markers. Industry reports show an average of around 30% acceptance (*https://oreil.ly/gXe-L*) for tools like Copilot. If your acceptance is, say, 5%, maybe the prompts need improvement or folks are using it for the wrong tasks. If it's 60%, that might actually be a red flag that people are overly trusting of it, unless it's well justified. Keep an eye on this. Also, note acceptance might vary by scenario (maybe high in test files, low in critical code).

Retention of AI-generated code
It's one thing to accept a suggestion initially, but do you end up modifying or deleting it later? The study linked earlier found developers kept 88% of the AI-generated code they accepted with minimal changes. High retention means the suggestions were solid (or at least harmless). Low retention (like if half of it gets rewritten later) might mean the AI often gives a draft that humans then have to clean up—which could be fine if that's expected, but it could also hint that the AI isn't saving as much time as it could.

Time to first suggestion
How quickly does the AI offer help when you start a coding task? If it takes five minutes of typing to get anything versus five seconds, that affects flow. Some tools measure the time from opening a file to the first suggestion accepted. Faster is generally better because it means AI is integrated into the flow and not causing delay.

Context usage
How often does the AI utilize in-project context in its answers? For instance, does it cite or reference in-repo functions and APIs (if the tool is capable of that)? If you see that suggestions frequently mention your internal APIs correctly, that's a good sign it's well-tuned. If it's always suggesting generic or wrong calls, the context integration might be failing. You could measure this qualitatively or via logs that show references.

QUALITY AND THROUGHPUT METRICS

Quality and throughput metrics measure the outcomes of using AI in terms of your team's actual work output and quality. These can include the following:

Task completion time
Take a set of tasks (maybe story points or specific types of tickets) and compare how long they take with AI versus without. For example, if implementing a standard CRUD (create, read, update, and delete) endpoint used

to take on average eight hours, and now, with AI assistance, it takes five hours, that's a tangible improvement. It's good to measure a baseline before AI and then after adoption. Some controlled experiments (like the one cited in "AI Agents: What They Can Do and How to Keep Them Tamed" on page 202) saw ~55% time reduction on a specific task (*https:// oreil.ly/qLZSu*), but your mileage will vary. Even a 10–20% improvement on average task time is huge over months.

PR cycle time (time to merge)
This is how long a pull request stays open before being merged. If AI helps with things like writing tests and catching issues earlier, you might see PRs get approved and merged faster. Also, if AI helps reviewers, the review cycle could shorten. Keep an eye on whether PRs are moving through the pipeline more quickly or with fewer review iterations after AI introduction.

Throughput (features/bugfixes per interval)
At a higher level, are you delivering more stuff? This can be tricky to measure (since complexity of work varies), but you could look at, say, the number of tasks or stories completed per sprint per developer pre- and post-AI. (Note: avoid relying solely on story points, as they can be inconsistent across teams and may not accurately reflect delivered value.) Or lines of code produced (not a perfect metric, but if dramatically more or less, it says something). One company's field study (*https://oreil.ly/QgVXx*) found an increase in pull requests per developer after adopting AI, implying more work got done in parallel.

Code quality metrics
This is key—speed means nothing if quality drops. Track *defect density* (bugs per 1,000 lines of code, for example) for AI-assisted code versus non-AI code. Also track *escaped bugs*: issues that weren't caught in testing and hit production. If AI is introducing subtle bugs, you might see a bump in production incidents in areas where it was heavily used. Conversely, maybe AI helps reduce bugs by catching things (e.g., if it writes tests that a human might have skipped, quality could improve). Data will tell. Microsoft's internal data, for instance, indicated no quality degradation in many cases and even improvements in build success rates (*https://oreil.ly/ QgVXx*) with AI usage—but you need to verify in your context.

Test coverage changes
> If you use AI to write tests, are you seeing your code coverage numbers go up? You can measure code coverage on AI-generated commits versus others. If each AI-aided feature comes with, say, 20% more tests, that's a positive quality indicator. On the flip side, ensure those tests are meaningful (we've all seen 100% coverage that still misses the point). Possibly measure the *mutation testing score* (how well tests catch injected faults) on AI-written tests versus human tests to gauge their effectiveness.

Security incident rates
> As a specific quality aspect, measure if the rate of security findings (from pen tests, bug bounties, automated scans) per line of code changes. If before AI you had X vulns per KLOC (thousands of source lines of code) and after AI it's 2X, that's a problem—maybe relating to vibe coding or insufficient guardrails. Ideally, with the security practices we outlined, this stays flat or even goes down (conceivably, if AI is always prompted for secure code, maybe it avoids some common mistakes humans make).

Tip

While the metrics in this section focus on internal development, don't neglect production and stability metrics. Recent DORA reports from 2024–2025 (*https://dora.dev*) have noted potential negative impacts on delivery stability with AI usage in some contexts, so it's essential to track production health alongside development speed.

One practical way to gather a lot of this data is to instrument your development process. Some AI tools provide dashboards (e.g., GitHub's metrics API can give suggestion acceptance stats). You might also extract info from your version control history (perhaps tagging commits that had AI involvement, then comparing metrics).

Now, measuring is great, but we have to be careful to interpret and act on the data correctly. This is where you put on your experiment-designer hat. Consider running a structured pilot experiment when rolling out AI. For example:

Baseline period
> For the first couple of weeks, have a small team work *without* the AI on some representative tasks, but measure all the preceding metrics. This is your baseline performance without the new tool (this might be current state if you haven't used it before).

Introduction with control group
> Enable the AI assistant for half of the team (randomly or for a volunteer group) for, say, a month, while the other half acts as a control (still without AI). Make sure both groups are doing comparable work (not one doing only hard stuff and the other easy stuff). This isolates the effect better.

Collect and compare
> See how the metrics differ between the AI group and the control. Are tasks closing faster for the AI group? Is their code quality similar, better, or worse? This will give you more confidence about causation (AI made the difference versus some other factor). In one enterprise study (*https://oreil.ly/gXe-L*), such an approach found the AI group indeed had higher satisfaction and similar or better code quality.

Survey the team
> Metrics are quantitative, but don't forget qualitative feedback. Ask the users how they feel: Do they think they're more productive? Less stressed or maybe more stressed? Do they trust the suggestions? Sometimes perception can highlight issues that raw metrics won't (e.g., maybe output is faster, but people feel less sure about the code, which could signal hidden issues).

Iterate based on findings
> Suppose you find that development speed improved, but code review time increased (maybe because reviewers are finding more issues in AI-written code). That points to adjusting your process: maybe more training on how to prompt better or adding an AI step for review, as discussed in "AI Agents: What They Can Do and How to Keep Them Tamed" on page 202. Or if you find certain types of tasks saw big improvements (like writing tests), but others didn't (like implementing complex algorithms), you can focus AI use where it helps most and not force it where it doesn't.

The goal is to treat the adoption of AI as a scientific experiment rather than a leap of faith. To track adoption effectively, establish clear mechanisms early: set up telemetry dashboards to monitor daily/weekly active users, create tagging conventions for AI-assisted commits (e.g., adding "AI-assisted" to commit messages), and schedule regular check-ins (weekly or bi-weekly) to review adoption rates and gather qualitative feedback from the team. This not only yields proof of value (or lack thereof) to inform decision making, but it also fosters a culture of continuous improvement in how you use the tool. Instead of "we bought this thing, hope it helps," you have "we tested this tool, here's how it helped and here's where we need to adjust."

One more benefit of measuring: it can guide coaching and best practices. If you see one team member's acceptance rate is way below others, maybe they need help with prompting or have a tougher environment to integrate with. If another's is super high, maybe they can share what they're doing with others (or maybe they're over-trusting—see "Where AI Shines (and Where You Still Need a Human Touch)" on page 177—which you could double-check).

Also, over time, you can keep an eye on trends. Perhaps initially AI helped a lot, but six months in, marginal returns dropped—could be people got lazy or stopped learning new features of the tool. Or maybe improvements compound as people discover new, clever uses. Ongoing metrics will tell the story.

In summary, don't fly blind. You wouldn't introduce a new server or service to production without monitoring; similarly, introduce AI to your dev process with monitoring of its own effectiveness. Measuring impact is what separates a fad from a truly effective practice. If the data shows improvement, you can double down confidently. If it shows problems, you can course-correct. Either way, you'll know where you stand—and so will the skeptics, which nicely leads into the next section about convincing others with data.

Once you've built that evidence base, the next step is practical: applying what you've learned to get even better results from AI day to day.

Prompt Patterns That Actually Work (Templates to Reuse)

By now we've talked a lot about what to do with AI and how to integrate it. Let's switch gears and get very concrete: actual *prompt patterns* you can use. These are like little recipes for common scenarios. The idea is to save you time so you're not always crafting prompts from scratch (and to share with your team so everyone benefits).

You can keep a file of such prompt templates in your repo or knowledge base. Think of them as starting points that you customize for each use case. Here are five prompt patterns that have proven effective in day-to-day engineering work:

Tests-first generator
When you want to generate tests for code (especially before implementation, as we discussed), your prompt could look like this:

> *You are a senior engineer familiar with our system. Write a set of unit tests (and property-based tests if applicable) for the following functionality: <describe functionality or user story>. Use our project's typical testing frameworks. Where relevant, reference any functions or modules by name. The tests should be comprehensive for edge cases and clearly fail (with understandable messages) until the functionality is correctly implemented. Do not assume any implementation details beyond what's described; focus on input-output behavior.*

Provide the assistant with any interface or spec info you have (function signatures, acceptance criteria). This prompt tells it to act as a test writer first and to ensure tests fail (so you know they're working). It's basically instructing the AI to think like a cautious senior dev: cover edge cases, name things clearly, etc. The bit about citing file paths or APIs is if your AI can see the codebase; it might then say, "using function X from module Y for setup," which is handy.

Secure scaffolder

For generating boilerplate code with security built in from the start, your prompt will look like this:

> *Create a scaffold implementation for <feature or service> using <framework/tech>. Important: incorporate security best practices: validate all inputs (e.g., check lengths, types, prevent SQL injection or script injection), perform output encoding for any user-facing text, avoid using any unsafe functions (like eval or raw SQL queries). Include structured logging (in our format) for key events, with sensitive data redacted. After writing the code, also produce a short security checklist explaining which OWASP-top-10 issues you mitigated and how (e.g., XSS—by encoding output).*

This prompt not only asks for the code but also a checklist, which serves two purposes: it forces the AI to reflect on security (making it more likely the code is safe) and it gives you a quick way to verify it didn't miss something obvious. If the checklist says "I mitigated SQL injection by using parameterized queries" and you see no database code in the output, that's a red flag (hallucination or mistake). But generally, this yields code that has extra guards, plus a nice summary that you can include in the PR description or design doc to show that you considered security.

Reviewer assistant

To help generate code review comments and summarize a diff, use this prompt:

> You are a code review assistant. Analyze the following diff (or describe the change) and do three things:
>
> (a) Summarize the key changes in a few sentences.
>
> (b) List any risky or complex parts of the change, especially things that could affect security, performance, or maintainability.
>
> (c) Suggest two to five specific code review comments with line numbers (if applicable) that a human reviewer might raise. These comments should reference our coding standards or best practices when relevant. Be polite and constructive.

Provide the diff text or a description of changes. The AI will then emulate a reviewer. It might say, for example:

> Change summary: Added profile picture upload feature including backend API and frontend UI. Risky parts: handling of image input (security), new dependency on image library (performance). Suggested comments: [Line 42] 'Consider limiting the file size to a configurable max to avoid large payloads.'

Use these suggestions as input—you (the human reviewer) make the final call on which comments to actually post, but this can catch things or help word them. It's also a great way to prep for a review if you're short on time: you get a quick brief of what to look at.

Migration planner

When you need a step-by-step plan to migrate tech (libraries, services, etc.), use this prompt:

> We need to migrate from <Library/Tech A> to <Library/Tech B>. Draft a safe, step-by-step migration plan. Include: necessary code changes or rewrites, ways to run A and B in parallel during transition if possible, any data migration needs, how to verify everything works

at each step, and a rollback plan in case issues occur. Emphasize minimizing downtime and risk. The output should be structured by phases (e.g., Phase 1: do X, Phase 2: do Y). Also note any gotchas or things to watch out for from similar migrations (you can infer common pitfalls).

The AI, if it has knowledge of both technologies, will outline something like this:

Phase 1: update dependency and set config to use new library in shadow mode, Phase 2: run both libraries side by side... Phase 3: switch traffic... Phase 4: remove old library.

It might mention telemetry ("monitor memory usage, since lib B might use more RAM"). This is great for ensuring you don't overlook a step. Of course, verify specifics, but it can serve as a first draft of a migration runbook. If external references are needed (maybe known issues migrating from X to Y), you could also prompt it to list references, which you then check.

Incident explainer

Using AI to help with post-mortems and blameless analysis would look like this:

Here is a timeline of an incident and some log excerpts: <provide incident data>. You are an incident analysis assistant. Please:

(a) Write a concise narrative of what happened during this incident in plain English, as you would in a post-mortem report.

(b) Identify the key contributing factors or root causes that led to the incident (list two to three).

(c) Propose two actionable, blameless remediation steps that would help prevent similar incidents in the future. These should be realistic and focus on system or process improvements (not pointing at individuals).

This prompt can take quite a bit of context (timeline of events, error messages). The AI will output a draft incident report. For example:

> *Incident Summary:* On 2025-05-01 at 09:00 UTC, service X experienced a 15-minute outage due to a memory leak that exhausted the container memory. The leak was introduced by a recent deployment...
>
> *Contributing Factors:* 1) Lack of memory usage alerts on service X. 2) The new image processing module wasn't covered by load testing...
>
> *Remediations:* Implement memory usage monitoring and alerting for service X. Add a load test for image processing to the CI pipeline to catch leaks before deployment.

This can save a lot of time in writing post-mortems and also ensure you cover the bases (timeline, causes, actions). Of course, you'll fact-check it against what you know and adjust wording, but it provides a solid starting structure.

These patterns have worked in the sense that they produce useful, actionable outputs that often only need minor tweaks. They encapsulate a lot of the advice from "Measuring Impact: How to Quantify AI's Effect Like an Engineer" on page 206: they frame tasks clearly, include constraints (especially security), and request structured outputs. You can modify these to fit your project's style (for instance, maybe you have an internal term for post-mortems, or a specific format for test names).

A good practice is to keep these patterns versioned. If you or a teammate refines a prompt and finds an even better way to ask it, update the template in your shared docs. Over time, you build an internal prompt cookbook that is tailored to your workflows, which is a real competitive advantage.

Also, remember that AI models change (a prompt that worked great on model version X might need tweaking on version Y), so occasionally revisit and test your prompt templates, especially after any major AI tool update. Encourage your team to contribute new patterns as they discover them. For example, someone might add "data analysis assistant"—a prompt to analyze a computerized system validation of metrics—if that proves handy.

These prompt patterns are like little power-ups. They embody effective prompting techniques and domain knowledge so you don't have to start from scratch every time. Use them, share them, and adapt them—they'll make your daily interactions with AI smoother and more productive.

Rolling AI Out to Your Team: A 90-Day Plan

If you're an IC, and not in a position to drive team-wide adoption, you can still introduce AI from the ground up. Start by using it yourself on low-risk tasks, document clear wins (time saved, bugs caught), and share those results informally with teammates. Offer to pair program with AI in team sessions to demonstrate its value. Once you've built credibility, propose a small pilot to your manager with specific metrics you'll track. Even without formal authority, demonstrating tangible benefits can help you become a catalyst for broader adoption.

Adopting AI in a team or organization isn't just flipping a switch. It's a change in tools and culture. It helps to approach it deliberately. I'll outline a pragmatic 90-day rollout plan for introducing AI assistance to a software team. This can be adapted based on team size or complexity, but it provides a rough timeline with milestones.

DAYS 0–30: ESTABLISH FOUNDATIONS AND GUARDRAILS

For the first month, focus on setup and understanding the baseline. That will look like the following:

Pick your pilot tools and integration points.
> There are many AI coding assistants out there (Copilot, CodeWhisperer, internal LLMs, etc.). Choose one to start with—ideally something that integrates with your team's IDEs or workflow. Also ensure it can work with your codebase size/language. Keep it simple; you can expand later, but initially minimize variables (one tool, a couple of languages). Get the necessary licenses or approvals.

Define data and security policies.
> Before anyone starts using the AI, set the ground rules: "Don't paste sensitive data into it," "Don't commit AI-generated code without review," etc. Configure the tool's settings for privacy (opt out of data sharing if possible, set up any available corporate controls like allowed repositories). Also figure out logging—e.g., will you capture all prompts? (You might not need to, but decide up front.) Basically, treat this like introducing any third-party software: do a mini threat model and compliance check. This might involve your security team, so start early.

Instrument metrics and gather baseline information.
> We discussed measuring in "Quality and Throughput Metrics" on page 207. In the first two to four weeks, measure how things are *without* much

AI (or with just a couple of early adopters). For example, have a subset of tasks done the old way and time them, measure code quality outcomes, etc. Also, set up whatever telemetry you can get from the tool (how to measure suggestions, etc.). If the tool has an enterprise dashboard, explore it now. You want a baseline to compare against. If you have historical data (like average PR merge time last quarter), record that too.

Begin with volunteers and small wins.
Identify a few engineers who are enthusiastic, or at least curious (maybe yourself plus a couple others) to start using the AI in low-risk areas. Maybe on internal tools or small features. Let them explore and start finding what works or not. Have them document any immediate issues or cool successes.

Facilitate lunch-and-learn kickoff and training.
Host a knowledge-sharing session about the AI assistant. Cover the basics of usage; maybe demonstrate one of the prompt patterns in "Prompt Patterns That Actually Work (Templates to Reuse)" on page 211. Emphasize that it's an experiment, not a mandate, so people feel open to give feedback. Share the policies decided, so everyone knows the dos and don'ts (for instance, highlight the privacy rule: "We're not feeding it prod data"). Encourage people to try it out in the coming weeks and share experiences.

By day 30, you should have the following: the tool in place, everyone aware of it, initial metrics captured, and some guardrails established. The team should feel like this is a structured rollout, not chaos.

DAYS 31–60: SCALE UP AND TRAIN THE TEAM

Now that the groundwork is laid, the second month is about getting more people on board and refining how you use the AI. This includes the following:

Expand usage patterns and share best practices.
Those early volunteers likely discovered some prompting tricks or identified which tasks the AI is great at versus where it stumbles. Compile this into a first-version prompt library or tip sheet. For example, you might codify a couple of the prompt patterns (tests-first, secure scaffolder, etc.) that seem relevant. Also, emphasize the context sandwich approach from earlier as a best practice. Run another short workshop or send a team-wide

email: "Hey, as you start using the AI, here's a cheat sheet of how to get good results."

Encourage AI-assisted code reviews.
Around this time, people have written some code with AI. Pair up reviewers who are comfortable with AI to leverage it during code reviews (like using the reviewer assistant prompt). This gets more folks seeing AI's value not just in coding but in quality control. It also prevents bottlenecks if some people are producing code faster (the review process won't get bogged down as much if AI helps reviewers catch up).

Pilot an agent or advanced use case with caution.
If you have interest in those AI agents or automation, this is a good time to try a very limited trial. For instance, pick a trivial but long-winded task (like updating a coding style across the repo) and let an AI agent attempt it. Keep the scope narrow and supervise the outcome. The goal is to assess if this is something worth integrating more. If it goes well (the agent's PR was fine after review), that's a cool success to share. If not, you learned something with minimal harm.

Institute security-first habits.
By now, ensure everyone is using the security prompts and checklists when they use AI for coding. You might update your PR template to include a checkbox: "AI used in this PR, security scan and prompts applied." Or automatically run additional SAST on AI-marked code as mentioned. This is the period to bake those guardrails into daily work. It's easier to start with them than to add them later after a scare. Also, if you haven't yet, update your CI to include those extra checks (test coverage, additional security scans for AI-generated code, etc.). Note: you don't need separate linters for AI code—the same linters should apply to all code. What differs is that you may want to run *additional* security or quality checks on AI-generated sections or flag them for extra human review. Essentially, by day 60, you want to have closed any gaps that popped up initially—for example, if someone found that the AI kept suggesting a dangerous function, maybe you added a lint rule to catch that pattern now.

Monitor metrics and gather feedback.
At the 60-day mark, do a quick analysis: how are the metrics looking for those who are using the AI versus before? Perhaps do a retro meeting: ask the team what's working and what's not. You might find, say, that AI really

helped with frontend code, but backend folks felt it was less useful because the AI lacked domain-specific knowledge of your systems. That could lead to actions (maybe get a fine-tuned model for the backend, or adjust expectations). Listen to any frustrations too (e.g., "It keeps suggesting old library calls, which is annoying"—maybe you can tweak the context it gets).

By day 60, ideally, most of the team is actively using the AI for some portion of their work, they have guidance on how to do it effectively, the early kinks are ironed out, and you have intermediate data indicating some positive signs (or at least clear areas to improve).

DAYS 61–90: OPTIMIZE AND DECIDE ON NEXT STEPS

In the final month of the rollout plan, focus on evaluating and solidifying the integration (or deciding to pivot if it's not delivering). This includes the following:

Compare metrics to baseline and objectives.
Now that you have about two months of data, do a thorough comparison. Did task completion times go down? Are PRs merging faster? Is quality holding up? Summarize this because you'll likely need to report it to leadership or to justify continued use. If something like "time to resolve bug tickets" improved by 20%, that's gold—capture it with numbers. If something didn't improve or worsened, be honest and dig into why.

Identify what worked and what didn't.
Perhaps you find that for certain types of work (like writing unit tests and boilerplate) the AI saved tons of time, but for creative design work it wasn't helpful. That's fine—use it where it works best. You might drop what adds noise—e.g., if the AI's suggestions for complex algorithm code were more trouble than help, you can decide as a team to not bother using it in that context. On the other hand, keep what moved—maybe code reviews went much faster thanks to AI checklists, so definitely keep that practice and make it standard.

Audit any concerning outputs (security, defects).
Before fully trusting the tool in more projects, do a mini-audit: look at the past two months of AI-generated code that has been merged. Did any critical bugs slip in? Any security near-misses? If yes, now's the time to tweak the process or training. If no, that builds confidence. Also verify compliance: ensure no one accidentally checked in a snippet with a weird

license by searching through the code for telltale signs. Basically, do a quality assurance pass on the AI's work so far.

Decide on wider rollout.
If the experiment shows clear benefits, you might plan to extend the use of AI to all teams or other projects. Conversely, if results were underwhelming or mixed, you could choose to refine or even roll back in areas. The 90-day checkpoint is a good time to make a call: double down, adjust, or in the worst case, pause usage. Often the result is, "This is promising, let's expand, but carefully." In which case you might allocate budget for more licenses, try a more advanced model, or train champions in each team to support their colleagues in using it.

Document learnings and finalize playbooks.
At the end of this pilot, consolidate everything you learned into documentation. Update the team's handbook with the dos and don'ts, the prompt library, the metrics outcome, etc. This way, if new engineers join or other teams ask how you did it, you have an effective AI usage guide ready. This also ensures the practices stick—e.g., if someone new starts next week, they will see that the established way to write code here is "use AI for X, Y, and Z, and always accompany with tests and security scans."

Share results and success stories.
Finally, celebrate the wins! If someone automated a gnarly refactor in two days that would've taken two weeks, share that story in a team meeting or company blog. This not only gives credit to those who embraced the change, but it also reinforces the value to any skeptics. Having hard numbers like "Our sprint velocity increased by 15% with no increase in bugs" can turn even curmudgeons into at least curious onlookers. Also share the cautionary tales in a constructive way: e.g., "We learned not to blindly trust it for XYZ—here's how we handle that now."

By day 90, you should have either a success case to keep building on (with evidence and refined processes) or a well-analyzed decision that perhaps the current approach/tool wasn't worth it (in which case, you pivot to another or wait for the tech to mature). In either scenario, you've handled it in a thoughtful, data-driven manner, which is exactly what effective engineers do.

Rolling out AI is as much about change management as it is about technology. This plan ensures that in three months, you move from uncertainty to clarity on how AI fits into your team, and you do so in a way that maximizes buy-in, minimizes risk, and focuses on outcomes.

A Checklist for Leaders: Evaluating AI Tools and Platforms

While this chapter is aimed at ICs, I think it's worth including a brief guide for those in tech lead or management positions who might be evaluating AI tools for a broader team or enterprise. Even as an IC, you might influence these decisions or want to understand how they're made, so it's worth reading this section for you as well.

Warning

Most companies already have extensive procurement and security checklists for evaluating any new tools or vendors. Work within those existing frameworks—don't try to bypass established processes. The following checklist complements your organization's standard evaluation criteria with AI-specific considerations.

Here's a procurement and architecture checklist for choosing and integrating AI in a software engineering org:

Integration and context
Does the tool seamlessly integrate with your development workflow? Specifically, can it plug into your IDEs, code editor, or repository browser so that it has direct access to your codebase and can provide context-aware suggestions? Tools that know your code (via indexing or APIs to fetch repo content) will be far more useful than those that don't. Check if it supports your languages and tech stack comprehensively. For example, if you do a lot of Python *and* Terraform, does it handle both?

Telemetry and measurement
What features does the platform have for measuring usage and impact? Look for a metrics dashboard or API—something that lets you track suggestion acceptance rates, user engagement, etc., per team or repository. If you're flying blind, it's not great. Ideally, the tool itself should give you some way to quantify its value (some enterprise offerings have this built in). If not, you'll have to build that, which is fine, but good to know in advance.

Privacy and data control

This is huge. Does the tool allow you to keep your code data private? For example, can you opt out of having your prompts used to train the vendor's models? Some tools might even offer an on-premises or self-hosted option so that nothing leaves your network. Evaluate what data (code, comments, etc.) it sends to the cloud and where it's stored. Also, does it have features to detect and block sensitive info in prompts? (Some enterprise solutions have filters that, say, prevent a sequence that looks like a password from being sent.) Make sure the tool's privacy posture aligns with your company's risk tolerance.

Security features

Beyond the security of the model itself, what does it offer to help you maintain secure code? For instance, does it have an "avoid insecure patterns" mode or a knowledge of Common Vulnerabilities and Exposures (CVE) patterns? Can it flag when a suggested code snippet might be copied from an insecure example? Also, on the admin side: does it support single sign-on for authentication, role-based access (maybe you only allow certain teams to use it initially), and audit logs of who used it when? If you're in a larger org, these enterprise features matter. Also check if it provides any liability or indemnity regarding code it suggests (some vendors may make promises about not giving you licensed code).

Governance and policy compliance

Can you enforce certain policies through the tool? For example, can you configure it to always provide citations for long outputs (to mitigate licensing issues), or to disallow usage in certain repos? Some tools might let you set organization-wide AI usage policies—find out. And does it align with frameworks like the NIST AI RMF (some vendors might market that they have features for each function, like govern/map). This is more about checking the vendor's maturity—if they can articulate how their tool supports governance, they've probably thought through things like audit logs, bias evaluations, etc., which might be important if you're using AI in production features.

Cost versus value

Obviously, consider pricing. Are you paying per seat, per token, or for a big enterprise license? And what does that translate to in terms of expected ROI? If it's per developer per month, calculate the yearly cost and think about how much time each dev needs to save for that to pay off. If the metrics you gather show, say, that each dev saves five hours a month and your dev's hourly cost is X, you can put a number on the value. Also consider model usage costs if applicable—some self-hosted or API-based models charge by usage (tokens). If your team uses it heavily, what's the projected monthly cost? Is there a risk of runaway usage incurring big bills (in which case, you'd want usage caps or monitoring)?

Regulatory fit

If you operate in regulated domains or regions, does the tool support compliance? For example, if the EU AI Act will require certain documentation for AI features by a certain date, can the vendor provide that or help with it? If you use AI in a way that might affect end users (like AI-generated code that influences how a user's data is processed), are you on track to meet any transparency or quality requirements of laws? This might involve working with legal, but from an engineering perspective, choose a tool that's transparent about how it works and gives you control (so you can explain or adjust it to comply with laws). If serving EU users, confirm how the vendor addresses EU AI Act obligations for providers versus general users of AI. You might not get all the answers (since some regs are new), but at least ask the questions—serious vendors will have some response.

Running through this checklist helps ensure you're not just enamored by a fancy AI demo, but making a sound decision that will hold up under real-world conditions (security, compliance, actual integration ease).

For example, imagine you're choosing between two coding assistant services: one might have a slight edge in code suggestion quality, but the other offers an on-prem deployment and robust admin controls. If you work at a bank, for example, you likely choose the latter for compliance reasons. Or maybe one tool integrates with your IDE and issue tracker, while another is a separate web app—the former will probably drive more adoption because engineers don't have to leave their flow.

Also, the evaluation shouldn't be one-time. After adoption, periodically revisit these criteria. A good cadence is this: evaluate frequently at the start (monthly for the first three to six months) to catch any issues early, then transition to less-frequent reviews (quarterly or annually) once the tool is stable and well-integrated. For high-risk or highly regulated environments, maintain more frequent reviews. Maybe the vendor releases a new version with improved privacy or other new features; or maybe new regulations come out and you need to adjust.

To summarize, leaders (and involved ICs) should evaluate AI platforms with the same rigor they'd evaluate any major piece of tech infrastructure. The preceding checklist questions can be used when talking to vendors or assessing open source options. It might even be worth scoring each area for multiple options if you're doing a request for proposal (RFP) or proof-of-concept for several tools. The choice you make can have long-term implications regarding how effectively and safely your team can use AI, so it's worth doing your homework upfront.

Bridging to What You Already Know (Connecting the Dots with Previous Chapters)

Throughout this book, we've touched on various aspects of being an effective engineer, from prioritization and communication to technical design and retrospectives. AI, as introduced in this chapter, isn't a standalone subject; it weaves into many of those topics. Let's briefly connect how practical AI usage amplifies or complements ideas from earlier chapters:

Understanding value and prioritization
> Earlier, we discussed connecting code to user sentiment and using data to drive what's valuable to work on. AI can form the bookends of a virtuous feedback loop here. For instance, Chapter 1 talked about focusing on delivering value (doing the right things). AI helps you gather and summarize user sentiment faster (maybe using natural language processing [NLP] to parse feedback or support tickets), so you can identify what features or fixes matter most. Chapter 8 covered prioritizing tasks or using metrics for prioritization. An AI assistant can analyze those metrics or even predict the impact (in a rough way) of certain backlog items.
>
> So you could use AI to help gather data and insights for team prioritization conversations—remember that engineers rarely prioritize work in complete isolation, so AI becomes a tool for informing collaborative decision making rather than solo choices. Then, after you ship, you use AI again to measure sentiment or outcomes (like analyzing app reviews) to feed back into the next cycle. In short, AI accelerates the build-measure-learn cycle: you build faster with AI, measure outcomes (with AI's help summarizing or highlighting patterns), learn what to do next, and use AI

to plan that work. It amplifies your effectiveness in chasing value, not just pumping out code.

Collaboration and code reviews

Chapters 2 and 10 talked about pair programming, getting early feedback, and not hoarding code until it's perfect. AI can serve as a kind of pair programmer that's always available. It encourages you to get quick feedback on code even if a human partner isn't around. You can ask the AI if there is a better way to do something. The AI-as-amplifier approach to code reviews dovetails with this nicely: instead of replacing human code reviews, we use AI to strengthen them. This can lower the cost of asking for a review because AI can pre-check some stuff so you're less hesitant to show early work. It's like having a nonjudgmental first-pass reviewer, making the actual human review more focused and less nit-picky. This encourages a culture of continuous feedback—you don't wait until a big lump of code is done; you can get AI feedback as you go, and your colleagues can rely on AI to assist them in reviewing partial work. It prevents the "hero coder" or "last-minute big PR" issues discussed in Chapter 5 because AI makes it easier to integrate feedback throughout.

Documentation and meetings: planning and async

Chapter 4 is about communicating effectively, writing stuff down, and running meetings, and Chapter 12 talked about retrospectives and continuous improvement. AI helps turn transient knowledge (meetings, discussions) into artifacts (summaries, action items). For example, earlier chapters have sidebars on summarizing PRDs or meeting notes quickly—we built on that in "Plan and Design with AI (Brainstorm, Then Draft an Architecture Decision Record)" on page 180 by using AI to not only summarize but to create actual to-dos and documentation.

Essentially, many pieces of advice, like "document your decisions" or "write good meeting notes," often fall by the wayside when we're busy. AI gives you a shortcut to do them. It can summarize a meeting recording or chat and produce decent minutes. It can draft an architecture decision record from a discussion. It can turn a design review meeting into an email summary for stakeholders. By doing so, it ensures knowledge doesn't get lost and everyone stays on the same page, reinforcing practices from those chapters.

And for retros (Chapter 6 covered learning from mistakes), an AI could help analyze incident logs (as we did with the incident explainer prompt in "Prompt Patterns That Actually Work (Templates to Reuse)" on page 211) or categorize a quarter's worth of bug reports to suggest process improvements. It injects a bit of automation into continuous improvement processes.

Bus factor, knowledge sharing, retrospectives

Chapters 5, 7, and 10 dealt with things like not having single points of failure (bus factor), doing blameless post-mortems, etc. AI can help democratize knowledge and reduce bus factor issues: if one person usually handles a tricky part of the code, AI can assist others by explaining that part or even coding within it. It's not a replacement for cross-training, but it lowers the entry barrier for someone to step into an unfamiliar area (the AI can help them search and understand it).

Chapter 7 is about mentorship and helping others—AI can augment mentorship by answering junior devs' questions quickly (like an interactive Stack Overflow), freeing seniors to focus on deeper coaching. And Chapter 10, which discussed retrospectives, ties with our use of AI for analyzing patterns and agentic chores: for example, if retrospectives revealed some repetitive toil, that's a candidate to hand to an AI agent (like writing a script to automate a deployment step). Also, AI can help gather data for retrospectives (like scanning commit messages for keywords to see if a certain type of issue keeps recurring).

The idea is that AI can continuously feed into process fixes and knowledge sharing, which keeps the team healthy and resilient. For bus factor specifically, here's an example of one fun way AI can help: if Bob is out and he was the only one who knew module X, an AI that's been trained on your code might help Alice navigate module X in Bob's absence, at least enough to handle a quick fix—essentially raising the AI factor of knowledge availability.

The common theme in all these cross-links is AI amplifies human-centric practices. It doesn't replace the need to prioritize, communicate, collaborate, learn, or reflect—it turbocharges those activities, when used right. The best practices from earlier chapters remain fully in play, and AI just greases the wheels.

So as you integrate AI, always tie it back to the fundamental goal: be more effective, not just more efficient. As emphasized in Chapters 1 and 4, effective engineers focus on outcomes and teamwork; use AI in service of those outcomes and to strengthen teamwork (e.g., sharing prompt libraries is a new kind of collaboration).

By bridging AI usage with these established practices, you ensure AI becomes a natural part of the team's culture rather than a gadget. It aligns the new capabilities with the values and habits you've already been cultivating as an effective engineer.

Building Consensus with Evidence: How to Have Effective Discussions About AI Adoption

You'll inevitably have discussions with colleagues or managers about whether and how to adopt AI in your engineering practice. These conversations are most productive when grounded in evidence rather than opinion or hype.

Instead of relying on a few dated studies, make this a habit: treat evidence like code—keep it up to date. The best arguments for (or against) AI-assisted development will evolve as models, practices, and regulations do. Here's how to stay credible and current:

Search for recent peer-reviewed or industry studies.
> Look for large-scale or enterprise-level evaluations of AI coding tools on platforms like arXiv (*https://arxiv.org*), ACM Digital Library (*https://dl.acm.org*), or Google Research (*https://research.google*). Focus on metrics like productivity gains, code quality, and developer satisfaction. Check sources like the DORA State of DevOps reports (*https://dora.dev*) and GitHub's research blog (*https://github.blog/category/research*) for the latest findings.

Track updates from the major tool vendors.
> GitHub, Google, OpenAI, Anthropic, and others frequently publish new data on adoption, accuracy, and impact. Bookmark their engineering blogs or research portals.

Watch independent research and audits.
> Companies like Stack Overflow, JetBrains, and Veracode regularly release reports on AI usage trends and security findings—often with fresh statistics each year.

Keep an eye on regulation and standards.
> Frameworks like the EU AI Act and NIST's AI Risk Management Framework will keep maturing. Understand how they apply to your projects and how your organization aligns with them.

Cite what's current.
When discussing AI's value or risks, use sources from the last 12 to 18 months. This not only strengthens your argument but also signals that your understanding is up to date.

By framing your discussions around verifiable, evolving data, you can turn subjective debates into informed decisions—the mark of a mature, evidence-driven engineering culture.

A Closing Note on Craft and Humanity

We've covered a lot of ground, and it's clear that AI, used well, can dramatically enhance your capabilities as a software engineer. But let's zoom out and remember why we're doing all this.

The most effective engineers, the ones this book celebrates, have something in common: they don't offload the core of engineering thinking to others. They embrace tools and automation to handle grunt work, but they remain deeply engaged in the creative and analytical process that only humans (for now) can do. AI is the newest, shiniest tool in our toolbox, but it's just that: a tool. A powerful one, yes, but not a replacement for the qualities that make an engineer truly effective.

What AI is allowing us to do is clear away obstacles so we can move faster and see farther. The "brush" is all those repetitive or incidental tasks (writing boilerplate, trawling through docs, formatting JSON, you name it) that suck up time and mental energy. By automating or accelerating those, you free up time and cognitive space for the uniquely human aspects of engineering: deciding what to build, empathizing with user problems, designing architectures at a high level, reasoning about trade-offs, and collaborating with others to solve complex problems.

In practical terms, if AI saves you two hours in a day that you'd normally spend writing tests or documentation, you can reinvest that time in higher-leverage activities—brainstorming a simpler design for the next feature, mentoring a teammate, or improving system resilience. These are the kinds of efforts where you add disproportionate value—"doing the right things" rather than just "doing things right." As discussed in the Preface and Chapter 1, being effective means doing the right things right. AI helps with both sides of that equation: it takes care of many of the routine things quickly and correctly, freeing up your bandwidth to focus on what's right to build next. But identifying those right things—and ensuring the final outcome truly is right—remains your responsibility.

So, use AI to write more code, but don't outsource your creativity or judgment. Use it to generate options, but you choose the option. Use it to critique a design, but you deliberate and decide. Use it to speed up writing, but you craft the narrative and ensure it's clear. Think of the AI as an extremely knowledgeable but naive intern: it can come up with lots of ideas and drafts, some brilliant, some flawed. You, the engineer, are the experienced artisan who shapes those into a coherent, robust solution.

The craft of software engineering—making elegant solutions, balancing trade-offs, and improving through feedback—remains as important as ever. AI won't reduce the need for craft; if anything, it will raise the bar. When everyone has access to AI helpers, the differentiator becomes who can leverage them most effectively to deliver value. That comes down to judgment and taste—knowing when to rely on the AI versus when to go back to first principles, knowing how to prompt it to get quality results, and knowing how to verify and test its outputs.

Finally, engineering is a team sport and a human endeavor at its core. AI can write code, but it can't (at least yet) go have a coffee with your product manager to brainstorm the next big feature inspired by a user anecdote. It can't replace the trust built among team members, or the excitement of collectively solving a hard problem at the whiteboard. Those human elements drive successful projects and fulfilling careers. As you weave AI into your work, keep those human connections strong—share knowledge, pair program (even if one part of the pair is an AI, involve another human from time to time, too), and do retrospectives that include feelings and team health, not just data.

In other words, adopt AI because it helps you be more of the engineer you aspire to be, not less. If you love designing systems, let AI free you from drudgery so you can design even more and better. If you pride yourself on clean code, use AI to handle menial code so you can focus on the tricky parts that require finesse. If you want to be a leader, use the time AI gives you to mentor others and align technology with business needs.

The future of software engineering isn't AI replacing engineers—it's engineers who know how to effectively harness AI replacing those who don't. By incorporating the practices from Chapter 13—pragmatic workflows, guardrails, continuous measurement, and a mindset anchored in effectiveness—you're ensuring that you'll be in that leading group. You'll write code faster, yes, but more importantly, you'll direct that saved energy into what only you can do: being creative, making judgment calls, and driving positive outcomes.

As you reach the end of the book, note that one thread runs through every chapter: effective engineers create outcomes, not activity. Tools evolve. Principles endure. Your edge is judgment, clear communication, and habits that compound. AI belongs in your toolbox, but you are accountable for what ships.

Here's what I hope you carry forward from the book:

Start with value.
> Tie work to user impact and business goals. If an effort is not moving a metric or a user need, rethink it.

Design before you build.
> Capture decisions with lightweight records, state trade-offs, and make failure modes explicit.

Tests make speed safe.
> Write tests early, use them to guide changes, and keep changes small and reversible.

Reviews are collaboration, not gatekeeping.
> Invite feedback early. Use checklists. Reserve human time for correctness, security, and architecture.

Measure what matters.
> Track cycle time, time to merge, escaped defects, and reliability. Let data guide where you adopt new tools.

Security and privacy are table stakes.
> Bake them into the path to production with scans, policies, and review, not as an afterthought.

Communicate in writing.
> Plans, decisions, and post-mortems reduce confusion and raise the bus factor across the team.

Share knowledge.
> Document prompts, playbooks, and patterns. Teach what you learn so the team improves faster than any one person.

Use AI as an amplifier.
   Let it handle scaffolding, summaries, and repetitive edits. Keep humans in the loop for intent, trade-offs, and risk.

Keep craft and teamwork at the center.
   Taste, judgment, and trust are still the force multipliers.

And here's my advice on what to do next:

This week

- Visit the companion website (*https://effective.addy.ie*) to check out the additional templates and resources I've created.
- Pick one workflow to augment with AI, tests, or automation. Good candidates: drafting unit tests first, summarizing a PRD into stories, or generating a review checklist.
- Define a simple personal scorecard: time to first useful change, time to merge, and one quality signal you care about. Record a baseline.

This month

- Run a small, low risk pilot using the patterns in this chapter. Capture the acceptance rate of suggestions, changes to cycle time, and any quality deltas. Add security prompts and scanners to the path to merge if they are not already there.
- Create or refine a prompt and checklist library in your repo. Keep it versioned. Make it easy for others to reuse.

The next 90 days

- Expand what worked. Drop what created noise. Document your results in a short write-up so your team can learn from the data.
- Raise the bus factor. Schedule one knowledge share, one joint design review, and one blameless post-mortem that turns into a concrete improvement.
- Audit guardrails. Ensure secrets stay out of prompts, scans run on every PR, and risky areas have tests and monitoring.

The next quarter (choose one)
- Never merge without a failing test first turning green.
- Add one metric or alert with every feature.
- Teach one thing you learned each sprint.

Tools will keep changing. Principles will not. Use AI and every other tool in the service of clear goals, sound engineering, and strong teams. That is how you stay effective, no matter what the future brings. Keep going, keep learning, and keep shipping.

Index

A

A/B testing (split testing), 104, 170
acceptance criteria, 135
accomplishment tracking, 74
action items, in retrospectives, 143-147
active listening, 162
adaptability, as ICs, 172-174
ADRs (architecture decision records), 180-182
Agile ceremonies, 135
AI (artificial intelligence), 225, 229-231
    adoption and behavior metrics, 206-207
    areas where human engineer should always be hands-on, 178-179
    async communication artifacts, 155
    attribution issues with, 199
    brag document creation, 75
    capabilities and management of, 177-179, 202-206
    code writing and review assistance, 20
    cognitive load reduction with summaries, 111
    complementing established knowledge, 224-227
    connecting code to user sentiment, 4
    context sandwich prompt structuring pattern, 193-194
    craft of engineering, 229-233
    debugging assistance, 25
    document summaries, 41
    effective discussions about adoption of, 227
    effective software engineering, 175-228
    embracing as collaborator, 167-170
    feeding context to, 192-195
    as force multiplier for thoroughness, 189
    governance and compliance, 176, 200, 222, 227
    hybrid ICs, 170-172
    knowledge silo detection, 48
    90-day rollout plan
        establishing foundations and guardrails, 216-217
        optimizing and deciding on next steps, 219-221
        scaling up and training team, 217-219
    not replacing human judgment, 175
    privacy, licensing, and compliance, 199-202

project management and status reporting, 91
prompt patterns, 193-194, 211-215
quality and throughput metrics, 207-211
research for accelerating architectural decisions, 33
retrospective analysis, 144
RMFs, 201-202
security, 176, 195-198
simulating system behavior, 168
structured pilot experiment, 209-210
testing and verifying outputs, 176
testing assistance, 22
tool and platform evaluation, 221-224
translating technical documentation for nontechnical audiences, 163
vibe coding, 198
work prioritization, 99
workflow enhancement with
    brainstorming and drafting ADRs, 180-182
    clean-up and communication, 188-190
    code reviews, 186-188
    example of, 190-192
    test-first approach, 183-186
    turning PRDs into work items, 182-183
AI Act, 176
Amazon, 103
analysis paralysis, 56-57
anti-patterns
  burnout, 110
  individual-level, 47-71, 226
    analysis paralysis, 56-57
    context-switching addiction, 60-62
    feedback resistance, 66-68
    hero complex, 50-51
    imposter syndrome paralysis, 69-70
    inability to delegate, 53-54
    knowledge silos, 48-50
    lack of visibility, 54-56
    meeting overload, 65-66
    moving forward from, 71-71
    not-invented-here syndrome, 57-59
    over-engineering, 51-53
    perfectionism and gold-plating, 59-60
    scope creep enablement, 62-63
    technical debt denial, 63-65
    tool obsession, 68-69
  team-level, 117-149, 225-226
    flaky product ownership, 130-137
    ineffective sprint retrospectives, 143-149
    knowledge silos, 117-124
    low bus factor, 137-142
    rubber stamping, 124-130
    vibe coding, 198
anxiety, 159
Appfire, 126
architecture decision records (ADRs), 180-182
artificial intelligence (see AI)
asynchronous communication, 154
audiences, adapting to different, 162

B

backlogs, 134, 182-183
backup assignees, 49, 121
benchmarking, 105, 202
boilerplate, generating with AI, 177, 184, 212
bottlenecks

inability to delegate, 53-54
knowledge silos, 117-124
team, 118
boundaries, 112-114, 153
culture of, 113
management, 45
remote work, 152-153
brag documents, 75, 83
branding, 76
breadth, 31-37
applying, 32-34
deciding on investment of, 36
defined, 31
versus depth, 35-36
developing, 32
hybrid ICs, 170-172
importance of, 31-32
staff engineers, 81
technical leadership roles, 31
bug fixing (see debugging and bug fixing)
burnout
anti-pattern, 110
cultivating sustainable careers, 114-115
example of, 115-116
importance of prevention, 108
managing energy, 109-111
physical and emotional warning signs of, 107-108
recognizing, 107-108
setting boundaries and saying "no", 112-114
10x myth, 111-112
work-related symptoms of, 108
bus factor, 48, 226
breaking down silos, 122
defined, 137
high, 137

increasing, 138-141
low, 137-142
example of, 141
over-specialization, 142
resilience as team value, 142
signs of, 137
persistence of, 138
business context
problem-solution alignment, 5
strategic awareness, 11
business goals
aligning with engineering goals, 100-101
connecting work to through AI, 100
business impact tracking, 14

C

careers
cultivating sustainable, 114-115
growth and leveling up, 73-85, 225
comparison of mid-level, senior, and staff engineers, 77-81
ICs versus EMs, 81-83
promotions, 73-75
self-advocacy, 83-85
unwritten rules of progression, 76-77
managing effectiveness at different stages of, 12-13
Center for Creative Leadership, 67
change control, 134
ChatGPT, 25
CI (continuous integration), 196
clarity
clean code, 20
communication, 12
documentation, 6

flaky product ownership, 131
clean code
    characteristics of, 20-20
    example of, 22
    good practices for, 21
Code Climate, 48
code debt, 21
code hoarding, 49
code ownership
    collective, 140
    retrospectives, 145
    spreading, 120
code quality metrics, 208
code reviews, 225
    accountability, 128
    adjusting workload to allow time for, 127
    assistance from AI, 186-188, 213, 218
    embracing, 23
    encouraging learning through, 130
    enforcing review of late changes, 134
    mentoring through, 93
    multiple reviewers and gating, 127
    productive versus effective, 9
    rubber stamping, 124-130
    setting expectations for, 126
    time-boxing, 130
    tools for, 129
    training for, 128
    two-way dialogue, 128
codebases, scaling, 34
collaboration, 225
    collaborative curiosity, 5
    cross-functional feedback, 15
    early involvement, 40
    educating each other, 40
    influence building, 12

influencing without authority, 42-44
    managing up, 44-46
    measuring success of, 15
    productive versus effective, 10
    technical insight in product discussions, 40
    working effectively with PM/design, 39-41
commits
    committing often when using AI, 185
    as storytelling, 24
communication
    AI for, 188-190
    aligning engineering with business goals, 101
    asynchronous, 154, 154
    avoiding flaky product ownership, 137
    becoming influential communicator, 157-159
    benefits of strong, 164
    in collaboration, 41
    cross-team, 91
    discussions about AI adoption, 227
    driving large initiatives without direct reports, 90-91
    early, 27
    effective discussions about AI adoption, 227-228
    example of, 165
    fighting context-switching addiction, 61
    fighting lack of visibility, 55
    fighting meeting overload, 65
    improving product ownership, 134
    influence building, 12
    influencing without authority, 43
    investing in, 156
    junior engineers, 26

leading without authority, 87
managing up, 44
mid-level engineers, 78
multiple channels for, 153
over-communicating, 152, 152
overcoming common obstacles, 159-161
about promotions, 74
remote work, 151-154, 156
respecting chain of, 45
senior engineers, 79
skills beyond public speaking, 161-164
technical data in, 105
tone of, 156
value of good, 165
vision, 102
competitive analysis, 11
completeness, definitions of, 135
complex topics, simplifying, 160
conflict resolution, 88, 91
consistency
clean code, 20
versus intensity, 116
and progression, 77
rubber stamping, 125, 126
context sandwich prompt structuring pattern, 193-194
context usage metric, 207
context-switching addiction, 60-62
benefit of avoiding, 62
culture fix, 61
remedy for, 61
signs of, 61
flaky product ownership, 132
continuous improvement practices, 16-17
continuous integration (CI), 196
credibility
building, 36, 41, 63, 87

influence without authority, 12
leading without authority, 87
cross-functional feedback, 15
cross-training
breaking down silos, 121
10x teams, 112
Cunningham, Ward, 35
customer understanding
journey mapping, 11
problem-solution alignment, 5

D

daily active user metrics, 206
data for decisions, 104-106
data literacy, 5
data-driven advocacy, 12
dead code, eliminating, 21
debugging and bug fixing, 24-26
AI agents for reproducing and isolating bugs, 203
escaped bugs, 208
practice to adopt, 23
productive versus effective, 9
rubber stamping, 124, 126
scientific method, 25
decision briefs, 180
decision-making, using metrics and data in, 104-106
deep in nothing, shallow in everything, 171
defaulting to transparency, 153
delegating
inability to delegate, 53-54
team effectiveness, 111
dependency upgrades and fixes, 203
depth, 29-31
applying, 32-34
versus breadth, 35-36

committing to, 30
deciding on investment of, 36
defined, 29
hybrid ICs, 170-172
leveraging, 30
three-step specialization process, 30
value of, 29-31
designing
with AI, 180-182
for scale, 32-34
DevOps, 123, 171-171
diligence, balancing with efficiency, 129
distributed work environments
challenges of, 151-152
example of, 156
strategies to thrive in, 152-156
document summaries, 41
documentation, 225
AI, 178, 188-190
breaking down silos, 120
good habits in, 26
increasing bus factor, 139
junior engineers, 26
long-term thinking, 6
90-day AI rollout plan, 220
post-merge phase, 188
showing consideration through, 26
and testing, 23
downstream feedback, 16
Drucker, Peter, vii-viii, 2
DZone Refcard, 127

E

effectiveness, 224
compared to efficiency, vii-viii, 1
compared to productivity, 8-10
craft of engineering, 229-231
delivering value, ix-x
foundation for advanced skills, 17-18
fundamental questions to ask, 2-3
lessons from book and what to do next, 231-233
long-term impact, 6-8
measuring and developing, 14-17
mindset, 10-13
outcomes versus outputs, 2-6
teams, 111-112
efficiency
balancing with diligence, 129
compared to effectiveness, vii-viii, 1
obsession with, viii
effort versus impact matrixes, 98
80/20 rule, 99
energy management, 109-111
engineering goals, aligning with business goals, 100-101
engineering impact spectrum, 3-4
engineering-product misalignment
addressing, 133-136
challenges of, 131-133
engineering-product alignment, 136
example of, 136
flaky product ownership, 133
overview of, 130-131
product-engineering relationship, 135
escaped bugs metric, 208
ethics, 84, 95-96
Evans, Julia, 83
experimentation mindset, 16
external solutions, rejecting, 57-59

F

fear-driven inaction, 69-70
feature development

balancing new features with system
  health, 7
productive versus effective, 8
YAGNI features, 20
feedback
  loop for insecure AI outputs, 197
  managing up, 45
  organizational context, 15
  and promotions, 74
  resistance to, 66-68
  360, 84
flaky product ownership
  addressing, 133-136
  causes of, 133
  challenges of, 131-133
  defined, 130
  engineering-product alignment, 136
  example of, 136
  overview of, 130-131
  signs of, 131
focus, lack of, 60-62

G

gatekeeping, avoiding, 121
git, 24
good intentions, 156
guardrails
  for AI, 204, 216-218
  for engineering-business goal alignment, 101

H

hero complex, 50-51
  avoiding, 51, 121
  culture fix, 51
  remedy for, 51
  signs of, 50

high cohesion principle, 21
high-impact work, identifying, 97-100
humans
  AI not replacing judgment of, 175
  connecting with, 154
  role in software engineering, 229-233
  supervising AI, 177-179
humility, 84

I

ICs (individual contributors)
  effectiveness anti-patterns, 47-71
    analysis paralysis, 56-57
    context-switching addiction, 60-62
    feedback resistance, 66-68
    hero complex, 50-51
    imposter syndrome paralysis, 69-70
    inability to delegate, 53-54
    knowledge silos, 48-50
    lack of visibility, 54-56
    meeting overload, 65-66
    moving forward from, 71-71
    not-invented-here syndrome, 57-59
    over-engineering, 51-53
    perfectionism and gold-plating, 59-60
    scope creep enablement, 62-63
    technical debt denial, 63-65
    tool obsession, 68-69
  future of, 225
    continuous learning and adaptability, 172-174
    embracing AI as collaborator, 167-170
    hybrid ICs, 170-172
    importance of communication skills, 157-158, 161

influencing product direction, 41
influencing without authority, 11, 42-44
lifelong path as, 173-174
versus management path, 81-83
real-world impact of work, 4
resilience as team value, 142
imposter syndrome paralysis, 69-70
inability to delegate, 53-54
inability to say "no", 62-63
incident explanations and summaries, 214
incident handling, 95-96
individual contributors (see ICs)
individual-level anti-patterns, 47-71
    analysis paralysis, 56-57
    context-switching addiction, 60-62
    feedback resistance, 66-68
    hero complex, 50-51
    imposter syndrome paralysis, 69-70
    inability to delegate, 53-54
    knowledge silos, 48-50
    lack of visibility, 54-56
    meeting overload, 65-66
    moving forward from, 71-71
    not-invented-here syndrome, 57-59
    over-engineering, 51-53
    perfectionism and gold-plating, 59-60
    scope creep enablement, 62-63
    technical debt denial, 63-65
    tool obsession, 68-69
industry awareness, 11
influence
    managing up, 44-46
    without authority, 11, 40, 42-44
    working with product and design, 39-41
introversion, 160
iteration mindset, 134

J

journey mapping, 11
junior engineers, 225
    documentation and communication, 26
    effectiveness, 13
    testing and quality mindset, 22-24
    version control and debugging discipline, 24-26
    writing quality code, 19-22

K

knowledge
    bridging from established practices to AI, 224-227
    technical depth and breadth
        deciding on investment of, 36
        designing for scale, 32-34
        hybrid ICs, 170-172
        importance of breadth, 31-32
        managing technical debt, 35-36
        value of depth, 29-31
knowledge sharing, 226
    benefits of strong communication, 164
    breaking down silos, 49, 120
    increasing bus factor, 138
    leading without authority, 88
    long-term thinking, 6
    measuring impact of, 14
    mistake handling, 96
    rubber stamping, 125
    stagnation of, 119
knowledge silos
    benefit of avoiding, 50
    breaking down, 49, 120-122
    causes of, 118
    cultivating learning culture, 123
    culture fix, 50

dangers of, 118-119
defined, 117
example of, 122
limiting ICs, 48-50
overview of, 117
signs of, 49, 119
siloed teams, 123

L

lack of visibility
    benefit of avoiding, 56
    communication fix, 55
    remedy for, 55
    signs of, 55
large language models (see AI)
lateral moves, 84
leadership
    breadth, 31
    driving large initiatives, 89-92
    earned, not given, 89
    EMs, 82
    ethical considerations and taking responsibility, 95-96
    ICs, 82, 226
    increasing bus factor, 140
    managing expectations with, 51
    mentorship and sponsorship, 92-94
    mid-level engineers, 13
    senior engineers, 79
learning and skill development
    avoiding burnout, 114
    continuous learning and adaptability, 172-174
    cultivating culture of learning, 123, 127, 130
    encouraging through reviews, 130
    future-proofing, 173
    lifelong, 114
    productive versus effective, 9-10
    skill gap analysis, 17
    T-shaped skills, 36
legacy code testing, 203
leveling guides, 74
linters, 23, 129
LLMs (see AI)
long-term success
    cultivating sustainable careers, 114-115
    example of, 115-116
    managing energy, 109-111
    recognizing burnout and stress, 107-108
    setting boundaries and saying "no", 112-114
    10x myth, 111-112
long-term thinking, 6
loose coupling principle, 21

M

machine learning (see AI)
macro-breaks, 109
management
    collaborating with, 44-46
    versus individual contributor path, 81-83
    thinking communication is for, 161
manager feedback, 15
Martin, Robert C. (Uncle Bob), 19
Matsudaira, Kate, 30
meeting overload, 65-66
mental health, 115
mentoring, 43, 92-94
    benefits of, 94
    breaking down silos, 121
    compared to sponsoring, 92

continuous improvement, 17
effective, 93
fighting imposter syndrome paralysis, 70
increasing bus factor, 140
leading without authority, 88
leveraging mentors, 85
and progression, 76
staff engineers, 81
metrics
adjusting, 104
AI adoption and behavior, 206-207
AI quality and throughput, 207-211
for decisions, 104-106
establishing key metrics, 104
90-day AI rollout plan, 216, 218
micro-breaks, 109
mid-level engineers, 225
compared to staff and senior, 81
documentation and communication, 26
effectiveness, 13
versus senior and staff engineers, 77-81
testing and quality mindset, 22-24
version control and debugging discipline, 24-26
writing quality code, 19-22
migration planning, 213
Minto, Barbara, 43
mistake handling, 95-96
ML (see AI)
morale issues
flaky product ownership, 132
knowledge silos, 119

N

narrative and storytelling, 163
National Institute of Standards and Technology (NIST) AI Risk Management Framework, 176, 201
networking, 17, 173
NFR (nonfunctional requirement) checklists, 181
90-day AI rollout plan
establishing foundations and guardrails, 216-217
optimizing and deciding on next steps, 219-221
scaling up and training team, 217-219
NIST (National Institute of Standards and Technology) AI Risk Management Framework, 176, 201
nonfunctional requirement (NFR) checklists, 181
North, Dan, 2
not-invented-here syndrome, 57-59
note-taking, 26

O

observability, 188-190
Open Worldwide Application Security Project (OWASP), 171, 179
OpenAI, 202
organizational context, 15
Orosz, Gergely, 31, 79
outcomes versus outputs
defined, 2
engineering impact spectrum, 3-4
identifying high-impact work, 98
overview of, 2
problem-solution alignment, 5-6
true outcomes, 2
over-communicating, 152
over-engineering, 51-53

over-specialization, 142
OWASP (Open Worldwide Application Security Project), 171, 179

P

pair programming, 54
    increasing bus factor, 140
    speed of, 175
patience, 84
peer feedback, 15, 84
perfectionism and gold-plating, 59-60
    benefit of avoiding, 60
    culture fix, 60
    never shipping, 59-60
    remedy for, 59, 113
    signs of, 59, 113
persistence, 84
personal branding, 76
personal time, 112
physical health, prioritizing, 110
planning processes, improving, 134
PMs (product managers), working with, 39-41
policy-as-code, 196
Pomodoro method, 61, 109
post-mortems, blameless, 96
PR cycle time (time to merge) metric, 208
Pragmatic Engineer, The, 31
PRDs (product requirements documents), 182-183
prioritization, 7, 110, 133
privacy
    checklist for AI selection and integration, 222
    hybrid ICs, 171
problem identification
    AI, 99

proactive, 7
productive versus effective, 9
    understanding the "why" behind requirements, 39
problem-solution alignment, 5-6
product managers (PMs), working with, 39-41
product ownership issues
    addressing, 133-136
    causes of, 133
    challenges of, 131-133
    engineering-product alignment, 136
    example of, 136
    overview of, 130-131
productivity
    compared to effectiveness, 8-10
    workspace for, 155
professionalism, 77
programming languages, 21
progression, unwritten rules of, 76-77
promotions
    overview of, 73-75
    self-advocacy for, 83-85
    and tenure, 73, 75
    tips for getting promoted, 74-75
prompt patterns, 193-194, 211-215
prototypes, 43
public speaking
    benefits of, 158-159
    building communication skills beyond, 161-164
    example of, 165
    overcoming common obstacles, 159-161
    overview of, 157-159
    strong communication, 164
    value of good communication, 165
Pyramid Principle, The (Minto), 43

Q

QA (quality assurance), 34
quality
    balancing with delivery pressure, 8
    compound effect of, 7
    metrics for AI, 207-211
    mindset of, 22-24
    rubber stamping effects on, 126
quality assurance (QA), 34

R

radical candor, 67
raises, 83-85
refactoring
    automated, 203
    clean code and refactorability, 20
    and testing, 23
reflection, 16, 144-147
regressions, preventing, 23
reliability, of senior engineers, 79
remote work
    challenges of, 151-152
    example of, 156
    strategies to thrive in, 152-156
requests for comments (RFCs), 180
resilience
    building into systems, 96
    as team value, 142
responsibility, taking, 95-96
retention of AI-generated code metric, 207
retrospectives (retros), 226
    celebrating improvements, 147
    as engine for continuous improvement, 148
    example of, 148
    ineffective, 143-149
    purpose of, 143
    reviewing previous, 145
    symptoms of ineffective, 143
    turning insights into impact, 144-147
RFCs (requests for comments), 180
RMFs (Risk Management Frameworks), 201-202
routines, establishing, 153
rubber stamping
    addressing, 126-129
    balancing efficiency and diligence, 129
    causes of, 125
    challenges of, 124-125
    consequences on quality, 126
    defined, 124
    encouraging learning, 130
    example of, 129
    overview of, 124
rubrics, 74

S

SAST (static application security testing), 196
saying "no", 62-63, 112-114
SBI (Situation-Behavior-Impact) model, 67
SCA (software component analysis), 196
scaffolding, generating with AI, 177, 184, 212
scaling
    designing for, 32-34
    systems, 32
    teams and codebases, 34
    usage of AI, 217-219
scope changes, 133
scope creep enablement, 62-63
security
    checklist for AI selection and integration, 222

as first-class concern with AI, 176
hybrid ICs, 171
90-day AI rollout plan, 216, 218
security incident rates, 209
self-advocacy, 83-85
self-discipline, 155
semantic search, 193
senior engineers
    compared to staff and mid-level, 81
    depth and breadth, 29-32, 36
    designing for scale, 32-34
    effectiveness, 13
    managing technical debt, 35-36
    versus mid-level and staff engineers, 77-81
sensitive data, 199
sentiment analysis, 4
shallow in everything, deep in nothing, 171
shipping, postponement of, 59-60
simplicity
    clean code, 20
    simplifying complex topics, 160
simulations, 105, 168
single responsibility principle, 20-21
site reliability engineers (SREs), 32, 34, 171
Situation-Behavior-Impact (SBI) model, 67
skill gap analysis, 17
soft skills, 172
software component analysis (SCA), 196
SOLID principles, 21
solution orientation, 40, 101
split testing (A/B testing), 104, 170
sponsoring, 85, 92-94
    benefits of, 94
    compared to mentoring, 92
    effective, 93
    and progression, 76

sprints
    flaky product ownership, 131
    ineffective retrospectives
        example of, 148
        overview of, 143-144
        retrospectives as engine for improvement, 148
        turning reflection into action, 144-147
    mid-sprint scope changes, 133
    sprint goals, 134
SREs (site reliability engineers), 32, 34, 171
staff engineers
    compared to mid-level and senior, 81
    versus mid-level and senior engineers, 77-81
    overview of, 80-81
stage fright, 159
stakeholders
    drafting release email for, 189
    feedback from, 16
    identifying and understanding, 42
    overpromising to, 131
static analysis and linters, 23, 129
static application security testing (SAST), 196
storytelling and narrative, 163
strategic prioritization, 7
strategic thinking, 224
    aligning engineering with business goals, 100-101
    balancing vision with execution, 102-103
    building effectiveness mindset, 10-11
    identifying high-impact work, 97-100
    using metrics and data in decisions, 104-106

stress, recognizing, 107-108
suggestion acceptance rate, 206
sustainable careers, 114-115
sustainable work cycles, 109
system health, 63-65
    balancing new features with, 7

T

T-shaped skills, 36, 171
task completion time metric, 207
team effectiveness anti-patterns, 117-149
    flaky product ownership
        addressing, 133-136
        causes of, 133
        challenges of, 131-133
        engineering-product alignment, 136
        example of, 136
        overview of, 130-131
    ineffective sprint retrospectives
        example of, 148
        overview of, 143-144
        retrospectives as engine for improvement, 148
        turning reflection into action, 144-147
    knowledge silos
        breaking down, 120-122
        causes of, 118
        cultivating learning culture, 123
        dangers of, 118-119
        example of, 122
        overview, 117
        signs of, 119
        siloed teams, 123
    low bus factor
        example of, 141
        increasing, 138-141
        over-specialization, 142
        persistence of, 138
        resilience as team value, 142
        signs of, 137
    rubber stamping
        addressing, 126-129
        balancing efficiency and diligence, 129
        causes of, 125
        challenges of, 124-125
        consequences on quality, 126
        encouraging learning, 130
        example of, 129
        overview of, 124
teams
    bottlenecks, 118
    effectiveness, 111-112
    resilience, 142
    scaling, 34
    siloed, 123
    10x, 111
    training to use AI, 217-219
technical communicators
    benefits of strong communication, 164
    example of, 165
    overcoming common obstacles, 159-161
    overview of, 157-159
    skills beyond public speaking, 161-164
    value of good communication, 165
technical credibility, 12
technical debt
    denial of, 63-65
    long-term thinking, 6
    managing, 35-36
    rubber stamping, 126
technical depth versus breadth
    prioritization scenario, 7

10x, 111-112
    deep experts, 30
    myth of, 109
    teams, 111
tenure, 73-75
    and promotions, 73
    value of, 75
test biases, 105
test coverage change metric, 209
testing
    automating, 23
    benefits of, 23
    mindset, 22-24
    test-first implementation approach, 183-186
tests-first generators, 211
thinking
    long-term, 6
    strategically, 10-11
360 feedback, 84
throughput metric, 208
time
    constraints, 160
    mismanagement, 65-66
    time-boxing reviews, 130
time to first suggestion metric, 207
time to merge (PR cycle time) metric, 208
tone of communication, 156
tool obsession, 68-69
    benefit of avoiding, 69
    culture fix, 69
    remedy for, 68
    signs of, 68
trust
    building with AI agents, 205
    flaky product ownership, 132
    leading as ICs, 42
    team effectiveness, 111

U
unit tests, drafted by AI, 184
unwritten rules of progression, 76-77
user feedback, 16
user risks, 95

V
vacations, 109, 112, 120
vanity metrics, 105
versatility, 31-32
version control, 24-26
vibe coding, 198
visibility
    of improvements, 146
    lack of, 54-56
    and progression, 76
vision, balancing with execution, 102-103

W
weekly active user metrics, 206
white knight syndrome, 50-51
work environments
    public speaking and communication skills
        example of, 165
        overcoming common obstacles, 159-161
        overview of, 157-159
        skills beyond speaking, 161-164
        strong communication, 164
        value of good communication, 165
    remote work strategies
        asynchronous communication, 154
        challenges, 151-152

establishing routines and boundaries, 153
example of, 156
fostering human connection, 154
investing in communication skills, 156
multiple communication channels, 153
over-communicating, 152
productive workspaces, 155
self-discipline and structure, 155
tone and good intentions, 156
workflow enhancement with AI
brainstorming and drafting ADRs, 180-182
clean-up and communication, 188-190
code reviews, 186-188
example of, 190-192
test-first approach, 183-186
turning PRDs into work items, 182-183
working groups, 90
workspaces, 155
writing well, 162

Y

YAGNI (you aren't gonna need it), 20, 52

About the Author

Addy Osmani has been an engineering leader at Google for 14 years, improving the developer and user experience for billions of users. Addy is the author of numerous books, including *Leading Effective Engineering Teams* (O'Reilly).

Colophon

The cover illustration is by Susan Thompson. The cover fonts are Gilroy Semibold and Guardian Sans. The text fonts are Adobe Myriad Pro, Adobe Minion Pro, and Scala Pro, and the heading font is Benton Sans.

O'REILLY®

Learn from experts. Become one yourself.

60,000+ titles | Live events with experts
Role-based courses | Interactive learning
Certification preparation | Verifiable skills

 **Try the O'Reilly learning platform free for 10 days.**